Snooker Year

Edited by Clive Everton

Virgin Books

First published in the United Kingdom in 1984 by
Virgin Books Ltd.
61–63 Portobello Road
London W11 3DD

U.K. Edition ISBN 0 86369 0513
Export Edition ISBN 0 86369 070 X

Printed in Great Britain by
The Thetford Press, Thetford

Bound by Skinner and Co, Cambridge

Typeset by Type Generation

Designed by Ray Hyden

Production services by
Book Production Consultants, Cambridge

Distributed by Arrow Books

Contents

The Editor

Clive Everton, snooker's senior and most authoritative journalist, is a BBC Television commentator, snooker correspondent of *The Guardian* and the *Sunday Times* and editor of *Snooker Scene*, the game's leading magazine.

Between winning the British Junior Billiards Championship in 1956 and turning professional in 1981, he was a top amateur at both billiards and snooker, twice reaching the semi-finals of the World Amateur Billiards Championship and winning the Welsh amateur title five times. He was six times a Welsh snooker international and in 1976 Midland Amateur Snooker champion.

He was recently the second winner of the Association of Snooker Writers' Services to Snooker Award.

Contributors

Steve Acteson is snooker correspondent of the Press Association

Alexander Clyde is snooker correspondent of the *Standard*

John Dee is snooker correspondent of the *Wolverhampton Express and Star*

Michael Gouge is snooker correspondent of the *Daily Express*

Alan Green is a member of the BBC sports commentary team and has covered a number of tournaments

Janice Hale is Assistant Editor of *Snooker Scene* and snooker correspondent of the *Daily Telegraph* and *The Observer*

John Hennessy is snooker correspondent of the *Daily Mail*

Graham Nickless is snooker correspondent of the *Daily Star*

Terry Smith is snooker correspondent of the *Daily Mirror*

Photographs

The editor would like to thank Benson and Hedges, David Muscroft, Graham Trott, BBC Hulton Picture Library, Neil Wigley, and Jim Latham for the use of photographic material in this book.

Introduction

Ten years ago a snooker yearbook would have been a very slim volume indeed. The World Professional Championship was the only professional event which took place annually, and even this was once or twice in doubt; a couple of sponsored events had come and gone; and, for all the popularity of *Pot Black*, it had yet to be proved that snooker could hold the attention of a mass television audience every day for anything between a week and a fortnight.

A snooker professional once spent most of his time playing club exhibition matches, as against only four or five weeks a year in tournament competition, a situation that has now been reversed.

The British circuit is these days so tightly crammed with tournaments that the leading players have little time for exhibitions, preferring to use scarce spare time to rest or practise.

The overseas circuit, hitherto spasmodic and unco-ordinated, is beginning to take shape, better organisation encouraging hopes that snooker's incredible domestic success may be reproduced elsewhere.

The proliferation of tournaments over the last decade has seen the British circuit's total prize money reach the staggering £2m that is at stake in the 1984-85 season, to be fought over by 116 professionals compared to the twenty or so who were in business in 1974.

Such expansion has created the need for a comprehensive and up-to-date reference book to marshal the multitude of new facts and statistics, a primary purpose of the *Benson and Hedges Snooker Year*, as well as to throw light on the top snooker personalities. It is not, however, a chronological history of the game. It concentrates, for the most part, on the immediate past, with supporting material from previous seasons to set in context the status of a tournament or player.

It is appropriate that this venture is supported by Benson and Hedges as the eponymous Masters tournament, instituted in 1975, makes the company snooker's senior sponsor.

Clive Everton

World Rankings

The world ranking list which will be in operation for the whole of the 1984-85 season is based on three years' performances in the Embassy World Championship, two years in the Jameson International, two in the Professional Players Tournament and one in the Lada Classic.

World rankings used to be determined solely by World Championship performances, but the Jameson International and PPT were designated ranking tournaments from 1983 onwards and the Lada Classic was also given this status last season.

However, to emphasise the importance of the game's blue riband event, double ranking points have been awarded in the Embassy World Championship since 1982.

In all tournaments except the World Championship, one ranking point is awarded for reaching the last 16, two for the quarter-finals, three for the semi-finals, four for the final and five for actually winning the event.

The World Professional Billiards and Snooker Association (WPBSA) stipulates that ranking tournaments must be open to all its members, a criterion which rules out such events as the Benson and Hedges Masters.

In addition to ranking points, there is a system of merit points which is chiefly significant in the lower reaches of the ranking list. Half a merit point is awarded for losing in the last 32 of a ranking tournament, and one merit point for losing in the last 32 of the Embassy World Championship (this applies only to players who were not exempted until that round so that neither points nor merit points can be awarded to a player simply for turning up).

In July 1984, the WPBSA decided that a three-year span of performances should be dropped. With the introduction of the Coral UK as a ranking tournament, and a sixth to be held in March (replacing the Yamaha International), it was felt that a two-year span of performances offered a more reliable guide to current form.

Therefore, the 1985-86 ranking list – which will be issued after the 1985 Embassy World Championship – will be based only on performances in this current season and in 1983-84.

Alex Higgins polishes the black

Ranking List

		Jameson International		Professional Players Tournament		Lada Classic	Embassy World Championship			Total
		1982	1983	1982	1983	1984	1982	1983	1984	
1	Steve Davis (England)	2	5	—	0	5	0	10	10	32
2	Tony Knowles (England)	5	1	0	5	2	2	6	0	21
3	Cliff Thorburn (Canada)	1	4	1	2	0	0	8	4	20
4	Kirk Stevens (Canada)	3	0	0	2	2	2	4	6	19
5	Ray Reardon (Wales)	1	1	5	1	0	4	2	4	18
6	Eddie Charlton (Australia)	0	3	3	1	2	3	4	2	18
7	Jimmy White (England)	1	0	4	0	1	3	0	8	17
8	Terry Griffiths (Wales)	2	3	2	1	2	0	2	4	16
9	Alex Higgins (Northern Ireland)	1	0	0	0	1	5	6	0	13
10	Tony Meo (England)	0	0	1	3	4	0	4	0	12
11	Dennis Taylor (Northern Ireland)	2	1	1	0	0	0	2	6	12
12	Willie Thorne (England)	0	2	0	3	0	2	2	2	11
13	John Spencer (England)	1	2	1	0	1	1	2	2	10
14	Bill Werbeniuk (Canada)	1	0	2	0	0	1	4	2	9
15	Doug Mountjoy (Wales)	0	2	0	0	0	1	2	4	8
16	David Taylor (England)	4	0	0	0	0	0	2	2	8
17	Silvino Francisco (South Africa)	—	2	—	1	1	2	0	2	8
18	John Virgo (England)	3	0	3	0	0	1	0	0	7
19	Joe Johnson (England)	0	0	2	4	0	0	0	0	6
20	John Parrott (England)	—	—	—	0	3	—	—	2	5
21	Mark Wildman (England)	0	0	1	1	3	1	1	1	5
22	Dean Reynolds (England)	1	0	2	0	0	1	0	0	4
23	Cliff Wilson (Wales)	2	0	1	1	0	0	0	0	4
24	Perrie Mans (South Africa)	1	0	0	—	—	1	2	0	4
25	Mike Hallett (England)	0	0	0	1	1	0	0	0	2
26	Dave Martin (England)	0	1	0	1	0	0	0	0	2
27	Eugene Hughes (Rep. of Ireland)	0	0	0	2	0	0	0	0	2
28	John Campbell (Australia)	—	0	—	2	0	—	0	0	2
29	Murdo McLeod (Scotland)	0	0	1	0	1	0	0	0	2
30	Neal Foulds (England)	—	—	—	0	0	—	—	2	2
31	Rex Williams (England)	0	0	0	0	1	0	0	0	1
32	Graham Miles (England)	0	0	0	0	0	1	0	0	1
33	Eddie Sinclair (Scotland)	0	0	1	0	0	0	0	0	1
34	Mike Watterson (England)	0	1	0	0	0	0	0	0	1
35	Mario Morra (Canada)	0	1	0	0	0	0	0	0	1
36	Jim Donnelly (Scotland)	0	1	0	0	0	0	0	0	1
37	Patsy Fagan (Rep. of Ireland)	0	0	0	0	0	1	0	0	1
38	George Scott (England)	0	1	0	0	0	0	0	0	1
39	Colin Roscoe (Wales)	0	0	0	0	1	0	0	0	1

£ Where Snooker's Prize Money Has Gone

		Langs Scottish Masters	Jameson International	Professional Players Tournament	State Express World Team Classic	Coral UK Championship
1.	Steve Davis	10,000	24,000	550	6,666	6,500
2.	Jimmy White	1,375	600	550	–	3,750
3.	Terry Griffiths	1,375	6,000	1,250	4,166	3,750
4.	Tony Knowles	5,000	1,500	12,500	6,666	2,000
5.	Tony Meo	1,375	600	5,000	6,666	2,000
6.	Cliff Thorburn	2,500	12,000	2,500	2,500	–
7.	Alex Higgins	2,500	600	150	2,500	12,000
8.	Eddie Charlton	–	6,000	1,250	1,750	–
9.	Ray Reardon	–	1,500	1,250	4,166	2,000
10.	Kirk Stevens	–	–	2,500	2,500	–
11.	Doug Mountjoy	–	3,000	150	4,166	1,250
12.	Willie Thorne	–	3,000	5,000	–	1,250
13.	John Spencer	–	3,000	550	–	1,250
14.	Dennis Taylor	–	1,500	150	2,500	1,250
15.	Bill Werbeniuk	–	600	550	2,500	–
16.	Joe Johnson	–	600	7,500	–	2,000
17.	John Parrott	–	–	550	–	700
18.	David Taylor	–	600	550	–	1,250
19.	Dave Martin	–	1,500	1,250	–	700
20.	John Virgo	–	600	550	–	700
21.	Silvino Francisco	–	3,000	1,250	–	–
22.	Mark Wildman	–	600	1,250	–	700
23.	Murdo McLeod	1,375	600	150	1,750	700
24.	John Dunning	–	–	150	–	700
25.	Mike Hallett	–	–	1,250	–	1,250
26.	Eddie Sinclair	–	600	150	1,750	225
27.	Warren King	–	–	150	1,650	–
28.	Rex Williams	–	–	550	–	700
29.	Neal Foulds	–	–	–	–	700
30.	Mario Morra	–	1,500	150	–	–
31.	Eugene Hughes	–	600	2,500	–	–
32.	Graham Miles	–	600	550	–	700
33.	John Campbell	–	–	2,500	1,750	–
34.	Tommy Murphy	–	–	550	2,500	700
35.	Mike Watterson	–	1,500	550	–	700
36.	Cliff Wilson	–	–	1,250	–	1,250
37.	Dean Reynolds	–	600	550	–	700
38.	Fred Davis	–	–	150	–	225
39.	Ian Black	–	–	150	1,750	700
40.	Colin Roscoe	–	–	150	–	–
41.	Jim Donnelly	–	1,500	150	–	225
42.	George Scott	–	1,500	550	–	–

Hofmeister World Doubles Championship	Lada Classic	Benson and Hedges Masters	Yamaha International Masters	Tolly Cobbold Classic	Benson and Hedges Irish Masters	Embassy World Championship	Total
12,500	18,000	6,000	12,000	7,000	12,295	44,000	115,555
5,000	2,000	35,000	1,000	1,250	1,025	22,000	73,550
1,500	3,500.	16,000	3,000	—	7,377	6,600	54,518
5,000	3,500	9,000	1,000	4,000	1,640	2,200	54,006
12,500	12,000	2,750	300	1,250	1,640	2,200	48,281
3,000	500	2,750	—	2,000	1,640	6,600	35,990
1,500	2,000	6,000	1,000	—	2,869	2,200	33,319
3,000	3,500	2,750	3,000	1,250	1,025	4,350	27,875
1,500	500	6,000	2,000	—	1,640	6,600	27,156
1,500	3,500	9,000	1,000	2,000	—	12,700	24,700
1,500	500	2,750	1,000	—	—	6,600	20,916
1,500	—	—	3,000	1,250	—	4,350	19,350
1,500	2,000	6,000	300	—	—	4,350	18,950
500	500	2,750	100	—	2,869	12,700	16,494
3,00	500	2,750	1,000	—	1,025	4,350	16,275
350	500	—	100	—	—	2,200	13,250
—	7,000	—	—	—	—	4,350	12,600
1,500	500	2,750	1,000	—	—	4,350	12,500
—	—	—	8,000	—	—	450	11,900
3,000	500	2,750	1,000	—	—	2,200	11,300
550	2,000	—	—	—	—	4,350	11,100
350	7,000	—	300	—	—	450	10,650
—	2,000	—	300	—	—	450	7,325
350	—	—	6,000	—	—	—	7,200
—	2,000	—	100	—	—	2,200	6,800
350	500	—	750	—	—	2,200	6,525
—	—	—	2,000	—	—	2,200	6,100
500	2,00	—	100	—	—	2,200	6,050
—	—	—	750	—	—	4,350	5,800
500	—	—	1,000	—	—	2,200	5,350
500	500	—	100	—	1,025	—	5,225
500	—	—	300	—	—	2,200	4,850
—	500	—	—	—	—	—	4,750
500	—	—	300	—	—	150	4,700
500	—	—	750	—	—	150	4,150
350	500	—	300	—	—	450	4,100
500	500	—	100	—	—	450	3,400
500	—	—	—	—	—	2,200	3,075
350	—	—	100	—	—	—	3,050
350	2,000	—	300	—	—	150	2,950
350	—	—	100	—	—	450	2,775
—	—	—	300	—	—	150	2,500

The Benson and Hedges Masters Trophy

Langs Scottish Masters

TOTAL PRIZE MONEY: £25,500
FIRST PRIZE: £10,000
ENTRIES: Eight invited
TELEVISION: BBC Scotland

Steve Davis started the 1983-84 season much as he had finished the previous, retaining the Langs Scottish Masters title in the same commanding style that he had won his second Embassy World Championship the previous spring.

He set a new tournament record break, 137, in beating the new Scottish champion Murdo McLeod 5-1 in the first round, defeated Alex Higgins 6-2 in the semi-finals and Tony Knowles 9-6 in the final.

Knowles, who had wriggled out of a losing position when Tony Meo led him 4-2 in the first round, looked as if he might be one of the players of the season when he overwhelmed Cliff Thorburn 6-2 in their semi-final, thus avenging the defeat Thorburn inflicted upon him in the World Championship semi-finals from two down with three to play.

Knowles also began the final very impressively; he won the first three frames, but Davis took the next five and retained the initiative from then on.

First round: Cliff Thorburn (Canada) beat Terry Griffiths (Wales) 5-1; Steve Davis (England) beat Murdo McLeod (Scotland) 5-1; Tony Knowles (England) beat Tony Meo (England) 5-4; Alex Higgins (Northern Ireland) beat Jimmy White (England) 5-3

Semi-finals: Knowles beat Thorburn 6-2; Davis beat Higgins 6-2

Final: Davis beat Knowles 9-6

Previous Years

In its three year existence, Scotland's leading international snooker event has gained each season in prestige and presentation. In its debut year, in the echoing vastness of the Kelvin Hall, Glasgow, it experienced all sorts of teething problems, although these were partly redeemed by the excitement of Jimmy White becoming the youngest ever winner of a professional tournament at the age of 19.

To achieve this, White beat three world champions, Ray Reardon, Steve Davis and Cliff Thorburn. He was to repeat his win over Davis, then the reigning world champion, in the final of the Northern Ireland Classic, a one-off event staged at the Ulster Hall, Belfast, two weeks later.

In 1982, the event was more effectively staged at the Holiday Inn, Glasgow. In 1983 there were large crowds for all sessions, with some full to capacity, at the Skean Dhu Hotel, Glasgow.

All four days of the event are televised by BBC Scotland.

1981
TOTAL PRIZE MONEY: £20,500
FIRST PRIZE: £8,000

Qualifying: Vic Harris (England) beat Ian Black (Scotland) 4-0

First round: Jimmy White (England) beat Ray Reardon (Wales) 5-4; Steve Davis (England) beat Doug Mountjoy (Wales) 5-0; Cliff Thorburn (Canada) beat Kirk Stevens (Canada) 5-1; Alex Higgins (Northern Ireland) beat Harris 5-3

Semi-finals: White beat Davis 6-5; Thorburn beat Higgins 6-2

Final: White beat Thorburn 9-4

1982
TOTAL PRIZE MONEY: £23,000
FIRST PRIZE: £9,000

First round: Dennis Taylor (Northern Ireland) beat Jimmy White (England) 5-4; Steve Davis (England) beat Tony Knowles (England) 5-4; Terry Griffiths (Wales) beat Ray Reardon (Wales) 5-3; Alex Higgins (Northern Ireland) beat Eddie Sinclair (Scotland) 5-1

Semi-finals: Davis beat Taylor 6-1; Higgins beat Griffiths 6-5

Final: Davis beat Higgins 9-4

Jameson International

TOTAL PRIZE MONEY: £85,000
FIRST PRIZE: £24,000
ENTRIES: Open to all professionals
TELEVISION: ITV

A change of venue from the Assembly Rooms, Derby, to Eldon Square Recreation Centre, Newcastle, saw Steve Davis regain the title he had lost in the previous year's quarter-finals to David Taylor.

So dominant was the world champion that he raised the spectre of going through the season undefeated. "He didn't murder me, he murdered the game", said his first opponent at Newcastle, Mike Watterson, after his daunting television debut had opened with a flawless Davis clearance of 120.

Following his 5-1 despatch of Watterson, Davis overwhelmed the South African Silvino Francisco 5-1 (allowing his opponent to score only twelve points in the last three frames), the Australian Eddie Charlton 9-2 and, in the final, Cliff Thorburn 9-4.

Thorburn qualified for the final after recovering from three down with four to play against Terry Griffiths, who missed a great chance to clinch the match when, leading 37-1 in the penultimate frame, he miscued on a simple black.

Griffiths thus suffered the same fate as befell his quarter-final opponent, John Spencer, who led him by two frames with three to play. Spencer himself had recovered from this position to beat defending titleholder Tony Knowles 5-4 in the last sixteen.

Willie Thorne enhanced his reputation by beating six-times world champion Ray Reardon in five straight frames before being beaten himself by Charlton 5-0 in the quarter-finals.

There were a number of early surprises: no less than

seven of the 16 players exempted until the intermediate round at Romiley Forum, Stockport, failed to qualify.

David Martin, recalling his run to the semi-finals two years previously, eliminated Alex Higgins 5-2; Mario Morra, a diminutive Canadian left-hander, beat Jimmy White 5-3; the veteran Liverpool professional George Scott overcame the gargantuan Canadian Bill Werbeniuk 5-3; the left-handed Glaswegian Jim Donnelly put out the previous year's runner-up, David Taylor, 5-3; and Kirk Stevens, the world's seventh-ranked player, missed his flight from Toronto and conceded his match to Francisco.

Qualifying

Group 1: Mike Watterson (England) beat Bert Demarco (Scotland) 5-3; Watterson beat Perrie Mans (South Africa) 5-4

Group 2: Tommy Murphy (Northern Ireland) beat Dessie Sheehan (Rep. of Ireland) 5-2; Willie Thorne (England) beat Murphy 5-2

Group 3: Rex Williams (England) beat Doug French (England) 5-1; Dean Reynolds (England) beat Williams 5-3

Group 4: Jim Donnelly (Scotland) beat Bernard Bennett (England) 5-1; Donnelly beat Cliff Wilson (Wales) 5-1

Group 5: Mike Darrington (England) beat Ian Williamson (England) 5-3; Silvino Francisco (South Africa) beat Darrington 5-2

Eddie Charlton

Group 6: Warren King (Australia) beat Ian Black (Scotland) 5-3; Graham Miles (England) beat King 5-3

Group 7: Dennis Hughes (England) beat Maurice Parkin (England) 5-0; Joe Johnson (England) beat Hughes 5-1

Group 8: Bob Harris (England) beat John Dunning (England) 5-3; Mark Wildman (England) beat Harris 5-2

Group 9: Dave Martin (England) beat David Greaves (England) 5-1; Martin beat Patsy Fagan (Rep. of Ireland) 5-0

Group 10: Roy Andrewartha (Wales) beat Clive Everton (Wales) 5-1; Eddie Sinclair (Scotland) beat Andrewartha 5-4

Group 11: Paul Medati (England) beat Vic Harris (England) 5-0; Murdo McLeod (Scotland) beat Medati 5-3

Group 12: Fred Davis (England) beat Billy Kelly (Rep. of Ireland) 5-1; Paddy Morgan (Australia) beat Jack Fitzmaurice (England) 5-4; Morgan beat Davis 5-3

Group 13: Mike Hallett (England) beat Colin Roscoe (Wales) 5-2; Mario Morra (Canada) beat Paul Watchorn (Rep. of Ireland) 5-3; Morra beat Hallett 5-3

Group 14: Geoff Foulds (England) beat Pascal Burke (Rep. of Ireland) 5-2; Eugene Hughes (Rep. of Ireland) beat Mick Fisher (England) 5-4; Hughes beat Foulds 5-1

Group 15: Matt Gibson (Scotland) beat Les Dodd (England) 5-1; George Scott (England) beat Pat Houlihan (England) 5-0; Scott beat Gibson 5-3

Group 16: Eddie McLaughlin (Scotland) beat John Campbell (Australia) 5-2; Ray Edmonds (England) beat Jack Rea (Northern Ireland) 5-1; Edmonds beat McLaughlin 5-1

Intermediate round

Dennis Taylor (Northern Ireland) beat Reynolds 5-3; Ray Reardon (Wales) beat McLeod 5-2; Thorne beat John Virgo (England) 5-2; Morra beat Jimmy White (England) 5-3; Doug Mountjoy (Wales) beat Wildman 5-4; Martin beat Alex Higgins (Northern Ireland) 5-2; Watterson beat Tony Meo (England) 5-3; Scott beat Bill Werbeniuk (Canada) 5-3; Terry Griffiths (Wales) beat Miles 5-2; Steve Davis (England) beat E. Hughes 5-1; Donnelly beat David Taylor (England) 5-3; Francisco w.o. Kirk Stevens (Canada) scr; Eddie Charlton (Australia) beat Johnson 5-2; Cliff Thorburn (Canada) beat Sinclair 5-0; John Spencer (England) beat Morgan 5-1; Tony Knowles (England) beat Edmonds 5-1

Competition Proper

First round: Griffiths beat Scott 5-0; Spencer beat Knowles 5-4; Thorburn beat Dennis Taylor 5-3; Mountjoy beat Martin 5-0; Charlton beat Morra 5-3; Thorne beat Reardon 5-0; Francisco beat Donnelly 5-1; Davis beat Watterson 5-0

Quarter-finals: Griffiths beat Spencer 5-4; Thorburn beat Mountjoy 5-2; Charlton beat Thorne 5-0; Davis beat Francisco 5-1.

Semi-finals: Thorburn beat Griffiths 9-8; Davis beat Charlton 9-2

Final: Davis beat Thorburn 9-4

Previous Years

ITV's desire to compete seriously with BBC on the Snooker front was an important factor in the establishment of the Jameson International in 1981. A couple of promoters, whose events ITV had covered, had been unable to maintain continuity of sponsorship or a high level of efficiency, two deficiencies which were overcome at a stroke through the involvement of Snookasport, who at that time had the Embassy World Championship, the State Express World Team Classic and the Coral UK Championship in their promotional portfolio.

To these events, Snookasport added not only the Jameson International but the Yamaha International Masters, both of which were covered by ITV.

In its second year, the Jameson became the first tournament other than the Embassy World Championship to be taken into consideration for ranking purposes, thus adding another incentive to the substantial prize money already at stake.

Steve Davis has won the first prize twice in three years. In 1981, his first win, he whitewashed Dennis Taylor 9-0 in the final after surviving very perilously 9-8 against Alex Higgins in the semi-finals.

He was beaten by David Taylor in the 1982 quarter-finals, when Tony Knowles came through to win his first major title. But Davis again dominated in 1983.

1981
TOTAL PRIZE MONEY: £66,000
FIRST PRIZE: £20,000

First round: Joe Johnson (England) beat Jim Wych (Canada) 5-2; Dave Martin (England) beat John Dunning (England) 5-2; Rex Williams (England) beat Jimmy White (England) 5-1; Tony Knowles (England) beat Mike Hallett (England) 5-2; Ray Edmonds (England) beat Eugene Hughes (Rep. of Ireland) 5-4; Jim Meadowcroft (England) beat Cliff Wilson (Wales) 5-4; Tony Meo (England) beat Eddie McLaughlin (Scotland) 5-2

Second round: Graham Miles (England) beat Johnson 5-3; Martin beat Bill Werbeniuk (Canada) 5-2; Williams beat Fred Davis (England) 5-0; Alex Higgins (Northern Ireland) beat Patsy Fagan (Rep. of Ireland) 5-3; John Spencer (England) beat Edmonds 5-3; John Virgo (England) beat Knowles 5-2; Kirk Stevens (Canada) beat Meadowcroft 5-1; Perrie Mans (South Africa) beat Meo 5-3

Third round: Miles beat Cliff Thorburn (Canada) 5-0; Martin beat Eddie Charlton (Australia) 5-2; Virgo beat Ray Reardon (Wales) 5-3; David Taylor (England) beat Stevens 5-0; Dennis Taylor (Northern Ireland) beat Williams 5-1; Higgins beat Doug Mountjoy (Wales) 5-1; Terry Griffiths (Wales) beat Spencer 5-2; Steve Davis (England) beat Mans 5-3

Quarter-finals: Martin beat Miles 5-1; Higgins beat Griffiths 5-2; Dennis Taylor beat Virgo 5-2; Davis beat David Taylor 5-1

Semi-finals: Dennis Taylor beat Martin 9-1; Davis beat Higgins 9-8

Final: Davis beat Dennis Taylor 9-0

1982
TOTAL PRIZE MONEY: £75,000
FIRST PRIZE: £22,000
Qualifying

Group 1: Ray Edmonds (England) beat Dennis Hughes (England) 5-0; Edmonds beat Graham Miles (England) 5-1

Group 2: Vic Harris (England) beat Dessie Sheehan (Rep. of Ireland) 5-3; John Virgo (England) beat Harris 5-2

Group 3: Mick Fisher (England) beat Tommy Murphy (Northern Ireland) 5-1; Fisher beat Fred Davis (England) 5-3

Group 4: Bernard Bennett (England) beat Marcus Owen (Wales) 5-2; Jim Wych (Canada) beat Bennett 5-0

Group 5: Mario Morra (Canada) beat Bert Demarco (Scotland) 5-2; Dean Reynolds (England) beat Morra 5-1

Group 6: Mike Watterson (England) beat Clive Everton (Wales) 5-1; Watterson beat Patsy Fagan (Rep. of Ireland) 5-1

Group 7: Eddie Sinclair (Scotland) beat Ian Anderson (Australia) 5-2; Sinclair beat Tony Meo (England) 5-3

Group 8: George Scott (England) beat Bob Harris (England) 5-4; Scott w.o. John Bear (Canada) scr

Group 9: Joe Johnson (England) w.o. John Phillips (Scotland) scr; Cliff Wilson (Wales) beat Johnson 5-4

Group 10: Eugene Hughes (Rep. of Ireland) beat Maurice Parkin (England) 5-2; Hughes beat Dave Martin (England) 5-4

Group 11: Chris Ross (Scotland) w.o. David Greaves (England) scr; Jim Meadowcroft (England) beat Ross 5-0

Group 12: Ian Williamson (England) beat Jim Donnelly (Scotland) 5-3; Billy Kelly (Rep. of Ireland) beat Geoff Foulds (England) 5-4; Kelly beat Williamson 5-1

Group 13: Colin Roscoe (Wales) beat John Dunning (England) 5-2; Doug French (England) beat Graham Cripsey (England) 5-1; Roscoe beat French 5-2

Group 14: Mike Hallett (England) beat Frank Jonik (Canada) 5-2; Mark Wildman (England) beat Matt Gibson (Scotland) 5-1; Wildman beat Hallett 5-2

Group 15: Jack Fitzmaurice (England) beat Ian Black (Scotland) 5-3; Les Dodd (England) beat Murdo McLeod (Scotland) 5-1; Dodd beat Fitzmaurice 5-3

Group 16: Rex Williams (England) beat Paul Medati (England) 5-3; Eddie McLaughlin (Scotland) beat Pat Houlihan (England) 5-2; Williams beat McLaughlin 5-1

Tony Meo

Competition Proper

First round: Tony Knowles (England) beat Sinclair 5-2; Reynolds beat Willie Thorne (England) 5-3; Steve Davis (England) beat Roscoe 5-0; Bill Werbeniuk (Canada) beat Wych 5-3; David Taylor (England) beat Fisher 5-1; Kirk Stevens (Canada) beat Watterson 5-3; Terry Griffiths (Wales) beat Williams 5-2; John Spencer (England) beat Edmonds 5-2; Dennis Taylor (Northern Ireland) beat Wildman 5-2; Virgo beat Eddie Charlton (Australia) 5-4; Perrie Mans (South Africa) beat Dodd 5-3; Jimmy White (England) beat Meadowcroft 5-1; Ray Reardon (Wales) beat Hughes 5-3; Cliff Thorburn (Canada) beat Scott 5-1; Alex Higgins (Northern Ireland) beat Kelly 5-3; Wilson beat Doug Mountjoy (Wales) 5-4

Second round: Davis beat Reynolds 5-0; David Taylor beat Werbeniuk 5-2; Stevens beat Mans 5-2; Griffiths beat Higgins 5-2; Dennis Taylor beat Thorburn 5-2; Wilson beat White 5-2; Virgo beat Spencer 5-4; Knowles beat Reardon 5-2

Quarter-finals: Virgo beat Dennis Taylor 5-3; David Taylor beat Davis 5-3; Knowles beat Wilson 5-4; Stevens beat Griffiths 5-3

Semi-finals: Knowles beat Stevens 9-3; David Taylor beat Virgo 9-5

Final: Knowles beat David Taylor 9-6

Professional Players Tournament

TOTAL PRIZE MONEY: £60,000
FIRST PRIZE: £12,500
ENTRIES: Open to all professionals
TELEVISION: None

Tony Knowles, winner of the Jameson International in 1982, took his second major first prize on the professional circuit by beating Joe Johnson 9-8. Such a desperately close finish had seemed highly unlikely when Knowles led 6-1.

Johnson's revival began with a total clearance of 135 in the last frame of the afternoon session, a new tournament record, and he eventually levelled the match at 8-8 with a run of three consecutive frames.

The Yorkshireman could not quite complete what would have been a marvellous victory but he could certainly look back on the tournament as by far the most successful of his five-year professional career. Wins over Jimmy White, Eddie Charlton, Cliff Thorburn and Tony Meo, all ranked in the world's top fifteen, helped him accrue four official ranking points for reaching the final.

The tournament, a promotional debut by the WPBSA's own promotions company, was full of surprises, none bigger than world champion Steve Davis's 5-2 second round defeat by the young Humbersider, Mike Hallett.

Willie Thorne, for the second tournament in succession, defeated Ray Reardon and went on to reach his first major semi-final before losing 9-7 to Knowles.

The young Dubliner, Eugene Hughes, eliminated former world champion Terry Griffiths to reach the quarter-finals. The tall, lean Australian John Campbell also enjoyed his best ever run in a major professional event by reaching the last eight before losing to Knowles.

Sizeable crowds were attracted to the tournament venue, Redwood Lodge Country Club, Bristol, and the whole event was so successful that the WPBSA's original determination to keep this a non-televised tournament wavered sufficiently for them to negotiate a television contract for it in the 1984-85 season with a change of title to Rothman's Grand Prix.

Ironically, the PPT came into being in 1982 largely as a means of re-distributing to its members — rather than paying it away in tax — the income which the WPBSA receives from television contracts.

Qualifying: George Ganim Jr. (Australia) beat Graham Cripsey (England) 5-4; Steve Duggan (England) beat Mike Darrington (England) 5-4; Tony Jones (England) beat Bill Oliver (England) 5-2; Doug French (England) beat Neal Foulds (England) 5-2; Bernard Bennett (England) beat Bert Demarco (Scotland) 5-4; Pascal Burke (Rep. of Ireland) beat Geoff Foulds (England) 5-4; Vic Harris (England) w.o. Paul Mifsud (Malta) scr; Paul Medati (England) beat Dennis Hughes (England) 5-1; Tommy Murphy (Northern Ireland) beat Paddy Browne (Rep. of Ireland) 5-2; John Parrott (England) beat Paul Watchorn (Rep. of Ireland) 5-0; Des Sheehan (Rep. of Ireland) beat Pat Houlihan (England) 5-2; Mario Morra (Canada) beat John Hargreaves (England) 5-0; David Greaves (England) beat Roy Andrewartha (Wales) 5-2; Warren King (Australia) beat Bob Harris (England) 5-3; Paddy Morgan (Australia) beat Matt Gibson (Scotland) 5-4

First round: Ray Reardon (Wales) beat Ganim 5-4; Cliff Thorburn (Canada) beat V. Harris 5-1; Jim Meadowcroft (England) beat Colin Roscoe (Wales) 5-4; Duggan beat John Dunning (England) 5-2; John Virgo (England) beat French 5-4; John Spencer (England) beat Ian Black (Scotland) 5-2; Willie Thorne (England) beat Clive Everton (Wales) 5-1; Cliff Wilson (Wales) beat Bennett 5-1; Terry Griffiths (Wales) beat Les Dodd (England) 5-3; Jimmy White (England) beat Ian Williamson (England) 5-2; Parrott beat Patsy Fagan (Rep. of Ireland) 5-2; Joe Johnson (England) beat Burke 5-3; Eugene Hughes (Rep. of Ireland) beat Eddie Sinclair (Scotland) 5-4

Second round: Reardon beat Duggan 5-2; Thorburn beat Meadowcroft 5-1; Thorne beat Spencer 5-1; Wilson beat Virgo 5-2; Griffiths beat Parrott 5-1; Johnson beat White 5-3; E. Hughes beat Werbeniuk 5-0; Charlton beat Fisher 5-4; Stevens beat Murphy 5-1; Martin beat Watterson 5-4; Wildman beat David Taylor 5-3; Campbell beat Miles 5-2; Meo beat Reynolds 5-0; Francisco beat Scott 5-1; Knowles beat Williams 5-4; Hallett beat Davis 5-2

Third round: Thorne beat Reardon 5-3; Thorburn beat Wilson 5-3; E. Hughes beat Griffiths 5-2; Johnson beat Charlton 5-0; Stevens beat Wildman 5-0; Campbell beat Martin 5-0; Knowles beat Francisco 5-0; Meo beat Hallett 5-3

Quarter-finals: Johnson beat Thorburn 5-1; Thorne beat E. Hughes 5-1; Meo beat Stevens 5-3; Knowles beat Campbell 5-3

Semi-finals: Knowles beat Thorne 9-7; Johnson beat Meo 9-6

Final: Knowles beat Johnson 9-8

Previous Years

The inaugural PPT was staged in the match arenas of two Birmingham clubs: the International Snooker Club, Aston, and the La Reserve Club, Sutton Coldfield, but was only indifferently supported by the public. Ray Reardon won his first major first prize since the 1978 Embassy World Championship by defeating Jimmy White in the final.

1982
TOTAL PRIZE MONEY: £32,000
FIRST PRIZE: £5,000

First round: Eddie Sinclair (Scotland) beat Fred Davis (England) 5-2; Jim

Meadowcroft (England) beat Bernard Bennett (England) 5-4; Mike Watterson (England) beat Jim Donnelly (Scotland) 5-4; Terry Griffiths (Wales) beat Colin Roscoe (Wales) 5-1; Alex Higgins (Northern Ireland) beat Doug French (England) 5-3; Ray Reardon (Wales) beat Tommy Murphy (Northern Ireland) 5-0; Bill Werbeniuk (Canada) beat Paddy Morgan (Australia) 5-3; Clive Everton (Wales) beat Patsy Fagan (Rep. of Ireland) 5-2; Cliff Thorburn (Canada) beat Paul Medati (England) 5-1; David Taylor (England) beat Ian Anderson (Australia) 5-1; Dennis Taylor (Northern Ireland) beat Ray Edmonds (England) 5-4; Jim Wych (Canada) beat Billy Kelly (Rep. of Ireland) 5-0; Rex Williams (England) beat Chris Ross (Scotland) 5-0; Perrie Mans (South Africa) beat Eddie McLaughlin (Scotland) 5-2; Willie Thorne (England) beat Bert Demarco (Scotland) 5-3; Mark Wildman (England) beat John Dunning (England) 5-4; Joe Johnson (England) beat Graham Miles (England) 5-1; Eddie Charlton (Australia) beat Dennis Hughes (England) 5-2; Frank Jonik (Canada) beat Doug Mountjoy (Wales) 5-3; Kirk Stevens (Canada) beat Eugene Hughes (Rep. of Ireland) 5-2; Tony Meo (England) beat Marcus Owen (Wales) 5-4; Cliff Wilson (Wales) beat Mario Morra (Canada) 5-2; Tony Knowles (England) beat Pat Houlihan (England) 5-4; John Virgo (England) beat Ian Black (Scotland) 5-2; Mike Hallett (England) beat Vic Harris (England) 5-3; Dave Martin (England) beat Matt Gibson (Scotland) 5-2; Jack Fitzmaurice (England) beat Dessie Sheehan (Rep. of Ireland) 5-1; John Spencer (England) beat Geoff Foulds (England) 5-1

Second round: Werbeniuk beat Jack Rea (Northern Ireland) 5-2; Sinclair beat Meadowcroft 5-3; Thorburn beat Everton 5-2; Griffiths beat Watterson 5-2; Reardon beat Higgins 5-2; Dennis Taylor beat David Taylor 5-1; Wildman beat Mans 5-4; Charlton beat Williams 5-2; McLeod beat Thorne 5-4; White beat Wych 5-0; Johnson beat Stevens 5-1; Meo beat Jonik 5-0; Wilson beat Knowles 5-4; Virgo beat Hallett 5-2; Spencer beat Martin 5-3; Reynolds beat Fitzmaurice 5-0

Third round: Werbeniuk beat Thorburn 5-2; Johnson beat Wildman 5-4; Reynolds beat Wilson 5-1; Virgo beat Spencer 5-1; Charlton beat Meo 5-3; White beat Dennis Taylor 5-3; Griffiths beat Sinclair 5-3; Reardon beat McLeod 5-2

Quarter-finals: White beat Griffiths 5-2; Virgo beat Johnson 5-1; Reardon beat Werbeniuk 5-3; Charlton beat Reynolds 5-2

Semi-finals: White beat Virgo 10-4; Reardon beat Charlton 10-7

Final: Reardon beat White 10-5

Ray Reardon helped Wales to victory in the 1983 State Express World Team Classic

State Express World Team Classic

TOTAL PRIZE MONEY: £60,000
FIRST PRIZE: £20,000
ENTRIES: National teams of three
TELEVISION: BBC

The State Express World Team Classic, won by England for the second time in three years through its trio of Steve Davis, Tony Knowles and Tony Meo, was created in 1979 as a result of the developing relationship between snooker and television. Its format was devised with television's requirements very much in mind and it received nine days' BBC coverage from the outset.

Team snooker, a new concept in the professional game, provided good entertainment and attracted highly respectable viewing figures. But it was felt that to spend the first six days cumbrously reducing the six teams to four for the knock-out semi-finals was an inappropriately prodigious use of television time.

The withdrawal of State Express from its British sports sponsorship commitments provided a suitable juncture for the WPBSA to review the situation on behalf of the sport. The WPBSA and BBC agreed to transfer the early season nine-day slot to the new Rothmans tournament (formerly the Professional Players Tournament) but to continue to televise the team event under new sponsorship, from the semi-finals onwards, later in the season.

Group A

Wales beat Canada 4-3
Doug Mountjoy lost to Cliff Thorburn 0-2; Ray Reardon lost to Bill Werbeniuk 0-2; Terry Griffiths beat Kirk Stevens 2-1; Mountjoy beat Stevens 2-1; Griffiths beat Werbeniuk 2-1; Reardon lost to Thorburn 0-2; Tie-break: Reardon beat Thorburn

Canada beat Australia 4-2
Werbeniuk lost to Eddie Charlton 1-2; Thorburn lost to Warren King 1-2; Stevens beat Campbell 2-1; Werbeniuk beat Campbell 2-0; Stevens beat King 2-1; Thorburn beat Charlton 2-1

Wales beat Australia 4-0
Reardon beat King 2-0; Mountjoy beat Charlton 2-1; Griffiths beat Campbell 2-1; Griffiths beat King 2-0

Group B

England beat Northern Ireland 4-1
Tony Meo beat Alex Higgins 2-1; Steve Davis beat Tommy Murphy 2-1; Tony Knowles beat Dennis Taylor 2-0; Meo lost to Taylor 0-2; Knowles beat Murphy 2-0

Northern Ireland beat Scotland 4-3
Murphy lost to Eddie Sinclair 0-2; Higgins lost to Ian Black 0-2; Taylor beat Murdo McLeod 2-0; Murphy beat McLeod 2-1; Taylor beat Black 2-0; Higgins lost to Sinclair 1-2; Tie-break: Higgins beat Sinclair

England beat Scotland 4-0
Davis beat Black 2-0; Meo beat Sinclair 2-1; Knowles beat McLeod 2-0; Knowles beat Black 2-0

Semi-finals

Wales beat Northern Ireland 4-1
Mountjoy beat Higgins 4-1; Reardon beat Murphy 2-1; Griffiths beat Taylor 2-0; Mountjoy lost to Taylor 0-2; Griffiths beat Murphy 2-1

England beat Canada 4-2
Meo beat Thorburn 2-0; Davis beat Werbeniuk 2-0; Knowles lost to Stevens 1-2; Meo beat Stevens 2-1; Knowles lost to Werbeniuk 1-2; Davis beat Thorburn 2-1

Final

England beat Wales 4-2
Davis lost to Mountjoy 0-2; Meo beat Reardon 2-0; Knowles beat Griffiths 2-1; Knowles beat Mountjoy 2-1; Meo lost to Griffiths 0-2; Davis beat Reardon 2-0

Previous Years

1979
TOTAL PRIZE MONEY: £27,500
FIRST PRIZE: £7,500

Group A: England (Fred Davis, Graham Miles, John Spencer) beat Rest of World (Perrie Mans, Jimmy van Rensberg, Patsy Fagan) 8-7; England beat Northern Ireland (Jack Rea, Alex Higgins, Dennis Taylor) 8-7; Northern Ireland beat Rest of World 8-7

Group B: Wales (Ray Reardon, Terry Griffiths, Doug Mountjoy) beat Canada (Cliff Thorburn, Kirk Stevens, Bill Werbeniuk) 9-6; Australia (Eddie Charlton, Gary Owen, Paddy Morgan) beat Canada 8-7; Wales beat Australia 9-6

Final: Wales beat England 14-3

1980
TOTAL PRIZE MONEY: £31,555
FIRST PRIZE: £9,000

Group A: Wales (Ray Reardon, Terry Griffiths, Doug Mountjoy) beat Canada (Cliff Thorburn, Kirk Stevens, Bill Werbeniuk) 10-5; Canada beat Rest of World (Jim Rempe, Eddie Sinclair, Perrie Mans) 9-6; Wales beat Rest of World 13-2

Group B: England (Fred Davis, John Virgo, David Taylor) beat Ireland (Alex Higgins, Dennis Taylor, Patsy Fagan) 11-4; Australia (Eddie Charlton, Ian Anderson, Paddy Morgan) beat England 8-7; Ireland beat Australia 10-5

Semi-finals: Wales beat Ireland 8-7; Canada beat England 8-5

Final: Wales beat Canada 8-5

1981
TOTAL PRIZE MONEY: £40,555
FIRST PRIZE: £12,000

Group 1: England (Steve Davis, John Spencer, David Taylor) beat Australia (Ian Anderson, Eddie Charlton, Paddy Morgan) 4-3; Northern Ireland (Tommy Murphy, Dennis Taylor, Alex Higgins) beat Australia 4-1; England beat Northern Ireland 4-3

Group 2: Wales (Ray Reardon, Doug Mountjoy, Terry Griffiths) beat Canada (Kirk Stevens, Cliff Thorburn, Bill Werbeniuk) 4-2; Wales beat Republic of Ireland (Patsy Fagan, Eugene Hughes, Dessie Sheehan) 4-0; Canada beat Republic of Ireland 4-2

Semi-finals: England beat Canada 4-2; Wales beat Northern Ireland 4-3 .

Final: England beat Wales 4-3

1982
TOTAL PRIZE MONEY: £50,555
FIRST PRIZE: £16,500

Group A: England (Tony Knowles, Steve Davis, Jimmy White) beat Northern Ireland (Alex Higgins, Tommy Murphy, Dennis Taylor) 4-3; Scotland (Eddie Sinclair, Jim Donnelly, Ian Black) beat Northern Ireland 4-1; England beat Scotland 4-1

Group B: Canada (Cliff Thorburn, Bill Werbeniuk, Kirk Stevens) beat Wales (Terry Griffiths, Doug Mountjoy, Ray Reardon) 4-3; Canada beat Australia (Eddie Charlton, Paddy Morgan, Ian Anderson) 4-0; Wales beat Australia 4-1

Semi-finals: England beat Wales 4-2; Canada beat Scotland 4-0

Final: Canada beat England 4-2

Coral UK Championship

TOTAL PRIZE MONEY: £60,000
FIRST PRIZE: £12,000
ENTRIES: Open to all professionals holding a UK passport*
TELEVISION: BBC

After two unsuccessful appearances in the final, Alex Higgins beat Steve Davis in extraordinary fashion 16-15 to win the Coral UK Championship at Preston Guild Hall, the home of the event since Coral's became its sponsor in 1978.

Davis, who had beaten Higgins with a session to spare in their world semi-final the previous spring, looked as if he was about to do the same when he whitewashed the Irishman 7-0 on the first afternoon.

With immense grit, Higgins won seven of the eight frames on the first evening, levelled at 11-11 the following afternoon and ultimately took the last two frames on the second evening to win the title.

Thus ended a modern fairy tale. Throughout the season Higgins had been desperately out of touch. His wife had instituted divorce proceedings and the threat of separation from the two children to whom he is devoted cast him into the depths of despair. It was only when reconciliation with his wife started to appear a definite possibility that his form began to improve.

Having dropped the first four frames to the Scottish champion, Murdo McLeod, in the first round, Higgins was watched by his wife in the evening session as he took the match 9-6.

He looked an altogether different player when he beat Paul Medati 9-1, Tony Knowles 9-5 and Terry Griffiths 9-4 to earn his place in the final.

So well did Davis play in the opening session of the final that Higgins could do little about it; but as soon as the world champion started to play like an ordinary mortal, Higgins regained his form and met the challenge.

*The W.P.B.S.A. decided in late summer 1984 that the event would be open to all professionals and would thus carry ranking points.

In spite of losing 9-4 to Davis in the quarter-finals, Tony Meo equalled the championship break record of 139, set by Graham Miles in 1978, and history was made in the first round when two survivors of the qualifying competition, Geoff and Neal Foulds, became the first father and son combination ever to compete in a major professional tournament.

Qualifying

Group 1: Joe Johnson (England) beat Matt Gibson (Scotland) 9-6

Group 2: Tony Jones (England) beat Eddie Sinclair (Scotland) 9-3

Group 3: Mark Wildman (England) beat David Greaves (England) 9-5

Group 4: Murdo McLeod (Scotland) beat Bernard Bennett (England) 9-0

Group 5: Mike Watterson (England) beat Clive Everton (Wales) 9-6; Watterson beat Fred Davis (England) 9-6

Group 6: Mike Darrington (England) beat Graham Cripsey (England) 9-3; Mike Hallett (England) beat Darrington 9-1

Group 7: Neal Foulds (England) beat Colin Roscoe (Wales) 9-2; Foulds beat Jim Meadowcroft (England) 9-2

Group 8: Vic Harris (England) beat Pat Houlihan (England) 9-6; Rex Williams (England) beat Harris 9-6

Group 9: Doug French (England) beat Jack Rea (Northern Ireland) 9-5; Dave Martin (England) beat French 9-3

Group 10: Geoff Foulds (England) beat Steve Duggan (England) 9-8; Foulds beat Les Dodd 9-7

Group 11: John Parrott (England) beat George Scott (England) 9-7; Parrott beat Mick Fisher (England) 9-0

Group 12: Roy Andrewartha (Wales) beat Bill Oliver (England) 9-1; John Dunning (England) beat Andrewartha 9-2

Group 13: Tommy Murphy (Northern Ireland) beat Bert Demarco (Scotland) 9-4; Murphy beat Jim Donnelly (Scotland) 9-4

Group 14: Paul Medati (England) beat Dennis Hughes (England) 9-3; Medati beat Ray Edmonds (England) 9-7

Group 15: Bob Harris (England) beat Eddie McLaughlin (Scotland) 9-8; Harris beat Jack Fitzmaurice (England) 9-3

Group 16: Ian Williamson (England) beat John Hargreaves (England) 9-4; Ian Black (Scotland) beat Williamson 9-6

Competition Proper

First round: Terry Griffiths (Wales) beat Martin 9-4; Hallett beat Graham Miles (England) 9-4; Johnson beat John Virgo (England) 9-6; David Taylor (England) beat N. Foulds 9-4; Tony Knowles (England) beat Jones 9-5; Doug Mountjoy (Wales) beat Watterson 9-2; Alex Higgins (Northern Ireland) beat McLeod 9-6; Medati beat Dean Reynolds (England) 9-3; Cliff Wilson (Wales) beat Williams 9-4; Ray Reardon (Wales) beat Harris 9-7; Dennis Taylor (Northern Ireland) beat Murphy 9-6; Jimmy White (England) beat Black 9-1; John Spencer (England) beat Dunning 9-7; Tony Meo (England) beat Parrott 9-7; Willie Thorne (England) beat Wildman 9-5; Steve Davis (England) beat G. Foulds 9-1

Second round: Griffiths beat Hallett 9-5; Johnson beat David Taylor 9-3; Knowles beat Mountjoy 9-5; Higgins beat Medati 9-1; Reardon beat Wilson 9-4; White beat Dennis Taylor 9-4; Meo beat Spencer 9-5; Davis beat Thorne 9-3; White beat Reardon 9-4; Griffiths beat Johnson 9-2; Higgins beat Knowles 9-5; Davis beat Meo 9-4

Semi-finals: Higgins beat Griffiths 9-4; Davis beat White 9-4

Final: Higgins beat Davis 16-15

Alex Higgins on his way to winning the Coral UK Championship

Previous Years

Mike Watterson's Snookasport Promotions, fresh from their successful, innovative staging of the 1977 Embassy World Championship, initiated an important new event at Blackpool Tower Circus with sponsorship from the manufacturers of Super Crystalate balls and with BBC television coverage of the final.

Despite poor attendances, not all that surprising at Blackpool in December, the event clearly possessed potential and the following year Coral Racing offered almost twice as much as Super Crystalate's £7,000.

With a prize fund increased to £12,500, television coverage of the semi-finals as well as the final and a move to a prestigious new venue, Preston Guild Hall, the event blossomed.

Doug Mountjoy's and John Virgo's names fell in beneath that of the first champion, Patsy Fagan, in the list of winners and in 1980 the Coral UK gave Steve Davis his first major title.

The prize money increased in stages to 1983's £60,000, and television coverage was extended to the last eight and then the last nine days. Davis won again in 1981 and Terry Griffiths and Alex Higgins in turn succeeded him, both in finals which went the full distance of 31 frames.

1977

(Super Crystalate UK Championship)
TOTAL PRIZE MONEY: £7,000
FIRST PRIZE: £2,000

First round: John Virgo (England) w.o. John Barrie (England) scr; Chris Ross (Scotland) beat Jack Karnehm (England) 5-4; Patsy Fagan (Rep. of Ireland) beat Jack Rea (Northern Ireland) 5-1; Jim Meadowcroft (England) beat Pat Houlihan (England) 5-1; Doug Mountjoy (Wales) beat Roy Andrewartha (Wales) 5-2; Willie Thorne (England) beat Bernard Bennett (England) 5-1; John Dunning (England) beat Maurice Parkin (England) 5-4; David Taylor (England) beat David Greaves (England) 5-4

Second round: Virgo beat Dennis Taylor (Northern Ireland) 5-2; Graham Miles (England) beat Ross 5-1; Fagan beat Fred Davis (England) 5-0; Meadowcroft beat Ray Reardon (Wales) 5-4; Mountjoy beat John Spencer (England) 5-3; Thorne beat Rex Williams (England) 5-4; Dunning w.o. John Pulman (England) scr; Alex Higgins (Northern Ireland) beat David Taylor 5-4

Quarter-finals: Virgo beat Miles 5-2; Fagan beat Meadowcroft 5-4; Mountjoy beat Thorne 5-4; Higgins beat Dunning 5-0

Semi-finals: Fagan beat Virgo 9-8; Mountjoy beat Higgins 9-2

Finals: Fagan beat Mountjoy 12-9

1978

TOTAL PRIZE MONEY: £12,500
FIRST PRIZE: £3,500

Qualifying: Willie Thorne (England) beat Bernard Bennett (England) 9-4; Roy Andrewartha (Wales) beat Pat Houlihan (England) 9-3; Doug Mountjoy (Wales) beat John Barrie (England) 9-5; Rex Williams (England) beat Terry Griffiths (Wales) 9-8; John Dunning (England) beat David Greaves (England) 9-3; John Virgo (England)

beat Ray Edmonds (England) 9-4; David Taylor (England) beat Maurice Parkin (England) 9-2; Jim Meadowcroft (England) beat Jack Rea (Northern Ireland) 9-5

First round: David Taylor beat Fagan 9-7; Virgo beat John Pulman (England) 9-3; Fred Davis (England) beat Dunning 9-2; Alex Higgins (Northern Ireland) beat Meadowcroft 9-6; Thorne beat Ray Reardon (Wales) 9-6; Graham Miles (England) beat Williams 9-8; Mountjoy beat Dennis Taylor (Northern Ireland) 9-4; Andrewartha beat John Spencer (England) 9-8

Quarter-finals: David Taylor beat Virgo 9-2; Higgins beat Davis 9-4; Miles beat Thorne 9-1; Mountjoy beat Andrewartha 9-4

Semi-finals: David Taylor beat Higgins 9-5; Mountjoy beat Miles 9-1

Final: Mountjoy beat David Taylor 15-9

1979

TOTAL PRIZE MONEY: £15,000
FIRST PRIZE: £4,500

First round: Jack Rea (Northern Ireland) beat Bernard Bennett (England) 9-8; Mike Hallett (England) beat Maurice Parkin (England) 9-1; John Dunning (England) beat David Greaves (England) 9-8

Second round: Willie Thorne (England) beat Roy Andrewartha (Wales) 9-4; Pat Houlihan (England) beat Rea 9-3; Steve Davis (England) beat Dunning 9-3; Patsy Fagan (Rep. of Ireland) beat Hallett 9-4; Bill Werbeniuk (Canada) beat Joe Johnson (England) 9-3; Ray Edmonds (England) beat Jim Meadowcroft (England) 9-3; Tony Meo (England) beat David Taylor (England) 9-7; Cliff Wilson (Wales) beat John Pulman (England) 9-7

Third round: Steve Davis beat Doug Mountjoy (Wales) 9-5; Terry Griffiths (Wales) beat Wilson 9-4; Alex Higgins (Northern Ireland) beat Houlihan 9-3; Fagan beat Graham Miles (England) 9-5; Werbeniuk beat John Spencer (England) 9-8; Dennis Taylor (Northern Ireland) beat Thorne 9-8; John Virgo (England) beat Meo 9-6; Edmonds beat Fred Davis (England) 9-6

Quarter-finals: Werbeniuk beat Edmonds 9-8; Dennis Taylor beat Fagan 9-6; Virgo beat Steve Davis 9-7; Griffiths beat Higgins 9-7

Semi-finals: Virgo beat Dennis Taylor 9-4; Griffiths beat Werbeniuk 9-3

Final: Virgo beat Griffiths 14-13

1980

TOTAL PRIZE MONEY: £22,500
FIRST PRIZE: £6,000

Qualifying

First round: Mike Hallett (England) beat Bernard Bennett (England) 9-4; Sid Hood (England) beat Chris Ross (Scotland) 9-3

Second round: Hallett beat Ray Edmonds (England) 9-8; Eddie Sinclair (Scotland) beat Kingsley Kennerley (England) 9-1; Mark Wildman (England) beat Cliff Wilson (Wales) 9-8; Jim Meadowcroft (England) beat David Greaves (England) 9-1; Roy Andrewartha (Wales) beat Tony Knowles (England) 9-8; Rex Williams (England) beat John Barrie (England) 9-1; Joe Johnson (England) beat John Dunning (England) 9-6; Tony Meo (England) beat Hood 9-5

Competition Proper

First round: Meo beat Pat Houlihan 9-1; Steve Davis (England) beat Hallett 9-1; Patsy Fagan (Rep. of Ireland) beat

Johnson 9-4; Sinclair beat Graham Miles (England) 9-5; Willie Thorne (England) beat Meadowcroft 9-1; Wildman beat John Spencer (England) 9-7; Williams beat Doug Mountjoy (Wales) 9-8; Andrewartha beat John Pulman (England) 9-6

Second round: Meo beat John Virgo (England) 9-1; S. Davis beat Bill Werbeniuk (Canada) 9-3; Dennis Taylor (Northern Ireland) beat Sinclair 9-6; Terry Griffiths (Wales) beat Fagan 9-8; Alex Higgins (Northern Ireland) beat Thorne 9-7; Fred Davis (England) beat Wildman 9-6; Ray Reardon (Wales) beat Andrewartha 9-3; Williams beat David Taylor (England) 9-7

Quarter-finals: S. Davis beat Meo 9-5; Griffiths beat Dennis Taylor 9-2; Higgins beat F. Davis 9-6; Reardon beat Williams 9-4

Semi-finals: Davis beat Griffiths 9-0; Higgins beat Reardon 9-7

Final: Davis beat Higgins 16-6

1981
TOTAL PRIZE MONEY: £40,000
FIRST PRIZE: £10,000

Qualifying

Group 1: Paul Medati (England) beat Eddie McLaughlin (Scotland) 9-5; Medati beat Jim Donnelly (Scotland) 9-7; Willie Thorne (England) beat Medati 9-6

Group 2: Mike Hallett (England) beat Vic Harris (England) 9-4; Hallett beat Dennis Hughes (England) 9-6; Hallett beat Patsy Fagan (Rep. of Ireland) 9-5

Group 3: Matt Gibson (Scotland) beat Jack Fitzmaurice (England) 9-6; Clive Everton (Wales) beat Gibson 9-7; Jimmy White (England) beat Everton 9-4

Group 4: Joe Johnson (England) beat Tommy Murphy (Northern Ireland) 9-1; Mike Watterson (England) beat Bernard Bennett (England) 9-4; Johnson beat Watterson 9-3; Johnson beat Cliff Wilson (Wales) 9-5

Group 5: Pat Houlihan (England) beat Kingsley Kennerley (England) 9-1; Houlihan beat Ian Black (Scotland) 9-4; Houlihan beat Jim Meadowcroft (England) 9-4

Group 6: Geoff Foulds (England) beat Bill Kelly (Rep. of Ireland) 9-7; Tony Knowles (England) beat Foulds 9-1

Group 7: Eddie Sinclair (Scotland) beat Mark Wildman (England) 9-8; Sinclair beat Sid Hood (England) 9-0; Dave Martin (England) beat Sinclair 9-7

Group 8: Rex Williams (England) beat Doug French (England) 9-3; Colin Roscoe (Wales) beat Murdo McLeod (Scotland) 9-7; Williams beat Roscoe 9-4; Williams beat John Dunning (England) 9-4

Competition Proper

First round: Thorne beat Ray Edmonds (England) 9-4; Kirk Stevens (Canada) beat Hallett 9-4; White beat John Virgo (England) 9-6; Johnson beat John Spencer (England) 9-5; Graham Miles (England) beat Houlihan 9-5; Knowles beat Fred Davis (England) 9-6; Alex Higgins (Northern Ireland) beat Martin 9-7; Tony Meo (England) beat Williams 9-8

Second round: Steve Davis (England) beat Thorne 9-2; Bill Werbeniuk (Canada) beat Stevens 9-7; White beat Dennis Taylor (Northern Ireland) 9-5; Ray Reardon (Wales) beat Johnson 9-7; Terry Griffiths (Wales) beat Miles 9-4; Knowles beat Doug Mountjoy (Wales) 9-6; Higgins beat David Taylor (England) 9-5; Meo beat Cliff Thorburn (Canada) 9-6

Quarter-finals: Davis beat Werbeniuk 9-5; White beat Reardon 9-8; Griffiths beat Knowles 9-5; Meo beat Higgins 9-4

Semi-finals: Davis beat White 9-0; Griffiths beat Meo 9-3

Final: Davis beat Griffiths 16-3

1982
TOTAL PRIZE MONEY: £50,000
FIRST PRIZE: £11,000

Qualifying

Group 1: Tony Meo (England) beat George Scott (England) 9-5

Group 2: Cliff Wilson (Wales) beat Eddie McLaughlin (Scotland) 9-6

Group 3: Dave Martin (England) beat Murdo McLeod (Scotland) 9-6

Group 4: Jim Meadowcroft (England) beat Dennis Hughes (England) 9-8

Group 5: Jim Donnelly (Scotland) beat Chris Ross (Scotland) 9-5

Group 6: Pat Houlihan w.o. John Dunning (England) scr

Group 7: Mike Hallett (England) beat Bert Demarco (Scotland) 9-1

Group 8: Billy Kelly (Rep. of Ireland) beat Jack Fitzmaurice (England) 9-0

Group 9: Geoff Foulds (England) beat Matt Gibson (Scotland) 9-3; Rex Williams (England) beat Foulds 9-7

Group 10: Vic Harris (England) beat Marcus Owen (Wales) 9-4; Joe Johnson (England) beat Harris 9-8

Group 11: Tommy Murphy (Northern Ireland) beat Clive Everton (Wales) 9-4; Eddie Sinclair (Scotland) beat Murphy 9-5

Group 12: Bob Harris (England) beat Graham Cripsey (England) 9-6; Harris beat Mike Watterson (England) 9-3

Group 13: Mick Fisher (England) beat Ian Black (Scotland) 9-3; Fisher beat Ray Edmonds (England) 9-8

Group 14: Les Dodd (England) beat Ian Williamson (England) 9-1; Dodd beat Doug French (England) 9-7

Group 15: Bernard Bennett (England) w.o. John Phillips (Scotland) scr; Paul Medati (England) beat Bennett 9-1

Group 16: Colin Roscoe (Wales) beat Jack Rea (Northern Ireland) 9-6; Mark Wildman (England) beat Roscoe 9-4

Competition Proper

First round: Steve Davis (England) beat Williams 9-6; Patsy Fagan (Rep. of Ireland) beat B. Harris 9-6; Terry Griffiths (Wales) beat Johnson 9-1; Dennis Taylor (Northern Ireland) beat Meadowcroft 9-7; David Taylor (England) beat Dodd 9-7; Meo beat Graham Miles (England) 9-4; John Virgo (England) beat Kelly 9-2; Doug Mountjoy (Wales) beat Houlihan 9-3; Ray Reardon (Wales) beat Wildman 9-5; Hallett beat Fred Davis (England) 9-7; Wilson beat Willie Thorne (England) 9-7; Jimmy White (England) beat Medati 9-7; John Spencer (England) beat Sinclair 9-8; Tony Knowles (England) beat Donnelly 9-6; Dean Reynolds (England) beat Fisher 9-6; Alex Higgins (Northern Ireland) beat Martin 9-7

Second round: S. Davis beat Fagan 9-3; Griffiths beat Dennis Taylor 9-7; Meo beat David Taylor 9-6; Virgo beat Mountjoy 9-5; Reardon beat Hallett 9-8; White beat Wilson 9-5; Spencer beat Knowles 9-6; Higgins beat Reynolds 9-8

Quarter-finals: Griffiths beat S. Davis 9-6; Meo beat Virgo 9-6; Reardon beat White 9-8; Higgins beat Spencer 9-5

Semi-finals: Griffiths beat Meo 9-7; Higgins beat Reardon 9-6

Final: Griffiths beat Higgins 16-15

Hofmeister World Doubles Championship

TOTAL PRIZE MONEY: £75,000
FIRST PRIZE: £25,000
ENTRIES: Open to all professionals
TELEVISION: ITV

A change of venue from the National Sports Centre, Crystal Palace, a vast, remote, cold sports hall inaccessibly sited on the outskirts of London, to the plush, modern, theatrical setting of the Derngate Centre, Northampton, made all the difference between the 1982 and 1983 Hofmeister World Doubles Championships.

On the table, the mixture was as before: Steve Davis and Tony Meo retained their title by beating Tony Knowles and Jimmy White 10-2, just as emphatically as they had won it the year before when they beat Terry Griffiths and Doug Mountjoy 13-2; but in every other respect the second championship was a class apart from the first.

The champions scored a runaway victory in the semi-finals before sweeping the table in the final. In their 9-1 semi-final defeat of Eddie Charlton and Bill Werbeniuk, a total clearance of 140 by Davis and a 56 clearance by Meo made the combined highest breaks by partners in the same match and fetched a £2,000 prize.

Runners-up Tony Knowles and Jimmy White beat Cliff Thorburn and John Virgo 9-7 in their semi-finals, which turned on an unusual incident. At 7-7 Knowles committed a foul and was asked by Virgo, who was due to play next, to play again. This in some way confused the Virgo/Thorburn partnership. Thorburn took the next shot, was penalised for playing out of turn and from the position left White won the frame with a break of 74.

Pre-qualifying: Bernard Bennett (England) and Pat Houlihan (England) beat Matt Gibson (Scotland) and Murdo McLeod (Scotland) 5-2; Steve Duggan (England) and John Hargreaves (England) beat Bill Oliver (England) and Paddy Browne (Rep. of Ireland) 5-1; George Scott (England) and John Parrott (England) beat Geoff Foulds (England) and Neal Foulds (England) 5-4; Bob Harris (England) and Mario Morra (Canada) beat Dessie Sheehan (Rep. of Ireland) and Eddie McLaughlin (Scotland) 5-2

Qualifying: Tommy Murphy (Northern Ireland) and Paddy Morgan (Australia) beat Pascal Burke (Rep. of Ireland) and Dave Martin (England) 5-4; Jack Fitzmaurice (England) and Vic Harris (England) beat Bennett and Houlihan 5-4; Jim Donnelly (Scotland) and Colin Roscoe (Wales) beat Warren King (Australia) and John Campbell (Australia) 5-3; Duggan and Hargreaves beat Dennis Hughes (England) and Billy Kelly (Rep. of Ireland) 5-0; John Dunning (England) and Bert Demarco (Scotland) beat Mike Hallett (England) and Graham Cripsey (England) 5-4; Ray Edmonds (England) and Jim Meadowcroft (England) beat Doug French (England) and Clive Everton (Wales) 5-2; Eugene Hughes (Rep. of Ireland) and Les Dodd (England) beat Scott and Parrott 5-2; B. Harris and Morra beat Mike Darrington (England) and Ian Williamson (England) 5-1

First round: Murphy and Morgan beat Ian Black (Scotland) and Eddie Sinclair (Scotland) 5-1; Dennis Taylor (Northern Ireland) and Rex Williams (England) beat Fitzmaurice and V. Harris 5-1; Tony Jones (England) and Silvino Francisco (South Africa) beat Donnelly and Roscoe 5-2; Graham Miles (England) and George Ganim Jr (Australia) beat Duggan and Hargreaves 5-3; Fred Davis (England) and Mike Watterson (England) beat Dunning and Demarco 5-3; Dean Reynolds (England) and Patsy Fagan (Rep. of Ireland) beat Edmonds and Meadowcroft 5-0; Hughes and Dodd beat Cliff Wilson (Wales) and Joe Johnson (England) 5-1; B. Harris and Morra beat Mick Fisher (England) and Mark Wildman (England) 5-2

Second round: Steve Davis (England) and Tony Meo (England) beat Murphy and Morgan 5-2; David Taylor (England) and Willie Thorne (England) beat Dennis Taylor and Williams 5-4; Eddie Charlton (Australia) and Bill Werbeniuk (Canada) beat Jones and Francisco 5-3; Alex Higgins (Northern Ireland) and Kirk Stevens (Canada) w.o. Miles and Ganim scr; Ray Reardon (Wales) and John Spencer (England) beat Davis and Watterson 5-2; John Virgo (England) and Cliff Thorburn (Canada) beat Reynolds and Fagan 5-2; Doug Mountjoy (Wales) and Terry Griffiths (Wales) beat Hughes and Dodd 5-3; Tony Knowles (England) and Jimmy White (England) beat B. Harris and Morra 5-4

Quarter-finals: Davis and Meo beat Taylor and Thorne 5-3; Charlton and Werbeniuk beat Higgins and Stevens 5-1; Thorburn and Virgo beat Reardon and Spencer 5-0; Knowles and White beat Mountjoy and Griffiths 5-0

Semi-finals: Davis and Meo beat Charlton and Werbeniuk 9-1; Knowles and White beat Thorburn and Virgo 9-7

Final: Davis and Meo beat Knowles and White 10-2

Previous Years

Doubles (or pairs) snooker has always been popular at amateur level but, apart from a couple of week-long challenge matches in the 1950's featuring Joe and Fred Davis, John Pulman and Walter Donaldson, the four best players at that time, it was an unknown quantity in terms of a professional tournament.

Sports Sponsorship International, promoters new to snooker, sensed that the rapid growth in the number of active professionals, from around a couple of dozen in 1978 to almost 100 in 1982, made a world doubles championship a realistic possibility.

ITV, seeking some variant of single-combat/knock-out tournaments in the pursuit of a wider involvement in professional snooker, agreed an authentic new world championship was worth a try and sponsorship was quickly forthcoming from Hofmeister.

The inaugural championship suffered from small crowds and an inappropriate venue, but its second year provided enough compensating success to assure it of maintaining a valued place in the calendar.

1982
TOTAL PRIZE MONEY: £60,000
FIRST PRIZE: £24,000
Qualifying

Group 1: Joe Johnson (England) and Cliff Wilson (Wales) w.o. Mario Morra (Canada) and Frank Jonik (Canada) scr; Johnson and Wilson beat Ray Edmonds (England) and Jim Meadowcroft (England) 6-4; Ray Reardon (Wales) and John Spencer (England) beat Johnson and Wilson 6-2

Group 2: Dave Martin (England) and Dennis Taylor (Northern Ireland) beat Les Dodd (England) and Doug French (England) 6-2; Terry Griffiths (Wales) and Doug Mountjoy (Wales) beat Martin and Dennis Taylor 6-0

Group 3: Fred Davis (England) and Paul Medati (England) beat John Dunning (England) and Bert Demarco (Scotland) 6-0; Alex Higgins (Northern Ireland) and Eddie Charlton (Australia) beat Davis and Medati 6-3

Group 4: Pat Houlihan (England) and Bernard Bennett (England) beat Eddie Sinclair (Scotland) and Ian Black (Scotland) 6-2; Dean Reynolds (England) and Mike Watterson (England) beat Houlihan and Bennett 6-3; Steve Davis (England) and Tony Meo (England) beat Reynolds and Watterson 6-3

Group 5: Mike Hallett (England) and Graham Cripsey (England) beat Murdo McLeod (Scotland) and Eddie McLaughlin (Scotland) 6-3; Hallett and Cripsey beat Patsy Fagan (Rep. of Ireland) and Geoff Foulds (England) 6-2; Kirk Stevens (Canada) and Jim Wych (Canada) beat Hallett and Cripsey 6-4

Group 6: Vic Harris (England) and Ian Williamson (England) beat Tommy Murphy (Northern Ireland) and Eugene Hughes (Rep. of Ireland) 6-1; Rex Williams (England) and Jack Fitzmaurice (England) beat Harris and Williamson 6-1; Graham Miles (England) and Bill

Werbeniuk (Canada) beat Williams and Fitzmaurice 6-5

Group 7: Jimmy White (England) and Tony Knowles (England) beat George Scott (England) and Dennis Hughes (England) 6-2; White and Knowles beat David Taylor (England) and Willie Thorne (England) 6-1

Group 8: Mick Fisher (England) and Mark Wildman (England) beat Clive Everton (Wales) and Colin Roscoe (Wales) 6-3; Fisher and Wildman beat Jim Donnelly (Scotland) and Matt Gibson (Scotland) 6-5; Cliff Thorburn (Canada) and John Virgo (England) beat Fisher and Wildman 6-2

Quarter-finals: Griffiths and Mountjoy beat Stevens and Wych 6-1; Davis and Meo beat Thorburn and Virgo 6-2; White and Knowles beat Reardon and Spencer 6-2; Higgins and Charlton beat Miles and Werbeniuk 6-3

Semi-finals: Griffiths and Mountjoy beat Charlton and Higgins 10-7; Davis and Meo beat White and Knowles 10-5

Final: Davis and Meo beat Griffiths and Mountjoy 13-2

Tony Knowles, runner-up with partner Jimmy White in last season's Hofmeister World Doubles Championship

Lada Classic

TOTAL PRIZE MONEY: £75,000
FIRST PRIZE: £18,000
ENTRIES: Open to all professionals
TELEVISION: ITV

Steve Davis, who made the first 147 maximum in a televised tournament in the 1982 event, retained the title which he won in 1983, by beating Tony Meo 9-8 in a highly dramatic final at the Spectrum Arena, Warrington, in January 1984.

At one stage he allowed Meo to score only 17 points in five frames as he went from 2-4 to 7-4, but the left-hander won the next three frames before Davis managed to take the last two for the match.

In the decider, Meo needed only a straightforward yellow to pink clearance to clinch his first major individual title but was cruelly distracted as he attempted the yellow by a spectator's untimely shout of 'Come on, Tony.'

Davis was also forced to deciding frames in order to beat Terry Griffiths 5-4 in the quarter-finals and John Parrott, the 19-year-old Merseysider, 5-4 in an epic semi-final, for which 2,000 spectators crammed into the event's magnificicent venue.

Parrott, in his first season as a professional, made his name with the television public with his victories over Doug Mountjoy, the reigning UK champion Alex Higgins and the world's fourth ranked player, Tony Knowles.

Mark Wildman, at the age of 47, enjoyed his best ever tournament, reaching the semi-finals with wins over John Virgo, Silvino Francisco and, after playing for four hours and 52 minutes, Eddie Charlton.

Rex Williams made the highest break of the tournament, 143, while losing to Meo in the second round, but in the qualifying rounds, Mario Morra, the left-handed Canadian, had come within four balls of winning the special prize for the maximum break of 147. He potted fifteen reds, fifteen blacks, yellow and green and the remaining four colours would have given him a Lada car.

Although only the 16-man final phase was televised, the event was for the first time open to all professionals and thus carried world ranking points.

Qualifying

First round: Geoff Foulds (England) beat Marcel Gauvreau (Canada) 5-2; Bert Demarco (Scotland) beat Matt Gibson (Scotland) 5-2; Neal Foulds (England) beat Pat Houlihan (England) 5-3; Mario Morra (Canada) beat Pascal Burke (Rep. of Ireland) 5-2; George Ganim Jr (Australia) beat Dennis Hughes (England) 5-2; Ian Williamson (England) beat Doug French (England) 5-1; John Hargreaves (England) beat Warren King (Australia) 5-3; Bill Oliver (England) beat Dessie Sheehan (Rep. of Ireland) 5-3; Paddy Morgan (Australia) beat Mike Darrington (England) 5-3; Tony Jones (England) beat Paul Mifsud (Malta) 5-3; Graham Crispey (England) beat Vic Harris (England) 5-4; John Parrott (England) beat Bernard Bennett (England) 5-0; Paddy Browne (Rep. of Ireland) beat David Greaves (England) 5-2; Paul Watchorn (Rep. of Ireland) beat Roy Andrewartha (Wales) 5-2; Steve Duggan (England) beat Bob Harris (England) 5-2; Paul Medati (England) beat Tommy Murphy (Northern Ireland) 5-4.

Second round: Eddie McLaughlin (Scotland) beat G. Foulds 5-1; George Scott (England) beat Demarco 5-2; N. Foulds beat Jack Rea (Northern Ireland) 5-1; Morra beat Clive Everton (Wales) 5-0; Colin Roscoe (Wales) beat Ganim 5-3; Frank Jonik (Canada) beat Williamson 5-1; Hargreaves beat Billy Kelly (Rep. of Ireland) 5-4; Oliver beat Jim Donnelly (Scotland) 5-4; Morgan beat Mike Watterson (England) 5-3; Jones beat Ian Black (Scotland) 5-0; John Campbell (Australia) beat Cripsey 5-3; Parrott beat Jack Fitzmaurice (England) 5-2; Ray Edmonds (England) beat Browne 5-1; Mick Fisher (England) beat Watchorn 5-4; Les Dodd (England) beat Duggan 5-2; Eugene Hughes (Rep. of Ireland) beat Medati 5-1

Third round: McLaughlin beat Willie Thorne (England) 5-3; Dean Reynolds (England) beat Scott 5-3; Cliff Wilson (Wales) beat N. Foulds 5-4; Silvino Francisco (South Africa) beat Morra 5-1; Roscoe beat Graham Miles (England) 5-2; Joe Johnson (England) beat Jonik 5-2; Mark Wildman (England) beat Hargreaves 5-1; Patsy Fagan (Rep. of Ireland) beat Oliver 5-2; Eddie Sinclair (Scotland) beat Morgan 5-2; Murdo McLeod (Scotland) beat Jones 5-2; Campbell beat Fred Davis (England) 5-0; Parrott beat Dave Martin (England) 5-1; Rex Williams (England) beat Edmonds 5-1; Jim Meadowcroft (England) beat Fisher 5-0; Mike Hallett (England) beat Dodd 5-1; E. Hughes beat John Dunning (England) 5-4

Competition Proper

First round: Kirk Stevens (Canada) beat McLaughlin 5-4; Terry Griffiths (Wales) beat Reynolds 5-2; Eddie Charlton (Australia) beat Wilson 5-0; Francisco beat Cliff Thorburn (Canada) 5-1; Roscoe beat Bill Werbeniuk (Canada) 5-4; John Spencer (England) beat Johnson 5-4; Wildman beat John Virgo (England) 5-2; Alex Higgins (Northern Ireland) beat Fagan 5-3; Steve Davis (England) beat Sinclair 5-1; McLeod beat David Taylor (England) 5-4; Jimmy White (England) beat Campbell 5-1; Parrott beat Doug Mountjoy (Wales) 5-4; Williams beat Ray Reardon (Wales) 5-4; Tony Meo (England) beat Meadowcroft 5-1; Hallett beat Dennis Taylor (Northern Ireland) 5-4; Tony Knowles (England) beat E. Hughes 5-1

Second round: Davis beat Spencer 5-1; Charlton beat White 5-3; Wildman beat Francisco 5-1; Knowles beat Hallett 5-3; Stevens beat McLeod 5-1; Griffiths beat Roscoe 5-2; Meo beat Williams 5-3; Parrott beat Higgins 5-2

Quarter-finals: Wildman beat Charlton 5-4; Davis beat Griffiths 5-4; Meo beat Stevens 5-2; Parrott beat Knowles 5-1

Semi-finals: Meo beat Wildman 5-3; Davis beat Parrott 5-4

Final: Davis beat Meo 9-8

Previous Years

Granada's wish to show its own home-produced tournament in its own area led to the promotion of the first Wilson's Classic in January 1980, which was won by John Spencer, and the second in December that year, which was won by Steve Davis.

The event was packaged into a seven-part series for weekly showing but press coverage of the matches, inevitable from any venue where the public is charged for admission, lessened its dramatic impact in comparison with tournaments which received live or, at least, same-day television coverage.

There was also a growing feeling that the event might appropriately be show in other regions but Wilson's, the Lancashire brewers, had nothing to gain from the tournament being shown outside Granada-land and decided not to renew their sponsorship.

Only at the eleventh hour were Lada, the Russian car

company, secured as sponsors for the January 1982 event by the promoters, Barwell Sports, whose snooker executive at the time, Simon Weaver, now promotes the event on his own account.

The precise extent of coverage outside Granada's area was uncertain when Lada agreed a sponsorship of £15,000, an arrangement which turned into the bargain of the year when Steve Davis, jet-lagged from a round-the-world trip, compiled against John Spencer the first 147 maximum (fifteen reds, fifteen blacks and all the colours) to be seen in a television tournament.

(By a supreme irony, Spencer had made a 147 in the Holsten Lager tournament, at Slough in January 1979, but during a period when the camera crew was absent owing to union regulations over hours. It is for this reason that camera crews always have sufficient manpower now to cover every frame.)

Davis's history-making break made the tournament's name and there was another bonus when Terry Griffiths beat Davis 9-8 on the final black in a memorable final.

The following year, as ITV decided to network the whole eight days of the event, Lada increased the prize money to £65,000 and extended the field from eight to sixteen. In 1984, this was further increased to £75,000 and the event was thrown open to all professionals, thus enabling players to earn world ranking points from it.

1982

TOTAL PRIZE MONEY: £15,000
FIRST PRIZE: £5,000

First round: Terry Griffiths (Wales) beat Cliff Thorburn (Canada) 5-1; Alex Higgins (Northern Ireland) beat Dennis Taylor (Northern Ireland) 5-1; Ray Reardon (Wales) beat David Taylor (England) 5-1; Steve Davis (England) beat John Spencer (England) 5-2

Semi-finals: Griffiths beat Higgins 5-1; Davis beat Reardon 5-4

Final: Griffiths beat Davis 9-8

1983

TOTAL PRIZE MONEY: £65,000
FIRST PRIZE: £16,000

First round: Eddie Charlton (Australia) beat John Virgo (England) 5-2; John Spencer (England) beat Ray Reardon (Wales) 5-3; Cliff Thorburn (Canada) beat Cliff Wilson (Wales) 5-3; Doug Mountjoy (Wales) beat Terry Griffiths (Wales) 5-1; David Taylor (England) beat Jimmy White (England) 5-3; Bill Werbeniuk (Canada) beat Alex Higgins (Northern Ireland) 5-4; Kirk Stevens)Canada) beat Tony Knowles (England) 5-0; Steve Davis (England) beat Dennis Taylor (Northern Ireland) 5-2

Quarter-finals: Spencer beat David Taylor 5-2; Werbeniuk beat Mountjoy 5-2; Stevens beat Thorburn 5-3; Davis beat Charlton 5-4

Semi-finals: Davis beat Spencer 5-4; Werbeniuk beat Stevens 5-2

Final: Davis beat Werbeniuk 9-5

Bill Werbeniuk had the 1983 Lada Classic snatched from his grasp by Steve Davis

Benson and Hedges Masters

TOTAL PRIZE MONEY: £115,000
FIRST PRIZE: £35,000
ENTRIES: Top 16 in world rankings
TELEVISION: BBC

Jimmy White's capture of the Benson and Hedges Masters brought him £35,000 and gave his career the boost it needed after he lost to Alex Higgins in the semi-final of the 1982 Embassy World Championship, having established a two-frame lead with three to play.

He won the first five frames of the final against an out-of-sorts Terry Griffiths and went on to win 9-5. Far more memorable, however, was his 6-4 semi-final win over Kirk Stevens.

He was leading 5-3 when Stevens compiled a 147 maximum, only the third ever seen on television and only the fourth ever in a professional tournament. This effort gave the Canadian a £10,000 jackpot for his 147 and £1,500 for a new tournament record but it did not help him to win the match.

White, who had earlier made a typically deft and speedy break of 113, produced another century (119) to clinch the match in which the standard of play at times took off into the realms of fantasy.

Stevens had earlier scored a notable quarter-final triumph over Steve Davis 5-3, after the world champion had led 3-1.

The defending champion, Cliff Thorburn, let slip a 4-1 lead over John Spencer in the first round and went down 5-4, but Spencer in turn was beaten 5-4 by Griffiths in the quarter-finals after leading 3-1 and 4-3.

First round: Tony Knowles (England) beat Dennis Taylor (Northern Ireland) 5-2; Ray Reardon (Wales) beat John Virgo (England) 5-3; John Spencer (England) beat Cliff Thorburn (Canada) 5-4; Terry Griffiths (Wales) beat Bill Werbeniuk (Canada) 5-1; Jimmy White (England) beat Eddie Charlton (Australia) 5-2; Alex Higgins (Northern Ireland) beat Doug Mountjoy (Wales) 5-2; Kirk Stevens (Canada) beat David Taylor (England) 5-1; Steve Davis (England) beat Tony Meo (England) 5-0

Quarter-finals: Griffiths beat Spencer 5-4; Knowles beat Higgins 5-1; White beat Reardon 5-3; Stevens beat Davis 5-3

Semi-finals: Griffiths beat Knowles 6-4; White beat Stevens 6-4

Final: White beat Griffiths 9-5

Previous Years

The inaugural Benson and Hedges Masters, which was staged at the West Centre Hotel, London, in 1975, was not its parent company Gallaher's first major venture into snooker sponsorship. Under the banner of another Gallaher brand, Park Drive, four four-man round robin tournaments were staged in 1971 and 1972 with the top two finishers in each meeting in a play-off recorded by BBC. Another Park Drive event was televised by Yorkshire TV.

All these events strengthened television sports departments' conviction that authentic competitive snooker over a reasonable spread of frames could make entertaining viewing.

The 1973 and 1974 Park Drive World Professional Championships had an even more dramatic long-term effect on the game. The decision to compress the 1973 Championship into a fortnight, instead of allowing it to ramble on for an entire season according to established practice, revitalised the whole event. There was television coverage only of the two finals but even this was, at the time, a substantial step forward for professional snooker.

The WPBSA chose to award the 1975 Championship to Australia and Park Drive never returned as sponsors, but the Benson and Hedges Masters very quickly established its own distinctive identity. It was played at the West Centre Hotel only once, but in 1976 its move to the New London Theatre, Drury Lane, established the link between theatre in the round and snooker, which has been strengthened with the choice of similar venues for other major events.

In 1979 the Masters moved again to Wembley Conference Centre, where it has since established several attendance records for professional snooker.

There were only ten competitors in the 1975 event and only the final was televised, but 16 invitations are now issued each year and BBC's cameras roll for the whole eight days. As befits the only major tournament staged in London, the Masters is magnificently mounted and generates the kind of atmosphere which produces dramatic matches. Cliff Thorburn said after winning the 1983 Masters title: 'After the World Championship, this is the Big Daddy.'

1975

TOTAL PRIZE MONEY: £5,000
FIRST PRIZE: £2,000

First round: John Pulman (England) beat Cliff Thorburn (Canada) 5-3; Alex Higgins (Northern Ireland) beat Bill Werbeniuk (Canada) 5-0

Quarter-finals: Eddie Charlton (Australia) beat Fred Davis (England) 5-3; John Spencer (England) beat Pulman 5-3; Ray Reardon (Wales) beat Graham Miles (England) 5-3; Rex Williams (England) beat Higgins 5-3

Semi-finals: Spencer beat Charlton 5-2; Reardon beat Williams 5-4

Final: Spencer beat Reardon 9-8

1976

TOTAL PRIZE: £5,200
FIRST PRIZE: £2,000

First round: Fred Davis (England) beat Cliff Thorburn (Canada) 4-2; John Pulman (England) beat Dennis Taylor (Northern Ireland) 4-2

Quarter-finals: Graham Miles (England) beat Alex Higgins (Northern Ireland) 4-1; Ray Reardon (Wales) beat Pulman 4-1; John Spencer (England) beat Davis 4-0; Eddie Charlton (Australia) beat Rex Williams (England) 4-1

Semi-finals: Miles beat Spencer 5-4; Reardon beat Charlton 5-4

Final: Reardon beat Miles 7-3

1977

TOTAL PRIZE MONEY: £5,200
FIRST PRIZE: £2,000

First round: Doug Mountjoy (Wales) beat John Pulman (England) 4-2; John Spencer (England) beat Dennis Taylor (Northern Ireland) 4-2

Quarter-finals: Ray Reardon (Wales) beat Rex Williams (England) 4-1; Graham Miles (England) beat Spencer 4-1; Alex Higgins (Northern Ireland) beat Perrie Mans (South Africa) 4-2; Mountjoy beat Fred Davis (England) 4-2

Semi-finals: Mountjoy beat Higgins 5-3; Reardon beat Miles 5-2

Final: Mountjoy beat Reardon 7-6

1978

TOTAL PRIZE MONEY: £8,000
FIRST PRIZE: £3,000

First round: John Pulman (England) beat Patsy Fagan (Rep. of Ireland) 4-2; Graham Miles (England) beat Fred Davis (England) 4-3

Quarter-finals: John Spencer (England) beat Pulman 4-2; Alex Higgins (Northern Ireland) beat Dennis Taylor (Northern Ireland) 4-3; Cliff Thorburn (Canada) beat Doug Mountjoy (Wales) 4-2; Ray Reardon (Wales) beat Miles 4-1

Semi-finals: Higgins beat Reardon 5-1; Thorburn beat Spencer 5-3

Final: Higgins beat Thorburn 7-5

1979

TOTAL PRIZE MONEY: £8,000
FIRST PRIZE: £3,000

First round: Doug Mountjoy (Wales) beat Fred Davis (England) 5-2; David Taylor (England) beat Patsy Fagan (Rep. of Ireland) 5-4

Quarter-finals: Alex Higgins (Northern Ireland) beat Eddie Charlton (Australia) 5-2; Perrie Mans (South Africa) beat Cliff Thorburn (Canada) 5-4; Mountjoy beat John Spencer (England) 5-0; Ray Reardon (Wales) beat Taylor 5-2

Semi-finals: Higgins beat Mountjoy 5-1; Mans beat Reardon 5-3

Final: Mans beat Higgins 8-4

Victory was Steve Davis's (left) in the 1982 Benson and Hedges Masters and Cliff Thorburn's (right) in 1983

1980

TOTAL PRIZE MONEY: £14,000
FIRST PRIZE: £4,500

First round: Cliff Thorburn (Canada) beat John Virgo (England) 5-3; Alex Higgins (Northern Ireland) beat Fred Davis (England) 5-1

Quarter-finals: Ray Reardon (Wales) beat Dennis Taylor (Northern Ireland) 5-3; Terry Griffiths (Wales) beat Thorburn 5-3; John Spencer (England) beat Eddie Charlton (Australia) 5-2; Higgins beat Perrie Mans (South Africa) 5-1

Semi-finals: Griffiths beat Spencer 5-0; Higgins beat Reardon 5-2

Final: Griffiths beat Higgins 9-5

1981

TOTAL PRIZE MONEY: £20,500
FIRST PRIZE: £6,000

First round: Perrie Mans (South Africa) beat Steve Davis (England) 5-3; Doug Mountjoy (Wales) beat Eddie Charlton (Australia) 5-0; Fred Davis (England) beat Kirk Stevens (Canada) 5-4; John Spencer (England) beat Dennis Taylor (Northern Ireland) 5-2

Quarter-finals: Alex Higgins (Northern Ireland) beat Mountjoy 5-1; Cliff Thorburn (Canada) beat Mans 5-4; John Spencer (England) beat Ray Reardon (Wales) 5-1; Terry Griffiths (Wales) beat F. Davis 5-2

Semi-finals: Higgins beat Thorburn 6-5; Griffiths beat Spencer 6-5

Final: Higgins beat Griffiths 9-6

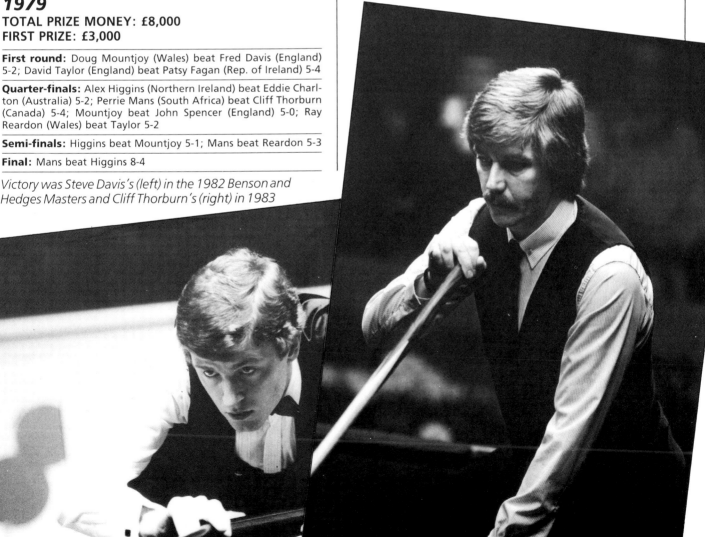

1982

TOTAL PRIZE MONEY: £27,250
FIRST PRIZE: £8,000

First round: Ray Reardon (Wales) beat Dennis Taylor (Northern Ireland) 5-3; Doug Mountjoy (Wales) beat John Spencer (England) 5-4; Tony Meo (England) beat David Taylor (England) 5-2; Eddie Charlton (Australia) beat Jimmy White (England) 5-4

Quarter-finals: Meo beat Cliff Thorburn (Canada) 5-0; Steve Davis (England) beat Mountjoy 5-2; Alex Higgins (Northern Ireland) beat Charlton 5-1; Terry Griffiths (Wales) beat Reardon 5-3

Semi-finals: Davis beat Meo 6-4; Griffiths beat Higgins 6-5

Final: Davis beat Griffiths 9-5

1983

TOTAL PRIZE MONEY: £55,250
FIRST PRIZE: £16,000

First round: Bill Werbeniuk (Canada) beat Alex Higgins (Northern Ireland) 5-4; Eddie Charlton (Australia) beat Tony Meo (England) 5-3; Terry Griffiths (Wales) beat Kirk Stevens (Canada) 5-3; Cliff Thorburn (Canada) beat Joe Johnson (England) 5-2; Ray Reardon (Wales) beat Dean Reynolds (England) 5-1; Doug Mountjoy (Wales) beat John Virgo (England) 5-1; Steve Davis (England) beat Mark Wildman (England) 5-2

Quarter-finals: Charlton beat Werbeniuk 5-3; Thorburn beat Griffiths 5-3; Reardon beat White 5-2; Mountjoy beat Davis 5-4

Semi-finals: Thorburn beat Charlton 6-5; Reardon beat Mountjoy 6-3

Final: Thorburn beat Reardon 9-7

Yamaha International Masters

TOTAL PRIZE MONEY: £65,000
FIRST PRIZE: £12,000
ENTRIES: Open to all professionals
TELEVISION: ITV

Three-man round robins with each match consisting of the best of only three frames is a format geared to producing surprises and two outsiders, Dave Martin and John Dunning, were fittingly involved in the final three-man group in 1984.

Despite the sprint format, however, Steve Davis completed a clean sweep of ITV's four networked tournaments by taking the £12,000 first prize.

He concluded his initial group with a break of 104 against the Manchester-based Irishman, Billy Kelly, before missing the fourteenth red which would have given him his second televised 147. But an even choicer slice of history appeared imminent in another group.

The deciding frame of the Kirk Stevens/Mike Watterson match began with Watterson conceding not only four points but a free ball, so creating the "extra" red which makes it possible for the normal 147 maximum break to be exceeded. Stevens nominated brown as his extra red, potted brown again as his colour and then potted eleven reds and eleven blacks. He took pinks with his next two reds to carry his break to 107 but failed on the penultimate red with a history-making 150 break in sight.

The first semi-final group provided an exciting finish: Terry Griffiths beat Warren King to put veteran Yorkshireman John Dunning through to the final on frames countback; the second semi-final group depended on the last frame, with Martin beating Eddie Charlton to go through; but Davis won the third semi-final group as convincingly as he was to win the final three-man round robin to secure the title for the third time in four years.

Pre-qualifying
(at Sheffield Snooker Centre)

Group A: Neal Foulds (England) beat John Parrott (England) 2-1; Parrott beat George Ganim Jr (Australia) 2-0; Tony Jones (England) beat Ganim 2-0; Jones beat Parrott 2-0; Foulds beat Jones 2-1; Foulds beat Ganim 2-0. **Qualifers: Neal Foulds, Tony Jones**

Group B: Warren King (Australia) beat Bert Demarco (Scotland) 2-0; Geoff Foulds (England) beat Bernard Bennett (England) 2-0; King beat Bennett 2-1; Bennett beat Demarco 2-0; Demarco beat Foulds 2-0. **Qualifiers: Geoff Foulds, Warren King**

Group C: Mario Morra (Canada) beat Paddy Morgan (Australia) 2-1; Morra beat David Greaves (England) 2-1; Paddy Browne (Rep. of Ireland) beat Greaves 2-1; Morgan beat Greaves 2-0; Morgan beat Browne 2-1; Morra beat Browne 2-0. **Qualifiers: Mario Morra, Paddy Morgan**

Group D: Marcel Gauvreau (Canada) beat Matt Gibson (Scotland) 2-0; Gibson beat Pat Houlihan (England) 2-0; Houlihan beat John Hargreaves (England) 2-0; Hargreaves beat Gibson 2-0; Hargreaves beat Gauvreau 2-0; Houlihan beat Gauvreau 2-0. **Qualifiers: Pat Houlihan, John Hargreaves**

Group E: Mike Darrington (England) beat Roy Andrewartha (Wales) 2-0; Bob Harris (England) beat Andrewartha 2-1; Harris beat Steve Duggan (England) 2-1; Darrington beat Harris 2-1; Darrington beat Duggan 2-1; Andrewartha beat Duggan 2-1. **Qualifiers: Mike Darrington, Bob Harris**

Group F: Doug French (England) beat Paul Watchorn (Rep. of Ireland) 2-0; Leon Heywood (Australia) and James Giannaros (Australia) scr. **Qualifiers: Doug French, Paul Watchorn**

Group G: Gino Rigitano (Canada) beat Bill Oliver (England) 2-1; Rigitano beat Dennis Hughes (England) 2-0; Paul Medati (England) beat Hughes 2-1; Hughes beat Oliver 2-1; Medati beat Oliver 2-1; Rigitano beat Medati 2-0. **Qualifiers: Gino Rigitano, Paul Medati**

Group H: Vic Harris (England) beat Pascal Burke (Rep. of Ireland) 2-0; Burke beat Dessie Sheehan (Rep. of Ireland) 2-0; Harris beat Sheehan 2-1. **Qualifier: Vic Harris**

Qualifying
(at Batley Leisure Centre)

Group 10: Jimmy White (England) beat Frank Jonik (Canada) 2-0; Jonik beat Rigitano 2-0; White beat Rigitano 2-0. **Qualifer: Jimmy White**

Group 11: Doug Mountjoy (Wales) beat Tommy Murphy (Northern Ireland) 2-1; John Bear (Canada) scr. **Qualifier: Doug Mountjoy**

Group 12: George Scott (England) beat Dennis Taylor (Northern Ireland) 2-1; N. Foulds beat Taylor 2-0; Foulds beat Scott 2-0. **Qualifier: Neal Foulds**

Group 13: John Virgo (England) beat Ian Black (Scotland) 2-0; Graham Cripsey (England) beat Black 2-0; Virgo beat Cripsey 2-1. **Qualifier: John Virgo**

Group 14: Tony Meo (England) beat Clive Everton (Wales) 2-0; Everton beat Morgan 2-0; Morgan beat Meo 2-0; Tie break: Morgan potted 30 balls, Meo 29, Everton 3.
Qualifier: Paddy Morgan

Group 15: Jack Fitzmaurice (England) beat John Spencer (England) 2-1; Spencer beat V. Harris 2-1; Fitzmaurice beat Harris 2-0.
Qualifier: Jack Fitzmaurice

Group 16: Willie Thorne (England) beat Eugene Hughes (Rep. of Ireland) 2-0; Jones beat Hughes 2-0; Thorne beat Jones 2-0.
Qualifier: Willie Thorne

Group 17: John Dunning (England) beat Dean Reynolds (England) 2-1; Watchorn beat Reynolds 2-1; Dunning beat Watchorn 2-1.
Qualifier: John Dunning

Group 18: Cliff Wilson (Wales) beat Mike Hallett (England) 2-1; Hallett beat Darrington 2-1; Darrington beat Wilson 2-0.
Qualifier: Mike Darrington

Group 19: Medati beat Graham Miles (England) 2-1; John Campbell (Australia) scr. **Qualifier: Paul Medati**

Group 20: Colin Roscoe (Wales) beat Joe Johnson (England) 2-0; French beat Johnson 2-0; French beat Roscoe 2-0.
Qualifier: Doug French

Group 21: Mark Wildman (England) beat Jim Donnelly (Scotland) 2-0; Morra beat Donnelly 2-0; Morra beat Wildman 2-0.
Qualifier: Mario Morra

Group 22: Eddie McLaughlin (Scotland) beat Patsy Fagan (Rep. of Ireland) 2-1; Fagan beat King 2-1; King beat McLaughlin 2-0.
Qualifier: Warren King

Group 23: Eddie Sinclair (Scotland) beat Ray Edmonds (England) 2-0; Edmonds beat Hargreaves 2-1; Sinclair beat Hargreaves 2-0.
Qualifier: Eddie Sinclair

Group 24: Mike Watterson (England) beat Murdo McLeod (Scotland) 2-1; McLeod beat G. Foulds 2-0; Watterson beat Foulds 2-0.
Qualifier: Mike Watterson

Group 25: Dave Martin (England) beat Mick Fisher (England) 2-1; Fisher beat B. Harris 2-0; Martin beat Harris 2-1.
Qualifier: Dave Martin

Group 26: Rex Williams (England) beat Les Dodd (England) 2-1; Dodd beat Houlihan 2-0; Houlihan beat Williams 2-0.
Qualifier: Les Dodd

Group 27: Billy Kelly (Rep. of Ireland) beat Jim Meadowcroft (England) 2-1; Ian Williamson (England) beat Meadowcroft 2-1; Kelly beat Williamson 2-0. **Qualifier: Billy Kelly**

Competition Proper
(at Derby Assembly Rooms)

Group 1: Ray Reardon (Wales) beat Darrington 2-0; Morro beat Darrington 2-1; Reardon beat Morra 2-0. **Qualifier: Ray Reardon**

Group 2: Steve Davis (England) beat Mountjoy 2-0; Mountjoy beat Kelly 2-0; Davis beat Kelly 2-0. **Qualifier: Steve Davis**

Group 3: Dunning beat Tony Knowles (England) 2-1; Knowles beat Dodd 2-0; Dunning beat Dodd 2-0. **Qualifier: John Dunning**

Group 4: Alex Higgins (Northern Ireland) beat Fitzmaurice 2-0; King beat Fitzmaurice 2-1; King beat Higgins 2-1.
Qualifier: Warren King

Group 5: Eddie Charlton (Australia) beat Virgo 2-0; Virgo beat Medati 2-0; Medati beat Charlton 2-1. **Qualifier: Eddie Charlton**

Group 6: Thorne beat Kirk Stevens (Canada) 2-1; Stevens beat Watterson 2-1; Thorne beat Watterson 2-1.
Qualifier: Willie Thorne

Group 7: Bill Werbeniuk (Canada) beat N. Foulds 2-0; Foulds beat French 2-1; French beat Werbeniuk 2-0.
Qualifier: Doug French

Group 8: Terry Griffiths (Wales) beat White 2-1; White beat Sinclair 2-0; Griffiths beat Sinclair 2-0. **Qualifier: Terry Griffiths**

Group 9: David Taylor (England) beat Morgan 2-0; Martin beat Morgan 2-0; Martin beat Taylor 2-0. **Qualifier: Dave Martin**

Semi-finals

Group 1: King beat Dunning 2-1; Dunning beat Griffiths 2-0; Griffiths beat King 2-1. **Qualifier: John Dunning**

Group 2: Charlton beat Reardon 2-0; Martin beat Reardon 2-0; Martin beat Charlton 2-1. **Qualifier: Dave Martin**

Group 3: Davis beat Thorne 2-1; Thorne beat French 2-0; Davis beat French 2-0. **Qualifier: Steve Davis**

Final

Martin beat Dunning 3-2; Davis beat Dunning 4-1; Davis beat Martin 3-0. **Winner: Steve Davis**

Previous Years

As the tournament circuit developed, variants of the traditional single-combat, straight knock-out format were sought. One such, the Yamaha International Masters, grew out of the British Gold Cup, which was instituted in 1980 by Snookasport and sponsored by three concerns within the industry, E.J. Riley (tables), Strachan (cloth) and Super Crystalate (balls).

With four, four-man round robin groups producing the qualifiers for the knock-out semi-finals, Alex Higgins had to beat Terry Griffiths 3-0 to win his group. He did so with the aid of breaks of 135 and 134 in the last two frames and went on to make a break of 132 in beating Ray Reardon 5-1 for the £4,000 first prize.

Between his round robin group and his semi-final, Higgins won the Tolly Cobbold Classic at Ipswich, travelling overnight from that success to reach Derby at 6.00 a.m., only five hours before beating Tony Meo 4-0 in the Gold Cup semi-final.

Such a scenario helped to establish the tournament's commercial potential and in 1981 the event returned to the Derby Assembly Rooms with a major sponsor, Yamaha Organs, who contributed a £30,000 prize fund and won itself four days' coverage by ITV. This, in fact, was the first major tournament to be fully networked by ITV on a daily basis, programming which had already produced impressive viewing figures for BBC.

Steve Davis won the event, retained the title in 1982 and regained it last season after Ray Reardon had taken first prize in 1983.

The format underwent various changes. Four-man groups spread over two sessions were replaced by three-man groups concluded in a single session and the group format itself was extended to the semi-finals and then, in 1984, to the final itself.

The event became a firm fixture at Derby and ITV covered the seven-day action in its entirety. Overall, however, it proved more popular with the public than with the players who felt that prize money and television exposure of such magnitude should not be devoted to such short matches.

With the WPBSA's asking price for major sponsorships

rising in relation to the value of television coverage, Yamaha withdrew for the 1985 event and the WPBSA felt a change of sponsor provided a suitable juncture to institute a ranking tournament on traditional lines.

1981

TOTAL PRIZE MONEY: £30,000
FIRST PRIZE: £10,000

Group 1: Doug Mountjoy (Wales) beat Ray Reardon (Wales) 3-0; David Taylor (England) beat Mountjoy 3-0; David Taylor beat Graham Miles (England) 2-1; Mountjoy beat Miles 3-0; Reardon beat Miles 3-0; Reardon beat David Taylor 2-1; Play-off: David Taylor beat Mountjoy

Group 2: Terry Griffiths (Wales) beat Bill Werbeniuk (Canada) 3-0; Kirk Stevens (Canada) beat Werbeniuk 2-1; Mike Hallett (England) beat Stevens 2-1; Hallett beat Werbeniuk 2-1; Griffiths beat Hallett 2-1; Stevens beat Griffiths 3-0

Group 3: Dennis Taylor (Northern Ireland) beat Alex Higgins (Northern Ireland) 3-0; Higgins beat Fred Davis (England) 3-0; Ray Edmonds (England) beat F. Davis 2-1; Higgins beat Edmonds 2-1; Dennis Taylor beat Edmonds 2-1; F. Davis beat Dennis Taylor 2-1

Group 4: Steve Davis (England) beat Cliff Thorburn (Canada) 2-1; S. Davis beat John Virgo (England) 3-0; Jimmy White (England) beat Virgo 2-1; S. Davis beat White 3-0; White beat Thorburn 3-0; Thorburn beat Virgo 2-1

Semi-finals: David Taylor beat Stevens 5-3; Davis beat Dennis Taylor 5-2

Final: Davis beat David Taylor 9-6

1982

TOTAL PRIZE MONEY: £32,500
FIRST PRIZE: £10,000

Group 1: Steve Davis (England) beat Bill Werbeniuk (Canada) 2-0; Kirk Stevens (Canada) beat Werbeniuk 2-1; Stevens beat Ray Edmonds (England) 2-1; Edmonds beat Werbeniuk 2-0; Edmonds beat Davis 2-1; Davis beat Stevens 2-0

Group 2: David Taylor (England) beat Cliff Thorburn (Canada) 2-1; David Taylor beat Alex Higgins (Northern Ireland) 2-1; Tony Meo (England) beat Higgins 2-0; David Taylor beat Meo 2-1; Thorburn beat Meo 2-0; Higgins beat Thorburn 2-1

Group 3: Terry Griffiths (Wales) beat Doug Mountjoy (Wales) 2-1; Mountjoy beat Jimmy White (England) 2-0; Graham Miles (England) beat White 2-1; Miles beat Mountjoy 2-0; Griffiths beat Miles 2-1; Griffiths beat White 2-1

Group 4: Dennis Taylor (Northern Ireland) beat Ray Reardon (Wales) 2-1; John Virgo (England) beat Dennis Taylor 2-1; Joe Johnson (England) beat Virgo 2-1; Dennis Taylor beat Johnson 2-0; Reardon beat Johnson 2-0; Virgo beat Reardon 2-0

Semi-finals:

Group A: Steve Davis beat Virgo 2-0; Virgo beat Edmonds 2-0; Edmonds beat Dennis Taylor 2-1; Virgo beat Dennis Taylor 2-0; Davis beat Dennis Taylor 2-1; Davis beat Edmonds 2-0

Group B: Griffiths beat David Taylor 2-0; Griffiths beat Thorburn 2-1; Thorburn beat Miles 2-1; Griffiths beat Miles 2-0; Miles beat David Taylor 2-0; Thorburn beat David Taylor 2-1

Final: Davis beat Griffiths 9-7

1983

TOTAL PRIZE MONEY: £47,550
FIRST PRIZE: £12,000

Group 1: Steve Davis (England) beat Bill Werbeniuk (Canada) 2-0; Jimmy White (England) beat Werbeniuk 2-0; White beat Tony Knowles (England) 2-0; Werbeniuk beat Knowles 2-0; Knowles beat Davis 2-1; White beat Davis 2-0

Group 2: Ray Reardon (Wales) beat David Taylor (England) 2-0; David Taylor beat Cliff Wilson (Wales) 2-1; Tony Meo (England) beat Wilson 2-1; David Taylor beat Meo 2-0; Meo beat Reardon 2-0; Reardon beat Wilson 2-0

Group 3: Doug Mountjoy (Wales) beat Alex Higgins (Northern Ireland) 2-1; Willie Thorne (England) beat Mountjoy 2-0; Thorne beat John Spencer (England) 2-0; Mountjoy beat Spencer 2-0; Spencer beat Higgins 2-0; Higgins beat Thorne 2-1

Group 4: Eddie Charlton (Australia) beat Kirk Stevens (Canada) 2-1; Terry Griffiths (Wales) beat Stevens 2-0; Griffiths beat Doug French (England) 2-1; French beat Stevens 2-0; Charlton beat French 2-0; Griffiths beat Charlton 2-0

Semi-finals

Group A: Griffiths beat White 2-0; Griffiths beat David Taylor 2-1; David Taylor beat Mountjoy 2-0; Mountjoy beat Griffiths 2-0; White beat Mountjoy 2-0; White beat David Taylor 2-0

Group B: Thorne beat Reardon 2-1; Davis beat Thorne 2-0; Davis beat Charlton 2-1; Thorne beat Charlton 2-1; Reardon beat Charlton 2-0; Reardon beat Davis 2-1

Final: Reardon beat White 9-6

Tolly Cobbold Classic

TOTAL PRIZE MONEY: £20,500
FIRST PRIZE: £7,000
ENTRIES: Invited
TELEVISION: Anglia

Steve Davis retained the 1984 Tolly Cobbold Classic at the Corn Exchange, Ipswich, with a very comfortable 8-2 final victory over Tony Knowles, but only after he had been within a ball of defeat against Kirk Stevens in their semi-final.

In what was almost a carbon copy of their Benson and Hedges Masters quarter-final, Stevens came from behind, 0-3 and 2-4 down, to level at 4-4. He led by 30 points with only one red remaining in the decider.

Eventually, the outcome depended on a twelve-shot duel on the final black which was resolved by the Canadian unsuccessfully attempting to double it and leaving it in a position from which Davis could pot it.

First round: Cliff Thorburn (Canada) beat Tony Meo (England) 5-4; Tony Knowles (England) beat Jimmy White (England) 5-1; Kirk Stevens (Canada) beat Eddie Charlton (Australia) 5-3; Steve Davis (England) beat Willie Thorne (England) 5-2.

Semi-finals: Knowles beat Thorburn 5-3; Davis beat Stevens 5-4

Final: Davis beat Knowles 8-2

Previous Years

In 1978, Ipswich promoters John Peachey and Ted Brown organised a four-man tournament (won by Patsy Fagan) at the Corn Exchange, Ipswich, which became the forerunner of the Tolly Cobbold Classic.

Anglia Television and Tolly Cobbold were involved for the first time the following year when Higgins won the last three frames to beat Ray Reardon 5-4 in the final.

The format, a four-man round robin with the top two finishers contesting the final, was repeated in 1980 when Higgins retained the title. It was also in operation in 1981, when Graham Miles won first prize, before an eight-man knock-out was instituted in 1982. It was this year that Steve Davis won the first of his hat trick of Tolly Cobbold titles.

The eight-man invitation, even, has been abandoned for the 1984-5 season and the Tolly Cobbold English Professional Championship inserted in its place.

1979
TOTAL PRIZE MONEY: £1,500
FIRST PRIZE: £600

Final: Alex Higgins (Northern Ireland) beat Ray Reardon (Wales) 5-4

1980
TOTAL PRIZE MONEY: £3,300
FIRST PRIZE: £1,500

Final: Alex Higgins (Northern Ireland) beat Dennis Taylor (Northern Ireland) 5-4

1981
TOTAL PRIZE MONEY: £5,400
FIRST PRIZE: £2,000

Final: Graham Miles (England) beat Cliff Thorburn (Canada) 5-1

1982
TOTAL PRIZE MONEY: £8,500
FIRST PRIZE: £2,000

First round: Graham Miles (England) beat Tony Meo (England) 3-0; Tony Knowles (England) beat David Taylor (England) 3-0; Dennis Taylor (Northern Ireland) beat Jimmy White (England) 3-1; Steve Davis (England) beat Willie Thorne (England) 3-0

Semi-finals: Davis beat Miles 5-2; Dennis Taylor beat Knowles 5-2

Final: Davis beat Dennis Taylor 8-3

1983
TOTAL PRIZE MONEY: £15,200
FIRST PRIZE: £5,000

First round: Bill Werbeniuk (Canada) beat Doug Mountjoy (Wales) 4-2; Terry Griffiths (Wales) beat Ray Reardon (Wales) 4-2; Steve Davis (England) beat Jimmy White (England) 4-3; Dennis Taylor (Northern Ireland) beat Alex Higgins (Northern Ireland) 4-2

Semi-finals: Griffiths beat Werbeniuk 5-3; Davis beat Taylor 5-1

Final: Davis beat Griffiths 7-5

Dennis Taylor, runner-up to Steve Davis in the 1982 Tolly Cobbold Classic

Benson and Hedges Irish Masters

TOTAL PRIZE MONEY: IR£45,000
FIRST PRIZE: IR£15,000
ENTRIES: Twelve invited
TELEVISION: RTE

Although he beat Terry Griffiths very easily in a 9-1 final, Steve Davis had to weather two tough matches to retain the Benson and Hedges Irish Masters title in one of snooker's very best venues, the sales ring of Goffs at Kill, Co. Kildare.

In the quarter-finals, Davis beat Tony Meo 5-4 having surprisingly missed the black which would have given him victory a frame earlier, and Alex Higgins pushed him to 6-4 in their semi.

The other semi-final provided a titanic struggle in which Griffiths, having trailed throughout, eventually overcame Dennis Taylor 6-5.

First round: Terry Griffiths (Wales) beat Bill Werbeniuk (Canada) 5-2; Dennis Taylor (Northern Ireland) beat Eugene Hughes (Rep. of Ireland) 5-1; Tony Meo (England) beat Jimmy White (England) 5-4; Alex Higgins (Northern Ireland) beat Eddie Charlton (Australia) 5-2

Quarter-finals: Taylor beat Cliff Thorburn (Canada) 5-2; Griffiths beat Tony Knowles (England) 5-0; Higgins beat Ray Reardon (Wales) 5-2; Steve Davis (England) beat Meo 5-4

Semi-finals: Griffiths beat Taylor 6-5; Davis beat Higgins 6-4

Final: Davis beat Griffiths 9-1

Previous Years

The Benson and Hedges Irish Masters, which receives extensive coverage from Radio Telefis Eireann, provides a unique mixture of tournament play and relaxed social atmosphere which makes it, for the top players, a popular last port of call on the circuit before the rigours of the Embassy World Championship.

Its venue, the sales ring at Goffs, Kill, Co. Kildare, just outside Dublin, might have been tailormade for snooker rather than bloodstock sales. Its 744 plush seats are set nearer the table than they are in many major tournament arenas, thus creating an especially intimate atmosphere.

Founded in 1978, the tournament initially comprised a combination of round robin groups and play-off semi-finals and final until a straight knock-out format was introduced in 1981.

John Spencer and Doug Mountjoy were the first two titleholders before Terry Griffiths achieved a hat trick of successes in 1980-82. Steve Davis could complete a hat trick in 1985.

1978

TOTAL PRIZE MONEY: £3,000
FIRST PRIZE: £1,000

Final: John Spencer (England) beat Doug Mountjoy (Wales) 5-3

1979

TOTAL PRIZE MONEY: £6,000
FIRST PRIZE: £2,000

Final: Doug Mountjoy (Wales) beat Ray Reardon (Wales) 6-5

1980

TOTAL PRIZE MONEY: £8,000
FIRST PRIZE: £2,500

Final: Terry Griffiths (Wales) beat Doug Mountjoy (Wales) 9-8

1981

TOTAL PRIZE MONEY: IR£15,000
FIRST PRIZE: IR£5,000

First round: Dennis Taylor (Northern Ireland) beat John Spencer (England) 4-2; Steve Davis (England) beat John Virgo (England) 4-3

Quarter-finals: Terry Griffiths (Wales) beat Kirk Stevens (Canada) 4-0; Cliff Thorburn (Canada) beat Doug Mountjoy (Wales) 4-0; Ray Reardon (Wales) beat Davis 4-2; Alex Higgins (Northern Ireland) beat Taylor 4-2

Semi-finals: Griffiths beat Thorburn 6-5; Reardon beat Higgins 6-5

Final: Griffiths beat Reardon 9-7

1982

TOTAL PRIZE MONEY: IR£25,000
FIRST PRIZE: IR£7,500

First round: Dennis Taylor (Northern Ireland) beat Dessie Sheehan (Rep. of Ireland) 5-3; Tony Meo (England) beat John Spencer (England) 5-3; Alex Higgins (Northern Ireland) beat Jim Wych (Canada) 5-3; Doug Mountjoy (Wales) beat Eugene Hughes (Rep. of Ireland) 5-4

Quarter-finals: Terry Griffiths (Wales) beat Meo 5-3; Ray Reardon (Wales) beat Taylor 5-4; Steve Davis (England) beat Mountjoy 5-2; Higgins beat Cliff Thorburn (Canada) 5-4

Semi-Finals: Griffiths beat Reardon 6-3; Davis beat Higgins 6-2

Final: Griffiths beat Davis 9-5

1983

TOTAL PRIZE MONEY: IR£35,000
FIRST PRIZE: IR£12,000

First round: Jimmy White (England) beat Dennis Taylor (Northern Ireland) 5-4; Tony Meo (England) beat Pascal Burke (Rep. of Ireland) 5-0; Doug Mountjoy (Wales) beat Tony Knowles (England) 5-1; Eddie Charlton (Australia) beat David Taylor (England) 5-4

Quarter-finals: Ray Reardon (Wales) beat Meo 5-4; Alex Higgins (Northern Ireland) beat White 5-2; Steve Davis (England) beat Charlton 5-1; Terry Griffiths (Wales) beat Mountjoy 5-4

Semi-finals: Reardon beat Higgins 6-3; Davis beat Griffiths 6-2

Final: Davis beat Reardon 9-2

British Circuit Tournaments continued on page 81

Masters of Snooker

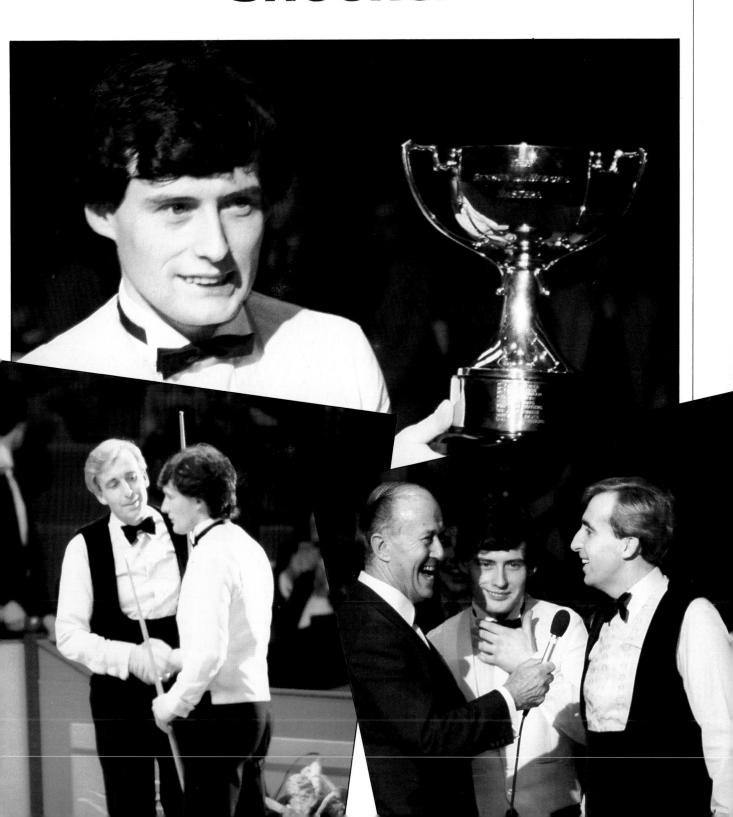

Steve Davis

(England)

BORN: 22.8.57
HOME: ROMFORD
WORLD RANKING: 1

It was an average sort of season for Steve Davis: he won almost everything.

First prizes in the Langs Scottish Masters and the Jameson International; for England in the State Express World Team Classic (with Tony Meo and Tony Knowles); in the Hofmeister World Doubles (with Meo); and in the Lada Classic, the Tolly Cobbold Classic, the Yamaha International Masters, the Benson and Hedges Irish Masters and pre-eminently the Embassy World Championship were set against only three defeats in the entire 1983-84 season — by Mike Hallett in the second round of the Professional Players Tournament, by Alex Higgins in the final of the Coral UK and by Kirk Stevens in the quarter-final of the Benson and Hedges Masters.

The nine first prizes (seven of them in single combat) in the 1983-84 season followed six (five) in 1982-83, six (five) in 1981-82 and five (five) in 1980-81. Since his first major title, the Coral UK in late 1980, despite the occasional loss and his aberrant 10-1 first round defeat by Tony Knowles in the 1982 Embassy World Championship, Davis has been unquestionably snooker's No 1.

In four extraordinary seasons he has lost only six matches consisting of the best of 17 frames or more. His defeats over the best of nine frames, still a chancy sprint in some respects, have been very infrequent. As he is still only 27, he has time to stake out his claim to be the greatest player in the history of the game even if such a claim can never be formally adjudicated.

Circumstances change. Joe Davis, who evolved virtually single-handed the complex break-building strategies and techniques which are taken for granted today, was so far ahead of the game and his contemporaries that most of his 14 championship successes were a formality. That era's best of 73 frames matches also insured him against a flash of inspiration from a lesser player, insurance which, over the best of nine or even seventeen, no modern champion can enjoy.

In the Age of Joe, snooker was a folk sport for amateurs while professionals played in showcase venues to a semi-regular coterie, remote in the main from the public at large. Joe himself would certainly have revelled in the television coverage of today, the media attention, the glitter and plush of the major arenas and, of course, the money. But broad as his shoulders were, he would have felt the pressures which tend to go with them.

With his force of personality, Joe would certainly have enjoyed a fair measure of success in the shorter matches of the Age of Steve, but it is difficult to envisage him accruing a better record than Steve's over the last four years.

One clear connection between them lies in Steve's intense early study — with his father, Bill — of Joe's classic

Snooker's No 1 in action and (right) triumphant in the Embassy World Championship

instruction books *How I Play Snooker* and *Advanced Snooker,* now regrettably out of print. As a teenager at Plumstead Common Working Men's Club, he was recognised as promising but in no way as a potential world champion. His dedication, allied to an analytical approach which enabled him to learn from his mistakes and enough self-discipline to perfect his cueing, transformed a sizeable talent into modern snooker's most consistently efficient practitioner.

A late developer in that he never won the British Junior Championship, Steve nevertheless won the corresponding billiards event. In his later years as an amateur he competed incessantly all over the country, accruing experience and prizes before he turned professional in September 1978.

Since there was no restriction on amateurs accepting prize money or exhibition fees, he had effectively been a professional since abandoning his A'levels in favour of playing full time under the management of Barry Hearn, his mentor and surrogate elder brother. Hearn, owner of a Romford snooker club, had seen Davis play there and immediately offered him a contract.

Steve Davis and referee John Street consider the position

He never won the English Amateur Championship but he did, a few months before turning professional, win the All England CIU Championship — reaching the billiards final for good measure — and the Pontins Open, receiving 30 start from the invited professionals. A year later he retained the Pontins Open, conceding 30 start.

In major tournaments, it took him a while to hitch his formidable technique to the knack of winning big matches, although in the 1979-80 season he reached the quarter-finals of both the Coral UK and the Embassy World Championships, beating Terry Griffiths, then the defending champion, in the latter to establish himself with Britain's television public.

After winning the Coral UK title the next season, his talent burst into full flower and his supremacy on the table was matched by a marketing operation, conducted by Hearn, of genuinely superstar proportions.

A £200,000, 3-year-contract with John Courage, containing a £20,000 increment for each UK or world title, and a £500,000 contract with Leisure Industries for miniature tables, also spread over three years, were two of the most startling items in a portfolio that also included agreements with E.J. Riley in the full size table and equipment market, three books, an instructional video and miscellaneous one-offs as various as chairing Anglia TV's *Sports Quiz* and appearing in the 'Gotta Lotta Bottle' milk promotion.

It is paradoxical that as Britain's highest paid sportsman he can love the game with the purity of a true blue amateur. An inhumanly demanding off-the-table schedule, aimed at maximising his commercial potential, depleted his inner resources so badly that he capitulated like a hollow man to Knowles in the 1982 Embassy World Championship. He has not made the same mistake again.

There is no need to. Free of money worries, he can arrange his life to the sole purpose of reaching peak form and concentration for major events. No one poses a foreseeable threat to his overall status as No 1, but it is possible that constant success may blunt the edge of his motivation.

You have to look hard for hairline cracks in his façade of invincibility, but one was perhaps revealed in the manner of his 16-15 defeat by Alex Higgins in the final of the 1983 Coral UK. He had established a 7-0 lead by the first interval, and possibly the very extent of this lead removed from some corner of his mind the sense of challenge on which every player thrives. When he needed to, he could not recover it.

Perhaps, too, a corner of his mind subconsciously hankers now for the supreme challenge, the supreme high of the last-frame decider. He won three in a row, against Terry Griffiths, John Parrott and Tony Meo to win the Lada Classic, another against Kirk Stevens in the Tolly Cobbold, and another against Meo in the Benson and Hedges Irish Masters. He lost in last-frame finishes to Stevens in the Benson and Hedges Masters and to Higgins in the Coral UK.

Looking back over the last four seasons, it is remarkable how often he has played a deciding frame as if he had been injected with a massive dose of mind-focusing, body-enhancing adrenalin. To put it another way, the knowledge, the technique, the hours of practice, the attention to detail in his preparation, his regulated life-style (not so regulated that he does not know how to enjoy himself) all strike sparks against the basic 'him or me' urge to survive so that the flame of winning inspiration is lit.

Clive Everton

Tony Knowles
(England)

BORN: 13.6.55
HOME: BOLTON
WORLD RANKING: 2

Tony Knowles, with his natural all-round sporting ability and athletic figure, was an appropriate choice for snooker's first representative on BBC-1's *Superstars*, but his elevation within his own game, from snooker star to superstar, during the 1983-84 season was no smooth process.

He began the season in fourth place in the world rankings after winning the 1982 Jameson International and reaching the semi-finals of the Embassy World Championship the following spring.

Largely through winning the Professional Players Tournament in October 1983, he progressed last season to second place in the rankings, although he did not gain any points from the Embassy World Championship, in which he lost to John Parrott in the first round, and only accrued two from the Lada Classic in which he also lost to Parrott and one, in early season, from the Jameson International, in which he lost to John Spencer.

With Steve Davis and Tony Meo, he comprised England's winning trio in the State Express World Team Classic; with Jimmy White, he reached the final of the Hofmeister World Doubles before losing to Davis and Meo; he beat Alex Higgins to reach the semi-finals of the Benson and Hedges Masters, having lost to him in the quarter-finals of the Coral UK; and he made the finals of two eight-man events, the Langs Scottish Masters and Tolly Cobbold Classic, both of which he lost to Davis.

Tony Knowles gets down to it.

As fine a season as this was (by anyone's standards, except possibly Davis's), it was overshadowed during the Embassy World Championship by publication under his name of a tawdry three-part extravaganza of sexual boastings in the *Sun,* for which he was subsequently fined £5,000 by the WPBSA for bringing the game into disrepute.

This alienated some, though not all, of his legion of female supporters and a large part of snooker's public in general. He also put pressure on himself by making some incautious predictions about his own success in the kind of ghosted columns beloved of the tabloids.

For all his talent, a question mark formed over the quality of his commitment to becoming No 1; he seemed more determined to pursue a hedonistic life-style based on the degree of his celebrity and the substance of his bank balance.

This is not to say that he did not try his very hardest when actually engaged in his matches, but the history of sport has shown that success is as dependent on peace of mind and correct preparation as it is on ability. Through some curious contradiction, Knowles sometimes talks obsessively about snooker, while apparently not being fully dedicated to it.

Although he won the first of his two British Junior titles in 1972 when he was only 16, Knowles was in some ways a relatively slow developer. After leaving art college he played snooker full time but his first really notable success did not come until October 1979 when, in the same week, he won the Pontins Autumn Open and was voted Player of the Series in the Home Internationals.

It was only at the second time of asking that his application for professional status was accepted. His first minor breakthrough in the professional ranks did not come

until he qualified for the television stage of the 1981 Embassy World Championship, in which he lost to Graham Miles in the first round.

Later in 1981 he broke through to the quarter-finals of the Coral UK by beating Doug Mountjoy, and in spring 1982 there came his amazing 10-1 win over Steve Davis in the Embassy World Championship when, jaded as Davis was, Knowles played with a steadiness and composure which proved that he was ready for the very highest class of competition. He went on to beat Graham Miles but lost 13-11 to Eddie Charlton in the quarter-finals after establishing a 9-5 lead.

A 5-4 loss to Davis in the Langs Scottish Masters after leading 4-2 was his start to the 1982-83 season. He immediately went on to notch up wins over Kirk Stevens and David Taylor in the last two rounds of the Jameson International to clinch his first major title.

He did not achieve much for the rest of the season, until in the Embassy World Championship, he not only beat Ray Reardon and Tony Meo but was within one frame of reaching the final before Cliff Thorburn, two down with three to play, beat him 16-15.

The ability through which Knowles has risen to second place in the world rankings should in no way be discounted. However, his losses in the Embassy World Championship to Charlton, Thorburn and, last season, Parrott each illustrate that he does not always make the most of his talent. The blemishes on his record, substantial as it is, have perhaps been too frequent for him yet to be envisaged as snooker's next No 1 with all the icy, committed professionalism which gaining that position requires.

Clive Everton

Cliff Thorburn

(Canada)

BORN: 16.1.48
HOME: TORONTO
WORLD RANKING: 3

Laid back, cool, patient, Cliff Thorburn is snooker's marathon man, except that he is indifferent to the clock. He is the only overseas player to have won the World Championship, a feat he only achieved in 1980, nine years after learning of its existence.

In the late 1960s and early 1970s, snooker in Canada was still in the world of *The Hustler*. It was a game played for money, either your own or a backer's, and Thorburn was part of that scene. If you didn't win, you were reduced to keeping body and soul together by washing dishes, picking cotton — anything, so long as you would get together enough money for another match.

In 1970, Thorburn saw Fred Davis and Rex Williams play in Toronto and only then realised there was another side to the game, tournaments featuring smartly dressed professionals who even had a governing body.

The following year, he played John Spencer in Canada and learned that a World Championship existed; in 1973 he made his first visit to Britain to play in it. Four years later, in 1977 he reached the final, but lost 25-21 to Spencer after leading by four frames. The following year, he reached the Benson and Hedges Masters' final for the first time.

A major tournament was then staged in Toronto, the Canadian Open, as part of the Canadian National Exhibition, a noisy combination of the Ideal Home Exhibition and a funfair. Between 1978 and 1980 he won the title three times.

With his success both at home and in Britain, he left the billiard halls behind him to gain sartorial elegance, a sophisticated image and, above all, a reputation as one of the toughest competitors in the game.

After winning the world title in 1980, Thorburn came to live in Britain but, cut off from his roots, his game suffered. The 1980-81 season was bad enough, the 1981-82 even worse: after reaching the final of the Langs Scottish Masters, the first event of the season, he did not win another match.

A drastic change was called for and Thorburn moved back to Toronto, deciding that it would be better to have the security of home even at the cost of commuting across the Atlantic several times a year.

His game immediately began to improve. On his second visit to Britain in the 1982-83 season — he had captained Canada to victory in the State Express World Team Classic on his first — he took the Benson and Hedges Masters with wins over Terry Griffiths, Eddie Charlton and Ray Reardon.

He returned to Toronto before coming back to Sheffield for the Embassy World Championship in which his qualities of endless concentration, tenacity and will-power resulted in a series of memorable wins which carried him to the final.

He made history by compiling the first 147 break in Championship history, a total clearance that contained no more than two difficult shots. That break earned him £10,000, plus £3,000 for the highest break; he later increased that by £15,000 for reaching the final. His total earnings were only £2,000 less than Steve Davis's for winning the title itself.

Equally memorable, though, were his marathons. His 13-12 second round victory of Griffiths supplied the Championship's latest ever finish (3.51 a.m.) to its longest ever session (6 hours 25 minutes).

In the next two rounds he was two down with three to play, but on both occasions he came through. In yet another final session of over six hours he beat Kirk Stevens 13-12 in the quarter-finals and, to reach the final, Tony Knowles 16-15.

But those three grinding, exhausting matches parched his inner resources and when he faced Davis in the final, there was nothing left to draw upon. The emotional and stamina wells were both dry. He lost 18-6.

His best performance last season was to reach the final of the Jameson International. He beat Dennis Taylor, Willie Thorne and, from three down with four to play, Griffiths; but once again the obstacle to the title was Davis. Thorburn went down 9-4.

After reaching the quarter-finals of the next competition, the Professional Players Tournament, Thorburn failed to win a match in the next three.

He survived two rounds of the 1984 Embassy World Championship, before losing to Jimmy White in the quarter-finals.

During the season, he tried speeding up (he was a little fed up with being described as "The Grinder"), but speed is not his natural game. Thorburn will never be a White or a Higgins but he will certainly remain one of the game's most determined and respected competitors. He will have his successes and when he is beaten it will only be the hard way.

Janice Hale

Kirk Stevens

(Canada)

BORN: 17.8.58
HOME: TORONTO
WORLD RANKING: 4

A victory over Steve Davis and three major semi-final appearances, with a televised 147 maximum in one, were the chief landmarks for Kirk Stevens in the 1983-84 season which saw him rise from seventh to fourth place in the world rankings after a long period of self-doubt.

Yet the 25-year-old Canadian, who belies his flamboyant public image in private, finished the season acutely self-critical. 'I could have won — I should have,' he said after losing a thrilling Embassy World Championship semi-final 16-14 to Jimmy White, though referee Jim Thorpe was convinced, as indeed were most observers, that no two players had ever served up such a feast of attacking snooker in one match at the Crucible.

But Stevens could not be consoled. 'I could have won — I should have,' he insisted. 'I played so well after a bad start and I felt all along I had the measure of Jimmy. I had already beaten Steve at Wembley, my safety game was really coming together and I honestly felt good enough to win the title this year.'

He had arrived back in Britain armed with the Canadian Professional title, albeit too late to take his appointed place in the season's first ranking tournament, the Jameson International.

He reached the Professional Players Tournament quarter-finals and the semi-finals of the Lada Classic, but it was not until the Benson and Hedges Masters at Wembley that he really made his mark on the season.

A comfortable first round win over David Taylor was followed by his finest victory, coming 3-1 down against Davis to win 5-3 with the sort of tough, relentless snooker he learnt in his late teens, when playing for big money — his own — in Canada and North America.

His semi-final against White in the Benson and Hedges Master foreshadowed their classic encounter at the Crucible: White made two centuries, Stevens made a 147 maximum and lost 6-4. Keenly as he wants to appear in his first major British final, he for once would not have exchanged winning for his 147: 'It was my proudest moment and nothing will ever rival it,' he said, 'For the first time I truly believed I could be world champion.'

He had come a long way since, as a 12-year-old, he challenged his great hero, Cliff Thorburn. He took 40 start but two $2-frames later he was broke. He made his first century break the same year, but now admits: 'I knew nothing about the game then and it took about 18 months before I was able to make another.'

He had come a long way even from his amateur days when, in 1978, he became the youngest player to appear in the World Amateur Championship semi-finals. He turned pro straight away and made his first professional break-

through in 1980, when he lost only 16-13 to Alex Higgins in their World Championship semi-final after beating John Spencer and Eddie Charlton. On the very first day of that Championship, against Graham Miles, he missed the final black for what would then have been a new Championship record of 143.

When Thorburn celebrated his 1980 world title success by moving to this country a few months later, Stevens came with him. But the grind of the exhibition circuit soon disillusioned both men and they returned to Canada after 15 months, Thorburn having been relieved of his crown and Stevens having failed to make the last eight at Sheffield.

The 1982 World Championship quarter-finals brought Stevens his first major clash with White, and the young Londoner took the opportunity to relieve him of his two-year-old distinction as the youngest ever semi-finalist: 'My game wasn't straight, and neither was my head,' admitted Stevens. 'I just didn't know which way to turn and I even considered going back into the construction business to earn a living.'

But he soldiered on, helping Thorburn and Bill Werbeniuk to win the State Express World Team Classic for Canada in October 1982 and reaching two major semi-

Kirk Stevens in play. Jimmy White sits out

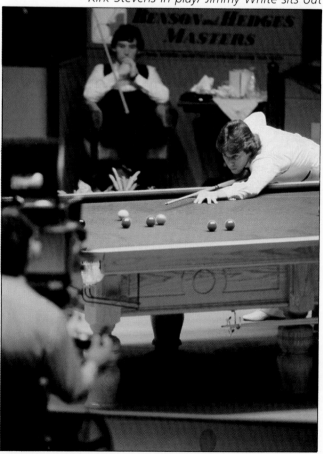

*Two more scenes from the epic Stevens/White 1984
Benson and Hedges Masters semi-final*

finals, the Jameson International and Lada Classic, before
being dealt another punishing blow: defeat by Thorburn in
the 1983 World quarter-final when victory seemed his at
two up with three to play.

A few months earlier he had moved to Chesterfield
under the management of Mike Watterson, chiefly known
as the promoter who brought the Embassy World Championship to the Crucible. The partnership was dissolved
after the 1983 Championship and Stevens once more
returned to Canada, this time with an arrangement that the
Salford club owner and manager, Geoff Lomas, would take
him under his wing for the 1983-84 season. In conjunction
with his associate Harvey Lisberg, Lomas, who already had
White and Tony Knowles on his books, provided him with a
home base and moral support.

'For the first time I could look out into the crowd and
know I had someone rooting for me.' said Stevens. 'Now I
have nothing to worry about except playing snooker. Geoff
takes care of everything else and, unlike others, under-
stands that I have to travel home to Canada from time to
time. I get very homesick and that's when my game suffers.'

John Hennessy

Ray Reardon

(Wales)

BORN: 8.10.32
HOME: STOKE
WORLD RANKING: 5

Ray Reardon looked back on the 1983-84 season as the worst of his career. He began the campaign as the world's worst No 2 and finished it as No 5 — by his own high standards, a disaster. In major tournaments, he beat only one player ranked in the top 16.

He started by suffering a humiliating 5-0 defeat by Willie Thorne in the second round of the Jameson International. Thorne again came out on top, this time 5-3, when they met in the third round of the Professional Players Tournament of which Reardon was the inaugural winner in 1982.

He captained Wales to the final of the State Express World Team Classic but failed to win a single frame in either of his matches against England. The Coral UK Championship saw him reach the quarter-finals before going out to Jimmy White. He went the same distance in the Hofmeister World Doubles with his partner, John Spencer, only to be beaten by the John Virgo/Cliff Thorburn combination. After losing to Rex Williams in the last 32 of the Lada Classic, he went out in the quarter-final groups of the Yamaha International Masters, an event he had won the previous year. Winner of the Welsh Professional Championship three times, he lost in last season's semi-final to Cliff Wilson and a crushing 13-2 defeat by Kirk Stevens ended his 1984 Embassy World Championship hopes in the quarter-finals.

Set against his six world titles, his four appearances in the Benson and Hedges final (albeit only once as the winner) and innumerable big prize money cheques, it was a travesty of his ability.

To many people — and for many years — Reardon has epitomised all that is cultured and gentlemanly in the professional snooker player, while remaining one of the game's tough competitors.

He came up the hard way. Born in Tredegar, almost at the top of the Rhymney Valley and in the heart of the South Wales coalfields, he took his place in the pits when the time came. But if mining was his living, snooker was what he lived for and he won the Welsh amateur title for six successive years, a sequence which began on his seventeenth birthday.

The mines were still waiting for him when his family moved to Stoke, but a roof fall that left him trapped for more than three hours before he was finally dug out was an experience which he had no inclination to risk again.

There were also risks at times in the City of Stoke police force: he was twice commended for bravery before he decided, displaying another kind of bravery, at the age of 35 to gamble on a career in professional snooker.

Ray Reardon gets his chin down; John Virgo tries to keep his up; referee John Smythe just watches

He had won the English Amateur Championship in 1964 — three years previously — and a subsequent trip to South Africa led to an introduction to Union Billiards representative Ken Shaw, who was in a position to offer him a professional tour. That offer convinced Reardon it was time to forfeit his amateur status.

He made his debut in the then disorganised and somewhat unrecognised, at least by the general public, World Championship in 1969 and suffered a single frame defeat at the hands of Fred Davis 25-24. He won the world title for the first time the following year, overcoming a semi-final challenge from reigning champion John Spencer and defeating John Pulman in the final.

Six months later, he lost his crown in Australia, where the event was being staged for the first time, beaten by Spencer in the semi-finals. It was 1972 before the World Championship was held again and he went out to Rex Williams in the quarter-finals; but in 1973, the first year the Championship was condensed into two weeks, Reardon beat his great rival of the period John Spencer 23-22 in the semi-finals, after trailing 12-19, and Eddie Charlton in the final to reclaim the title.

Four more world crowns came his way: he retained the title in Manchester in 1974; in Melbourne, the following year, he came from six frames down with only nine to play

to beat Eddie Charlton 31-30; in 1976 he made it four in a row with a victory at Wythenshaw; 1977 saw him lose the crown to Spencer in the quarter-finals, but he won it back, his sixth in all, at Sheffield's now famous Crucible Theatre in 1978.

Little did anyone then think that it would be October 1982 before he won another major first prize, the Players Professional Tournament in Birmingham. He was always hard to beat, and because of his achievement and personality he remained a box office attraction; but problems in finding, and then adjusting to, a new cue underminded his confidence and his results were patchy.

Hard practice was the only answer and his 1981-82 campaign ended with defeat by only two frames, 18-16, by Alex Higgins in the Embassy World Championship final. Then came three first prizes (PPT, Welsh and Yamaha) and two second (Benson and Hedges Masters and Benson and Hedges Irish Masters) in the 1982-83 season before all the ground he had made up in these years was lost again.

Michael Gouge

Breaking off: Reardon below, Virgo inset

Eddie Charlton
(Australia)

BORN: 13.10.29
HOME: SYDNEY
WORLD RANKING: 6

If the BBC ever needs anyone from snooker for an over 50's *Superstars* event, Eddie Charlton is their man. His pleasure in playing no less than nine sports competitively made him reluctant to concentrate on snooker and he was 37 before he turned professional; but the physical conditioning of those early years has helped him, at the age of 54, not only to maintain his standard but, he thinks, improve it.

In fourteen attempts at the world title in the last fifteen years, Charlton has eight times reached the semi-finals, at least, without ever winning it.

'You can't win it unless you're fit,' he said after one of the daily six-mile runs he still undertakes at the brisk pace at which he carried the Olympic flame for a stage in the 1956 Melbourne Games. Until last year he was still putting his shoulders and upper body through the rigorous exercises he did as a member of the crew which won the Australian Surf Rowing title in 1950.

His deeply hooded eyes look like a boxer's and in his youth they were. He won three tournaments as an amateur and boxed an exhibition with Dave Sands, who was then world middleweight champion. Cricket, tennis, golf, squash and speed roller-skating were also in his program-me and he spent the last decade of his eighteen-year soccer career in First Grade. Recently he took up ice-skating.

A comparison with his fellow Australian Ron Clarke, the great even-paced runner who broke world records but who was invariably outsprinted on the run-in when Olympic titles were at stake, is irresistible. Day in, day out, "Steady Eddie" plays to a high standard: but his sixth place in the world rankings has been achieved without ever winning a major tournament in Britain and for the least three seasons, the period over which world rankings are assessed, without ever reaching a final.

'I lost to Steve in six tournaments the last two seasons and he went on to win all of them,' he points out, reasonably enough. 'Tony Knowles has won two major titles but in the Jameson final in 1982 he played David Taylor and in the PPT in 1983 he played Joe Johnson, who are good players but not the tops.' The Jameson semi-final and the Lada Classic quarter-finals were Charlton's best runs in 1983-84.

Snooker players carry scar tissue in their minds as surely as boxers carry it round their eyes. They have to resist the psychological jabs which fate, circumstances and their opponents direct at it. The world title has slipped tantalisingly out of Charlton's reach so often that, if he is ever to win it, he will have to overcome the doubts that fester in the emotional wounds of near-misses.

Eddie Charlton, the great competitor

'looking down the gun barrel'

He looked a certainty to reach the final in Australia in 1970. He was to play another Australian, Warren Simpson, who had beaten him only once in the preceding six years. Driving to their semi-final, Charlton was involved in a serious car accident. The couple in the on-coming car were badly hurt. He was not, but said: 'I just couldn't play.' He lost 27-22.

In the 1973 world final, played over the best of 75 frames in Manchester, he led Ray Reardon 7-0. At the start of play on the fourth evening it was 27-25 to Reardon but with television lighting, much cruder then than now, in operation for the first time, Charlton won the first three frames to lead 28-27. Reardon, obviously affected by the lighting, complained about it. The interval was taken early and some lights were switched off. On the resumption, Reardon won the next three frames and was never behind again.

In the best-of-61-frames final in Melbourne in 1975, Charlton led 29-25 going into the final session and was 22 points in front with only the last four colours remaining in the first frame of the evening. Brown was on its spot; the cue-ball lay a few inches from the middle pocket, offering an almost straight pot.

'I could have just pushed the brown in and Ray would have needed two snookers, but then I thought that that wasn't the way to play,' said Charlton afterwards. 'I brought the cue-ball off the baulk and side cushions for the blue but the brown wobbled in the jaws and stopped, overhanging the edge of a pocket.' If the brown had dropped, Charlton would have been five up with six to play, but Reardon snatched the frame and went on to win 31-30.

'That sort of thing affects you, no doubt about it,' he said. 'It works the other way as well, of course.' When Willie Thorne missed what would have been a match-winning black in 1979, Charlton beat him from three down with four to play. In the next round, he beat Cliff Thorburn from four down with five to play.

If a player is on the threshold of winning a match or a crucial frame, it is hard to cope with having the door of success slammed in his face. Even when the scoreboard had Thorburn still in the dominant position against Charlton, Thorburn afterwards confessed: 'The feeling that I was going to lose came over me like a tidal wave.'

Meanwhile, 1979 at the Crucible gave Charlton his 'biggest disappointment of all.' With Reardon and Spencer, six times and three times champion respectively, already beaten, there was no one left who could remotely match Charlton's experience and record. But, after the last sixteen frames of their semi-final had run all afternoon and, with a brief interval, until 1.40 a.m., Terry Griffiths, in his first professional season, beat him 19-17.

Leading 17-16, Charlton snookered Griffiths with one red remaining. 'I walked back to my seat thinking for the first time 'I've got him',' said Charlton. 'Even if he hits the reds there's a good chance it'll finish where I can pot it and win the frame. This would put me two up with three to play and after all the amount we'd played and the lateness of night and all, I felt Terry wouldn't be able to beat me three out of three. On top of that, Dennis Taylor was through to the final and Dennis had never beaten me. What happens? Terry not only hits the red but flukes it in the middle pocket.'

Later, Griffiths fluked the brown with an incredible baulk cushion to middle pocket double and twice saw the blue go safe in attempting to pot it before his third attempt levelled the score at 17-17.

'I think it's fair to say that with a bit of luck I could have won the Championship three times but I also have to say that the reason I haven't won it is because I wasn't good enough. If I had been, I wouldn't have needed the luck,' says Charlton.

Charlton, with his straight as a gun-barrel cueing, prepares his body in such a way as to reduce as far as possible the pressure on his mind: he does not smoke; he drinks little and leads an athletic life; he takes his portable fruit-blender, in which he constantly crushes fresh fruit into fortifying drinks, everywhere; and he practises for three to five hours a day.

He plays billiards very little but, at Portsmouth last March, he contested with Mark Wildman a desperately close final in the Strachan World Professional Championship, through whose 114-year history only 13 players have ever gained the symbolic immortality which is conferred on those whose names appear on the championship roll.

As the last few hundred seconds of the five-hour final ticked away, Charlton came to the table for what proved to be the last time, 87 behind with eight minutes to play.

Briefly, he was in perfect position; suddenly, he was struggling to score. At one point, unable to decide between tricky alternatives, he occupied a full, agonising minute without striking a ball. He was still in play with 54 — one point for each year of his age — when time ran out.

Clive Everton

Jimmy White

(England)

BORN: 2.5.62
HOME: WIMBLEDON
WORLD RANKING: 7

Few of BBC's viewing millions will ever forget Jimmy White's remarkable performance in the 1984 Embassy World final against Steve Davis.

At 22 years and five days, he failed by only two frames to become the youngest ever champion, but the way he fought back from 4-12 at the end of day one to force a desperate finish on day two captivated a nation.

White, who used to skip school in Tooting to learn his snooker trade, admitted that his 16-14 semi-final win over Kirk Stevens had taken it all out of him, as he struggled on that first day: 'I just wasn't in the game.'

That all changed spectacularly on the second day as White reeled off the frames to produce a final night of almost unbearable tension. Journalists wrote and re-wrote their stories, but no fairytale ending was ever published as Davis edged to his third title by an 18-16 margin.

White drowned his sorrows in a few drinks and returned home with his wife, Maureen, to join their young daughter. He took with him a £22,000 runners-up cheque — just right for a family about to move into a £100,000 house in Wimbledon's stockbroker belt.

Among the other money White is investing in his new house is the £35,000 he picked up for winning the Benson and Hedges Masters title at Wembley early in 1984. Throw in a few more cheques and White had collected £73,550 in prize money in the 1983-84 season — second only to Davis.

The Masters victory came in front of a capacity crowd at the Wembley Conference Centre, when White hammered Welshman Terry Griffiths 9-5 in the final. His form was as exceptional as it had been in beating Stevens 6-4 in the semi-finals, during which he made two centuries and the Canadian a 147.

But take away these two tournaments and the rest of the season, with only one ranking point from three events, could never be counted an outstanding success. He did reach the Coral UK semi-finals and with Tony Knowles the final of the Hofmeister World Doubles but his manager, Geoff Lomas, publicly slated his young star.

Nevertheless, White has come a long way since those early days when his father, Tom, used to take him as an 11-year-old to play snooker at Balham United Services Club. He took to the game immediately: 'He was a natural,' says Tom.

He has always been heading for the top: he was only 16 when he became the youngest ever winner of the English Amateur title, making a break of 130 in the final down in the depths of Cornwall; at 18 he travelled halfway round the world to become the youngest ever world amateur champion in Tasmania; in 1984 he went to Sheffield knowing it was his last chance to become the youngest ever world professional champion.

Alex Higgins, who collected his first world title when he was nearly 23, had beaten him from two down with three to play in a great semi-final in 1982, but last spring he was a nervous, excited onlooker during the final with Davis, always cheering and encouraging White.

'I wanted Jimmy to win badly. He's my sort of player. He's like me, the crowd love him and his style,' proclaimed Higgins.

Away from the bustling Sheffield snooker madhouse, in his quiet country retreat in the Peak District at Castleton (aptly named Hope Valley), White was soon expressing hopes for the future.

And these are in no way unrealistic: in only three and a half seasons as a professional, his successes include first prizes in the Langs Scottish Masters and Northern Ireland Classic in 1981 (beating Davis in both); two second prizes in 1982, in the PPT and Yamaha International Masters; and a string of semi-finals and quarter-finals. Everyone knows White has it in him to be world champion one day.

Terry Smith

Danger: genius at work!

Terry Griffiths
(Wales)

BORN: 16.10.47
HOME: LLANELLI
WORLD RANKING: 8

For the first time since he turned professional in 1978, Terry Griffiths failed in the 1983-84 season to land one of the major titles on offer on the circuit. By this — and only by this — high standard, it was the worst of his career.

He reached the finals of both the Benson and Hedges Masters events in England and Ireland, only to lose to Jimmy White and Steve Davis respectively.

'It may have been the worse season I've ever had' says Griffiths, 'but I still finished third in the money list behind Steve and Jimmy. If it hadn't been for Steve I would have won a lot more too. Anyway there wasn't much else to win after him.'

The jinx was on Griffiths at the season's start when Cliff Thorburn knocked him out of both the Jameson International (semi-finals) and Langs Scottish Masters (first round). In the Professional Players Tournament his reputation took another blow when he found himself a shock second-round loser to Eugene Hughes, even though the Irishman had forfeited the first frame for late arrival.

Certainly the season had not started well for a player much maligned in the media for his slow play and it did not help when his tactics were scrutinised by all and sundry. It was clear that he tried to quicken the pace against Alex Higgins in their semi-final of the Coral UK Championship, but that only made the game more difficult for him and he lost 9-4.

Smooth cueing (right); a problem with the half butt (below)

The New Year looked as if it might bring Griffiths a change of fortune when he reached the Benson and Hedges final at Wembley, but unfortunately "Whirlwind" White truly lived up to his nickname that day.

After their titanic Lada Classic quarter-final battle, in which Davis beat him 5-4, Griffiths might have been expected to have given the world's No 1 a better run for his money in the Benson and Hedges Irish Masters final: but he lost 9-1. 'I was murdered,' said Griffiths.

Their Embassy World Championship quarter-final at Sheffield was much tighter, but Davis still won 13-10.

Terry Griffiths works out his options

Apart from the *Pot Black* title there was no addition to the Griffiths trophy cabinet in 1983-4. 'It's still better than working,' he said in his matter-of-fact manner, bearing in mind that Llanelli had known him as a postman, bus conductor and insurance clerk before he became famous. 'From Llanelli League to World Champion,' said Terry's father, Martin, after Griffiths had astounded everyone, and become a hero to millions overnight, by beating Perrie Mans, Alex Higgins, Eddie Charlton and Dennis Taylor to land the Embassy World Championship in his first attempt in 1979.

The following season, Griffiths coped admirably with the transformation in his public and personal life. He won the Benson and Hedges Masters, the first of what was to be a hat trick of Benson and Hedges Irish Masters titles, and also reached the finals of the Canadian Open and the Coral UK.

But his defence of the world title in 1980 lasted only one match — he lost 13-10 to Davis after conceding the opening seven frames. Davis was to haunt Griffiths for the next two years.

He hammered him 9-0 in the 1980 Coral UK semi-final and 16-3 in the 1981 final, the first of five consecutive major finals they contested that season. Griffiths scraped home 9-8 on the final black in the Lada Classic; Davis took the Benson and Hedges Masters 9-5 and the Yamaha International 9-7 before the Welshman won the Benson and Hedges Irish Masters 9-5. The surprise of the 1981-82 season was that they both lost in the first round of the Embassy World Championship.

Despite their rivalry, they teamed up in Barry Hearn's managerial stable, a move which worked wonders for his finances and which helped a more relaxed Griffiths to beat Davis on the way to collecting the Coral UK crown for the first time with a terrific 16-15 final victory over Higgins.

Frequently as he has been involved in the later stages of tournaments, that was Griffith's last major success. 'Yes, I have had my downs,' he admits. 'But everytime I look at my house and drive my Mercedes I think to myself — so what?'

Graham Nickless

Alex Higgins
(Northern Ireland)

BORN: 18.3.49
HOME: MANCHESTER
WORLD RANKING: 9

Mercurial, flamboyant, unstable, trouble-torn, tempestuous are only a few of the adjectives which have described Alex Higgins during his 13 years as a professional snooker player.

He exploded on to the mainland British scene in 1971, and it took him from January of that year until February 1972 to win the then season-long, round-the-country World Professional Championship by beating John Spencer in the final. It was a decade before he was to win the title again, ten years which spanned snooker's re-birth and subsequent growth into a major sport.

In that cold February week in 1972, the centre of snooker, the folk sport, was Selly Park British Legion, a small club (unpretentious or grotty according to your point of view) in the suburbs of Birmingham. The six-day final coincided with an industrial dispute and there were power cuts to add to the chaos that had already been created by the tiered seating — chairs on top of beer crates — and the excitement that, in retrospect, was caused by the emergence of something new in snooker.

The novelty was youth, and not of the boy-next-door style either. Snooker had hitherto been a staid game, requiring thought and patience whether played in the local league or by a professional.

Higgins can hardly be said to have been wanting in thought. Some of the shots he played were of such originality and brilliance that the word genius was attached to him; and the speed of his thought processes, so quick that he seemed to sprint over the long distance of that final, made the label stick all the harder, and won him the nickname "Hurricane".

In the 1930s, boxing had been the traditional sporting escape route; but now here was a youth from the backstreets of Belfast who had learnt his snooker the hard way, playing for money, mostly in a sleazy billiard hall called the Jampot on the Donegal Road.

He crossed the Irish Sea to try his luck in Lancashire and the folklore began: 'I'm a snooker player. I play for money. Who'll play me?' is the legendary account of his arrival.

Soon, with the world title under his belt and the game beginning to grow, his antics brought snooker to the notice of the media. Snooker, lucky to be represented in the results round-up, overjoyed to be given two paragraphs on the sports pages, began to command more space — frequently for the new champion's off-the-table activities.

Called, on more than one occasion, to account for his behaviour to the committee and later the board of the WPBSA, Higgins has been reprimanded, fined, and made to forfeit world ranking points, but whatever his misdemeanours or outbursts he has remained the game's biggest box office attraction.

In the Higgins corner

His virtuosity on the table can induce in a crowd a hush so tense that it threatens, any second, to break into mass hysteria. Indeed, the tendency to play to audiences rather than for victory became one of his most self-destructive traits.

Nevertheless, he won the Benson and Hedges Masters in 1978 and 1981, the British Gold Cup in 1980 and was runner-up twice in both the Coral UK in 1980 and 1982 and the Benson and Hedges Masters in 1979 and 1980.

He reached two world finals, in 1976 and 1980, but lost to Ray Reardon and Cliff Thorburn respectively, the latter beating him after Higgins had lost four frames in succession from a 9-5 lead.

After his victory over Steve Davis in the 1980 world quarter-final, he did not beat him again in competition until the Coral UK final last season. In spite of his eventual defeat, Davis dominated the game with his steadiness, composure and brilliance, albeit of a more controlled and predictable variety. He was in no hurry to get anywhere; Higgins wanted to conquer the world in case, next time he blinked, there was no world left to conquer.

Higgins did not have to beat Davis in his bid to recapture the world title in 1982: Tony Knowles did that for him in the first round. With Davis and Terry Griffiths, the season's other dominant player (who also failed to survive his first match), out of the running, the cards were really falling his way. He got past Doug Mountjoy 13-12, Willie Thorne pressed him to 13-10 and in the semi-finals the "Hurricane" met the "Whirlwind", snooker's other fast, fluent genius, Jimmy White, who was out to supplant him in the record books as the youngest ever world champion.

Two up with three to play, White was on the verge of making the final, but instinct took over in the heat of the battle and Higgins, in a display of death or glory potting, made a clearance of 69 to save the match, which he eventually took 16-15.

From 15-15 in the final he won three straight frames — with a total clearance of 135 in the last — to beat Ray Reardon 18-15 and become the self-styled "People's Champion" amid emotional scenes featuring his wife and baby daughter.

If the added responsibility of paternity had helped him regain the world title, it did not help him sustain his form. The following season, he reached the final of the Coral UK (losing 16-15 to Griffiths) with performances that were not Higgins at his most distinguished.

But much worse was to follow. Just before the start of the 1983-84 season, his marriage began to disintegrate and he suffered a series of ignominious defeats in the early part of the circuit, losing 5-2 in the first round of the Jameson International to Dave Martin and by the same score-line to Mike Watterson in the first round of the Professional Players Tournament.

However, stability was to re-enter his life during the Coral UK Championship at Preston Guild Hall in November 1983. His estranged wife, Lyn, suddenly arrived to watch him play,

differences were resolved and, with his emotional equilibrium restored, he reached the final.

The awesomely cool figure of Steve Davis stood between him and the title. Davis had drubbed him several times in the past and looked like doing so again when he won the first of the four sessions 7-0. But Higgins the battler, Higgins the winner, won seven of the eight frames on the first evening and eventually triumphed 16-15.

The emotion on which he thrives so much was not to be rekindled in the rest of the season. He lost 5-2 to John Parrott in the Lada Classic, 5-1 to Tony Knowles in the Benson and Hedges Masters. His best performance was in the Benson and Hedges Irish Masters where he beat Bill Werbeniuk and Ray Reardon before losing 6-4 to Davis in the semi-finals. His sojourn at Sheffield for the World Championship was brief as he lost 10-9 to the 20-year-old Londoner, Neal Foulds, in the first round.

For all his hell-raising image, some of it justified, he needs the security of a home life and family to which he can escape from the emotional high so necessary to his finest performances.

Janice Hale

A tricky rest shot; Tony Knowles hovers for the outcome

Tony Meo

(England)

BORN: 4.10.59
HOME: MORDEN
WORLD RANKING: 10

Tony Meo shocked his friends and supporters when he announced after his surprising first round defeat by Silvino Francisco in the 1984 Embassy World Championships: 'I'm just a loser.'

Allowances had to be made for his bitter disappointment, but if one swallow doesn't make a summer then one bad result — albeit in the most important tournament of the season — doesn't make a loser. After all, both Alex Higgins and Tony Knowles also fell at the first hurdle in Sheffield.

The fact is that Meo made tremendous strides last season and came agonisingly close to winning his first major title, the Lada Classic. He was within a straightforward yellow to pink clearance of beating Steve Davis for the £18,000 first prize and the title when he was distracted by a supporter's untimely cry of 'Come on, Tony.' The yellow, which would have put him in a frame and match winning position, went wide of the pocket and a couple of minutes later he was a 9-8 loser.

Despite that cruel setback and his subsequent failure against Francisco, Meo had a splendid season. He soared from 24th in the ranking to tenth, finished fifth in the money list with over £48,281 in prize money and had a share in two major titles, the Hofmeister World Doubles with Davis, repeating their success of the previous season, and the State Express World Team Classic with Davis and Knowles.

Meo is still without that elusive first major title of his own, but he proved last season that he is now a force to be reckoned with in the game. Events away from the snooker table helped to strengthen his character. October 1983 was to be a traumatic month in which, as husband, father and home owner, he discovered the true meaning of responsibility, having just turned 24.

First, his three-year-old daughter, Gina, contracted meningitis. Within a few days, her eleven-month-old brother, Tony junior, was stricken by gastroenteritis, a serious illness in an infant, and the two children were soon in the same ward of St. Thomas's Hospital, London. Meo, and his wife, Denise, were spending more time at the hospital than in their new three-bedroomed semi in Morden in suburban Surrey.

Their torment lasted only a couple of weeks. Both children began to make rapid recoveries without any after-effects but while Tony Meo, father, was in turmoil, Tony Meo, professional snooker player, had a living to earn.

He carried on manfully: although he lost to Mike Watterson in the last 32 of the Jameson International at Stockport, he reached the semi-finals of the Professional Players Tournament at Bristol and then helped Davis and

Knowles to an England victory in the State Express World Team Classic at Reading.

The month ended with a burglary at the Meo residence, when thieves stole snooker trophies, a video recorder, jewellery and shoes: 'Lucky they didn't steal anything important . . . like my cue,' Meo managed to joke.

That cue, seven years old and made of ordinary ash, had helped the dapper left-hander establish himself in snooker's top bracket with a series of consistent, gutsy performances.

Two quarter-finals and two semi-finals in the Coral UK and a quarter-final in the 1983 Embassy World Championship are among the performances with which Meo has forced his way into snooker's elite. Before last season ended disappointingly for him with two more losses to Davis, 5-0 in the Benson and Hedges Masters and 5-4 in the Benson and Hedges Irish Masters, and that first-round defeat in the World Championship by Francisco, he was able to say: 'After what happened to me and my family this last year, I hope I've got my priorities right. I've done OK on the table; I've played consistently and got some good results. But when you boil it down, snooker's only a game. I play it for a living but the important thing is to make your family secure. Nothing can compare with your own flesh and blood.'

Barry Hearn, the manager whose astute and forceful approach has helped his number one charge, Davis, earn a fortune (not forgetting the fortune he has earned for himself), has also done wonders for Meo's self-confidence.

Tony Meo and Steve Davis: partners below; rivals opposite

The very fact that Hearn had enough faith in Meo to take him on in 1982 — along with the mature and self-reliant Terry Griffiths — was a compliment in itself.

Hearn believes in winners and he can afford to be choosy. He is fond of using the word 'class' and his skilful psychology has transformed a somewhat naive and undisciplined young man into a smoothly efficient and thoroughly professional member of the prosperous 'Romford Family'.

Hearn boomed: 'Tony made tremendous strides in 1983. He learned a great deal about how to conduct himself and discover how to be hard when you're out there all on your own under the television lights. The way he came through his domestic problems and still produced winning snooker showed how much he has matured. He's a good professional and I can't think of any higher praise. It's not something I would say about some other players.'

With the cushion of Hearn's protective approach, Meo last season spent less time in the seedy, smoke-filled snooker halls of South London where he grew up and more time on the road with his thoroughly professional stablemates Davis and Griffiths.

Although they remain friends, he saw less of the blissfully talented but woefully undisciplined Jimmy White, who shared a desk with him at Tooting's Ernest Bevin Comprehensive School on the rare occasions when the pair of them had not defected to one or other of the local snooker halls.

London born and bred as he is, his Italian parentage accounts for the characteristically Italian blend of charm and emotion. He cries every time he sees his favourite films — *Rocky I, II* and *III* — and, on reflection, he may draw inspiration from the moral of that saga: everyone has it in him to be a winner if the ability, the courage and the determination is there.

Alexander Clyde

Dennis Taylor

(Northern Ireland)

BORN: 19.1.49
HOME: BLACKBURN
WORLD RANKING: 11

In years to come Dennis Taylor may well have cause to consider the 1983-84 season, and in particular the 1984 Embassy World Professional Championship, as an important turning point in his career.

The performances of the jovial Ulsterman at the Crucible determined whether he would remain in the elite of the world's top 16. 'I hadn't worked out my position in detail but I knew I was in trouble, especially if I lost to Joe Johnson in the first round,' he recalls. The consequences of failure were serious indeed. 'It's not simply a matter of pride, financially it would have been disastrous. You could lose £30,000 over a year and it would also have meant I'd have had to qualify for all the major events.'

Taylor responded superbly to the pressure: he reached the last four, his best performance in the Championship since he lost the final to Terry Griffiths back in 1979 after reaching two of the previous four semi-finals. His ranking, once in peril, actually improved and once more he was back in the world's top dozen.

'Almost as important to me was my attitude before the semi with Steve,' says Taylor. 'I was happy at getting that far but I wasn't satisfied to leave it at that. I was hungry to win the title, more to the point I believed I could and that's why I was so disappointed to lose. I'm not one of these players who go into matches with Davis thinking they're going to get hammered. He is the most consistent player in the world but, if you play well and, critically, if you take the few chances he gives you, then you can beat him. I missed a simple red in the thirteenth frame, the score went 8-5 instead of 7-6 and that was that.'

Nevertheless, the wins over Johnson, John Parrott and Doug Mountjoy had retrieved a season which, till then, had been dismal. Apart from the Benson and Hedges Irish Masters in which he lost 6-5 to Griffiths in the semi-finals, Taylor had not got beyond the second round in any competition. A string of fine results in the Professional League, in which he finished runner-up to John Virgo, provided some consolation, but not enough.

He has twice beaten Alex Higgins and once Patsy Fagan to win the Irish title, but second prize in the Jameson International has been his best performance in five years in major tournaments, albeit with quite a few semi-finals and quarter-finals thrown in.

Three studies of the Association of Snooker Writers 1984 Personality of the Year

In fact, a major title is the only symbol of success which snooker has denied him. He lives with his wife, Patricia, and his three children, Denise, Damian and Brendan in a magnificent three-storey house (with snooker room, of course) on the outskirts of Blackburn, his adopted town.

In the driveway one of the two cars is a Mercedes Coupé with personalised number plate — CUE 82.

He has come a long way since, at 17, he left Coalisland, Co. Tyrone, to live with his aunts in Darwen, Lancashire. Like many others who have crossed the Irish Sea from west to east, he was looking for a job:

'I'd been working in the local pipe factory but there was a spot of bother — nothing to do with me — and the whole shift was sacked! I was offered my job back later but I decided to try elsewhere.'

He had been playing snooker at Gervin's Club in Coalisland since he was nine. By 14 he'd won the town's senior billiards and snooker championships, but there was no yardstick to measure his ability by and when he went to England he left his cue behind: 'I thought the players would all be that much better — they weren't.'

Soon he built a reputation in the North of England and received invitations to play John Spencer (who had already won the first of his world titles) in a 'Find a Champion'

competition run by the *Lancashire Evening Telegraph*. Taylor feels Spencer was instrumental in his being accepted into the professional ranks at the end of 1972. At first he found it hard going but soon he realised that he could supplement his snooker by using his ready wit in his club exhibitions.

'I think humour plays a big part in the game. Many of the newer players are like robots. They don't know when to smile. Some don't know how to. People are there to be entertained. Everyone enjoys a laugh. I try to provide it but I always hold back in tournament play. It could easily put other players off.'

Taylor could make a more than comfortable living on the periphery of the game and has just signed a new three-year contract as a commentator with ITV, a role he thoroughly enjoys. But it is all secondary to his ambition to win titles rather than be recognised as a nice guy who loses in the end. There would surely be no more popular winner.

Alan Green

Willie Thorne

(England)

BORN: 4.3.54
HOME: LEICESTER
WORLD RANKING: 12

The 1984-85 season is the first of Willie Thorne's nine-year professional career in which he will not have to negotiate the minefields of the qualifying competitions. He has finally broken into the world's top 16 — at No 12, an improvement of six places on the previous season.

It is a mystery to the game's devotees why he has taken so long. Having followed up his 1973 British Junior Championship success by beating John Spencer, then almost at his peak, in the 1975 Canadian Open, great things were expected of this tall, elegant player whose seemingly effortless break-building has made him such a crowd-pleaser.

But his only first prize of note came four years after turning professional when he beat Steve Davis and Cliff Wilson on the way to toppling Terry Griffiths on the final black of the Pontins Professional tournament. He won the title again last May beating John Spencer in the final after accounting for Terry Griffiths and Tony Knowles.

A string of injuries and illnesses has held up Thorne's progress. He broke both ankles in a go-karting accident just before the 1982-83 season began and was hospitalised by food poisoning before the 1983 Embassy World Championship. He fell down some stairs before the 1983 Coral UK.

Nevertheless, eleven world ranking points, seven of them earned last season, have put Thorne finally into the top echelon.

In the Jameson International he beat John Virgo — now back in the qualifying ranks himself — in the first round and then destroyed Ray Reardon 5-0 before he himself was demolished 5-0 in the quarter-finals by Eddie Charlton.

'My mind was already on a semi-final with Steve Davis,' said Thorne. 'I had forgotten I had to win the quarter-final first and I could not believe what was happening to me against Eddie. As for the early years, well, perhaps I was just too young. I could never get my mind right at the right times. Part of the problem was undoubtedly the qualifying. I would get peaked up for the qualifiers, then there would be this gap before the tournament proper and I would relax and think: 'Well, I'm there now'.'

He added to his two ranking points from the Jameson International three from the Professional Players Tournament by reaching the semi-finals through wins over Spencer, Reardon and Eugene Hughes before he lost 9-7 to Knowles in the semi-finals. A desperate 10-9 first round win over Virgo in the Embassy World Championship gave him two more ranking points before he lost 13-11 to Cliff Thorburn. His best World Championship performance has so far been a place in the 1982 quarter-finals in which he made a break of 143, his highest in competition, although he has made over 20 maximums in practice.

Willie Thorne: among the elite at last

Thorne earned nearly £25,000 from tournaments alone last season. He was assured of £27,500 in 1984-85, even were he to lose in the first round of every tournament his new status entitles him to play in. He was able to look forward to a trip to the Canadian Masters in October 1984 and his first Benson and Hedges Masters appearance at Wembley in January 1985. Through reaching the last 16 of the Embassy World Championship, he received an automatic invitation to compete in *Pot Black* for the fourth time.

Away from the tables, Thorne has a new house in Oadby, Leicester, is a fervent supporter of Leicester City FC and has taken up Golf. He has been on the board of the WPBSA for the last two years and recently became a summariser on the BBC commentary team, a role he fills only after he has been eliminated from a tournament. The Willie Thorne Snooker Centre in Leicester has been open four years and now boasts 2,000 members and 24 tables.

Steve Acteson

John Spencer

(England)

BORN: 18.9.35
HOME: RADCLIFFE
WORLD RANKING: 13

John Spencer's satisfaction in moving from sixteenth to thirteenth place in the rankings after the 1983-84 season was overshadowed by the threat to his career posed during the summer by persistent double vision.

Until the end of last season, the system in all WPBSA tournaments was that the No 1 seed would play the No 16, the No 2 the No 15 and so on, a pattern which, in the last 16, always projected last season a clash between Spencer and the defending titleholder.

He beat two of them, Tony Knowles in the Jameson International and Cliff Thorburn in the Benson and Hedges, by narrow 5-4 margins and after trailing 2-4, only to lose subsequently to Terry Griffiths in both events after leading 4-2 and 4-3 respectively. The most formidable defending champion of all, Steve Davis, beat him in both the Lada Classic and the Embassy World Championship.

Spencer's current status, respectable as it is, bears little comparison to that which he enjoyed when he won the world title at his first attempt in 1969 and at his third, in Australia, in 1970 before losing at his fourth to Alex Higgins in the 1972 final.

His record in the next three World Championships, in which his best performance was to lose 23-22 to Ray Reardon in the 1973 semi-final (after leading 19-12), did not match up to his performances in other tournaments: he won the Park Drive 2000 three times out of four, both Norwich Union Opens and the first Benson and Hedges Masters in 1975.

Inexplicably, he lost the edge, and at times more than the edge, of his form although there were still isolated successes — in the first Benson and Hedges Irish Masters in 1978, the first Wilsons Classic, forerunner of the Lada, in 1980, and most notably in the Holsten Lager in 1979 when his break of 147, albeit without the television cameras in operation, was disqualified for record purposes because of over generous pockets.

Some say that he was never the same player after his cue was broken in a car accident in 1974. It was pinned together so well that he actually won his next tournament with it but it soon became clear that the life and resilience had gone out of it.

He became the first player to win the world title using a two-piece cue but even this great effort in 1977 owed more to his knowledge, experience and fighting qualities than the easy inspiration of his 1969 and 1970 successes. In some curious way, the rhythm and timing of his cue action was not quite so sweet and, even more seriously, it lost its natural straightness.

The ghastly sequence of results which then ensued included six consecutive first-round losses in the Coral UK and only three match wins in the Embassy World Cham-

John Spencer ponders his position

pionship since he last won it in 1977.

However, as his Bolton club, Spencers, became progressively better established he regained some of his appetite for the game and began to make his presence more felt. His easygoing nature and fondness for practical jokes make it hard to tell how disappointed he has been by his descent from the top of the professional game to a precarious place in its leading echelon.

It is also easy to forget that, in contrast to most new professionals today, he was 33 before he left the amateur ranks and now, at the age of 49, motivation is harder to sustain.

The degree to which he did motivate himself in the 1983-84 season hinted at his renewed sense of enjoyment in the game, a pleasure not easily attained or sustained if life is felt to be full of pressures. He is a senior member of the board of the WPBSA and is one of BBC Television's contract summarisers.

Clive Everton

Bill Werbeniuk

(Canada)

BORN: 14.1.47
HOME: VANCOUVER
WORLD RANKING: 14

Voted Personality of the Year by the Association of Snooker Writers after the 1982-83 season, the best of his career, Bill Werbeniuk sank from eighth to fourteenth in the world rankings after the 1983-84 season, one of his very worst.

His performances between the two seasons gave no hint of the disasters to come. He beat Dennis Taylor, Alex Higgins and Tony Knowles before losing to Cliff Thorburn in the final of the Winfield Australian Masters in Sydney and he won the Winfield New Zealand Masters, a *Pot Black*-style sprint event, in Auckland.

He had reason to think that his efforts during the 1982-83 season would be matched or even bettered in the next ten months but he began to have problems with his cue, lost confidence and 13-5 to Terry Griffiths in the second round of the 1984 Embassy World Championship, after which he announced that he had played with it for the last time. It has now become a memento permanently stored in his Vancouver home.

'The cue was starting to fall apart,' said Werbeniuk. 'I just didn't feel right using it and to try and put things right I had an inch taken off.' This proved to be a mistake and he was never at ease with the cue again.

Assessment. . .

. . .inspection. . .

. . .execution

In 1982-83 Werbeniuk grossed over £30,000 from major events, reaching the final of the Lada Classic with wins over Alex Higgins, Doug Mountjoy and Kirk Stevens and making the highest break, 101, of the tournament. However, he lost the first prize to Steve Davis 9-5.

He also reached the semi-finals of the Tolly Cobbold Classic (beating Mountjoy) and the last eight of the Benson and Hedges Masters (beating Higgins) and Professional Players Tournament (beating Thorburn).

The icing on the cake was his part in Canada's capture of the State Express World Team Classic for the first time, in harness with Thorburn and Stevens. The big man lost only once in the entire competition.

He finished off the season by losing only 13-11 to Alex Higgins in the quarter-finals of the Embassy World Championship after leading by two frames at the start of the final session.

On medical advice, he drinks steadily before and during any match to overcome a nervous disorder which causes his cue arm to tremble. He cannot hold it still even when drinking a cup of coffee. Usually, Werbeniuk spends a couple of hours before a match 'downing' half a dozen cans of lager, topping up at the rate of roughly a pint a frame during the match itself.

He was leading Higgins 9-7 at the end of the penultimate session, but another slow match brought a two-hour delay. By the time he got back to the table he admitted that he could not line a shot up with his usual accuracy. Until the Canadian started working the drink out of his system, which took about half-an-hour, the adrenalin would not flow. By then, Higgins had won three frames in a row and Werbeniuk was never able to recover the advantage.

'There are times when the alcohol can get to me. When that happens I lose co-ordination and it can cost me a frame or two but it never lasts for more than 30 minutes and it doesn't occur too often.'

About this 19-stone heavyweight's 1983-84 season, the least said the better. His earnings from major events dropped to around the £22,000 mark as he failed to progress beyond the second round in any of them, apart from the Hofmeister World Doubles, in which he partnered Eddie Charlton to the semi-finals.

He began the 1984-85 season with a new cue. Only time will tell whether it has helped him regain his old form and confidence.

John Dee

Doug Mountjoy
(Wales)

BORN: 8.6.42
HOME: EWYAS HAROLD
WORLD RANKING: 15

Now that Doug Mountjoy is pulling pints as well as potting balls, he is happier then he has been for six years.

Deciding that he needed another financial string to his bow, he crossed the Welsh border into Herefordshire to run the Temple Bar Inn in Ewyas Harold in March 1984.

'That move took the pressure off me,' he said. 'It gave me security in the money sense. I knew that I didn't just have my snooker to rely on. There's a snooker table at the pub. I work during the lunch time, practise in the afternoon and then pull pints again at night. It's a perfect arrangement. And, of course, I can take time off when I want for all the snooker events. I started enjoying my snooker for the first time in six years. I couldn't wait to get out there and play.'

That had not been the case in the early part of the 1983-84 season when Mountjoy earned only one point in the first three ranking tournaments. He had been struggling for consistency, but in March won his third Strongbow Welsh Professional title by beating Terry Griffiths and Cliff Wilson. He moved to his new pub and rose from eleventh and last to fourth in the Professional League before reaching the last eight of the Embassy World Championship with wins over Mike Hallett and Neal Foulds, a performance which enabled him to stay in the top 16 despite falling three places.

Mountjoy has been among snooker's elite since he won the 1977 Benson and Hedges Masters, his first professional event. He had already won the Welsh amateur title twice and the 1976 World Amateur Championship in Johannesburg.

He won the Coral UK Championship in 1978 and the Welsh Professional title in both 1980 and 1982 before his third success last season. In 1981 he lost to Steve Davis in the final of the Embassy World Championship, but had beaten Willie Thorne, Dennis Taylor and Ray Reardon to get there. His 145 break against Reardon in the semi-finals was a Championship record until it was superseded by Cliff Thorburn's 147 in 1983.

Terry Smith

David Taylor
(England)

BORN: 29.7.43
HOME: MANCHESTER
WORLD RANKING: 16

David Taylor entered his sixteenth year as a professional in sixteenth place in the world rankings. He had begun the 1983-84 season tenth in the world and ended it grateful to have held on to his place in the top 16 by the skin of his teeth.

He lost to Jim Donnelly in the first round of the Jameson International, to Mark Wildman in the second round of the Professional Players Tournament and in the second round of the Coral UK Championship to Joe Johnson.

A 5-4 loss to Murdo McLeod in the final qualifying round (the only one he had to play) of the Lada Classic preceded a first round defeat in the Benson and Hedges Masters and he only kept his place in the top 16 by virtue of a 10-5 win over Canadian newcomer Marcel Gauvreau in the first round of the Embassy World Championship, before Kirk Stevens knocked him out 13-10.

Born in the Cheshire village of Bowden, Taylor discovered snooker when he was 14. He visited a local snooker club with half a dozen friends and found after a few weeks that he could give them a start of 60 points a frame and still win. His amateur career soon blossomed and in 1968 he won not only the English Championship but the World Amateur title in Sydney.

He turned professional immediately; however, he was anything but an instant hit. For the first ten years of his professional career, he was almost professional in name only.

It was a difficult time. He had already quit his first job as a hairdresser to become a swimming instructor and consequently give himself more time to practise his snooker. But it was not working. There were then only a couple of tournaments a year — nothing like the plethora which exists today — and there was not very much exhibition work about.

Taylor spent most of the summer months of the 1970s following the well-trodden path of most other professional snooker players by giving exhibitions at a host of holiday camps. In mid-1974, he was again 'on duty' at a holiday camp. He had not made a century break for months, and he decided it was time to move back to Manchester from Bacup on the outskirts. It was to be the start of better things.

Even so, it was a long, hard road. He spent anything up to seven hours a day at the table and put himself under the wing of Roy Lomas, a famed money-match player, who had never been able to win a major amateur title. Lomas soon spotted the flaws in his game and worked with him until Taylor started to make an impression on professional snooker.

It was in the Coral UK Championship of 1978 that he made people sit up and take notes. He beat defending champion Patsy Fagan in the first round and went on to eliminate John Virgo and Alex Higgins on his way to the final, which he lost to Doug Mountjoy.

His growing confidence helped him defeat Ray Reardon to reach the semi-finals of the 1980 Embassy World Championship and he was runner-up to Steve Davis in the Yamaha International Masters in 1981 and to Tony Knowles in the 1982 Jameson International, an event that saw him eliminate Davis in the quarter-finals. He also performed a memorable feat on the exhibition circuit when in June 1978, at Butlins in Minehead, he made three consecutive total clearances of 130, 140 and 139.

Michael Gouge

Silvino Francisco
(South Africa)

BORN: 3.5.46
HOME: CAPE TOWN
WORLD RANKING: 17

Silvino Francisco is, in seventeenth place, the highest-ranked South African on the circuit, after accruing six of his eight ranking points in the 1983-84 season.

His best win was over Cliff Thorburn which took him to the last 16 of the Lada Classic, a stage he also reached in the Professional Players Tournament and the Embassy World Championship, in which he beat Tony Meo. He was a quarter-finalist in the Jameson International, receiving a walkover from the absent Kirk Stevens and beating the left-handed Glaswegian Jim Donnelly.

One more win in a ranking tournament would have given him a place in the top 16. In retrospect, his best chance of achieving it was against Ray Reardon at the Crucible.

He was poised to take the lead at 8-8 but attempted to make doubly sure of it by potting a blue which would have left Reardon needing three snookers. He rolled it when he should have punched it and Reardon, who had been looking extremely vulnerable, not only won that frame but the next four as well to win the match 13-8, exactly the same score as that by which he had beaten Francisco in their world quarter-final two years before.

As an amateur, Francisco was sometimes overshadowed by his elder brother, Mannie, who had been runner-up in both the World Amateur Billiards and World Amateur Snooker Championships in his time. However, he lost some of his edge after Silvino beat him to reach the semi-finals of the 1976 World Amateur Snooker Championship in Johannesburg. Silvino himself won five South African amateur titles at snooker and three at billiards.

Mannie is now a professional too, although he has never played in Britain as one. His son, Peter, gave the Francisco family a third representative in the professional ranks when he was granted professional status in May 1984.

John Virgo

(England)

BORN: 3.4.46
HOME: GUILDFORD
WORLD RANKING: 18

The worst year of John Virgo's career, punctuated by illness, injury and disappointing results, was capped by the cruellest of ironies: he won the inaugural Professional Snooker League only to find there was no money in the kitty for prizes, no golden cue to celebrate his success, no £18,000 first prize and no national publicity of any note.

Even allowing for the non-participation of the three Barry Hearn management clients — Steve Davis, Terry Griffiths and Tony Meo — and for the withdrawal of Kirk Stevens halfway through, it was no mean feat to top the League with seven wins, two draws and only one defeat in his ten matches. It was a record which should have set him up nicely for his Embassy World Championship first round match against Willie Thorne.

Instead, he bowed out 10-9 and Thorne replaced him in the top 16 of the world rankings, an exchange of status which meant that Thorne, not Virgo, would compete in the 1985 Benson and Hedges Masters.

Leading 9-8, Virgo only needed to pot one more ball for victory and two precious ranking points, but he went in-off the black from a safety shot to give the frame to Thorne. It was virtually the death knell to a season in which he had not secured a single ranking point.

A few months earlier at Northampton, Virgo and Cliff Thorburn were level at 7-7 against Tony Knowles and Jimmy White in the semi-finals of the Hofmeister World Doubles. Knowles committed a foul and was asked by Virgo, who was due to play next, to play again. This somehow confused the Thorburn/Virgo partnership, for Thorburn came to the table next and potted a red, dislodging the black and some other reds into pottable positions.

A foul was rightly awarded for playing out of order and White, from the position Thorburn would have had, made a frame-winning break of 74. 'It never rains but it pours,' was Virgo's only response after White and Knowles had gone on to win 9-7.

Realistically, he says: 'I suppose over the last year or so I've lost some of my battling qualities, for whatever reason — life getting a bit easier perhaps. But I've had plenty of chances and with the seeding system based on four tournaments now, I'm sure I'll be back in the top 16 next season. Playing in the qualifiers should give me the incentive to get back to basics.'

Despite his setbacks, he is never short of work on the exhibition circuit. His wickedly funny impersonations of the world's leading professionals have been enjoyed by millions of TV viewers and have served to keep him in the limelight even when he has been an early loser in the tournaments.

He first made his mark on the game 22 years ago when he won the British Under 16 Championship and three years later he was the Under 19 champion. He steadily built a reputation as one of the North's top amateurs and played fifteen times for England.

But it was a full decade before he made his mark on the game again at national level by winning the British Pairs Championship with Paul Medati in 1976 and reaching the final of the northern section of the English Amateur Championship.

Virgo joined the pro ranks in 1977, travelling south two years later after he had reached the semi-finals of the 1979 Embassy World Championship, in which he lost to Dennis Taylor.

He joined Henry West's Kingston stable along with Patsy Fagan and two then-teenagers, Tony Meo and Jimmy White, in a squad billed as the Magnificent Seven.

He won the Coral UK Championship at Preston in December the same year but even that success was not without trauma. Leading Terry Griffiths 11-7 overnight and needing just three frames to secure his first major title, Virgo arrived at the venue 20 minutes late because he had mistaken the starting time and was promptly docked two frames.

When Griffiths won the opening two frames to level the match, Virgo looked finished but somehow steeled himself to win 14-13. 'If I'd lost that one I think it would have ruined me forever,' he says, even now.

Immediately, he won the Bombay International and the following autumn reached the final of the ill-fated Champion of Champions at the New London Theatre, Drury Lane, where again there was no prize money. Even his keen sense of humour might be hard-pressed to appreciate that, out of all snooker's affluent tournaments, he has played some of his best snooker in the only two serious financial disasters there have been.

John Hennessy

Joe Johnson
(England)

BORN: 29.7.52
HOME: BRADFORD
WORLD RANKING: 19

Joe Johnson has reached nineteenth place in the world rankings without ever having won a match on television. Indeed, he had never qualified for the televised phase of the Embassy World Championship until the spring of 1984 — and then he was beaten 10-1 by Dennis Taylor.

His high ranking is attributable chiefly to his inspired run to the final of the 1983 Professional Players Tournament, beating Jimmy White, Eddie Charlton, Cliff Thorburn and Tony Meo on the way, before losing 9-8 to Tony Knowles.

Up until then, his best performance had been a victory over Kirk Stevens in 1982's PPT, like 1983's untelevised.

Apart from a few glimpses of him sitting down in the edited highlights of his group in the 1983 Yamaha International Masters, he had not appeared on television at all as a professional until his victory over David Taylor put him into the televised quarter-finals of the 1983 Coral UK in which he lost to Terry Griffiths.

However, the 140 break, still a world amateur record, which he made in 1978 just before he went to Malta to finish runner-up in the World Amateur Championship, is safely recorded for posterity on the tapes of Tyne Tees.

John Parrott
(England)

BORN: 11.5.64
HOME: LIVERPOOL
WORLD RANKING: 20

John Parrott suddenly emerged as a new nation-wide hero after two remarkable performances on television in the Lada Classic and Embassy World Championship. Starting the season as just another young hopeful dreaming of the big time, he ended it ranked twentieth in the world.

He qualified for both the Professional Players Tournament and the Coral UK Championship, only to make quick exits to experienced professionals Terry Griffiths and Tony Meo respectively. All the same, this young man, tipped by so many experts to become 'the new Steve Davis' was already making an impression in the right circles.

In January the 19-year-old Liverpudlian's career really took off as he faced Alex Higgins in the first round proper of the 1984 Lada Classic before a packed, excitable Spectrum Arena audience in Warrington.

Despite trailing 0-56, Parrott won the opening frame on the black and went on to lead 4-0. The UK champion pulled two frames back but Parrott's 5-2 win was soon sending

Fleet Street into a flap as newspapers vied with each other for the corniest headline.

Tony Knowles, reported to have said: 'I will stuff the Parrott,' met the teenager in the quarter-finals and went the same way as Higgins, a 5-1 loser.

It took Steve Davis to see off the Young Pretender but not before a dramatic semi-final had gone to the final frame with Davis snatching victory with a 71 break.

Parrott had nevertheless arrived. He fell to earth in his pre-qualifying group of the Yamaha International Masters, but dropped only five frames in three matches in the Embassy World Championship qualifying section at Bristol, walloping the South African champion Perrie Mans 10-1 to earn a first round meeting with Knowles at Sheffield.

Surely the No 4 seed and Professional Players champion would put the record straight this time. It was not to be. Parrott never allowed him to take charge and for the second time in this amazing season sent the Bolton glamour-boy packing 10-7.

The unimpressionable Irishman, Dennis Taylor, gave Parrott more to think about in the next round and after a disastrous second session the teenager was left with the proverbial mountain to climb. And he nearly made it, pulling back from a huge deficit to lose eventually by a creditable two-frame margin, 13-11. So Parrott's magical season ended with his father, Alan, and his business manager and confidant, Phil Miller, both delighted with his progress.

Parrott was 12 when his father introduced him to snooker: 'We were going for a game of bowls. It started raining so Dad suggested we went down to the local club for a game of snooker instead,' he recalls.

His remarkable talent did not take long to shine through. Within six weeks he had claimed his first half-century break and he was soon playing in the Garston League.

His father gave him his first coaching, George Scott took off some of the rough edges, and later Frank Callan, the man who helped Steve Davis perfect his cue action, arrived on the scene; Liverpool businessman Miller was always on hand to offer advice.

It was obvious that Parrott was destined for television's bright lights when, as the 1981 Pontins Junior champion, he returned a year later to win the Pro-Am event, beating Ray Reardon 7-4 (helped by a 25 point start).

He left Liverpool Comprehensive with 6 O' levels. Between February 1982 and July 1983, when he turned professional, he won 15 tournaments, gaining valuable TV exposure by winning *Junior Pot Black* and chalking up overseas experience by winning two Zimbabwe Opens.

In his first year as a professional he showed, on and off the table, that he is the stuff of which world champions are made.

Graham Nickless

Mark Wildman

(England)

BORN: 25.1.36
HOME: PETERBOROUGH
WORLD RANKING: 21

A former British Junior champion at both billiards and snooker, an English amateur snooker international and English amateur billiards champion in 1968, Mark Wildman experienced little success in his last ten years in the amateur ranks before turning professional in 1979.

However, his change of status rekindled his ambitions and refocused his concentration on the game, although he continued to work, until early 1984, as an executive with United Dominions Trust, the city finance house.

By this time, his newly-opened Court Snooker Centre in Peterborough was sufficiently well established to allow him to give his full attention to the game. His work with the ITV commentary team supports his activities on the table.

He reached the final of the World Professional Billiards Championship in 1980 and 1982, before taking the title in March 1984 at Portsmouth by a mere 33 points in a desperately close finish against Eddie Charlton. In January 1983 he also won the UK Professional Billiards title.

By adding to his world and UK billiards titles a series of useful performances on the snooker circuit, he established a claim to be the game's leading all-rounder. He beat the South African, Perrie Mans, to earn a place in the 1983 Benson and Hedges Masters, a performance which gave him his first world ranking point.

He also reached the last 16 of the Professional Players Tournament in 1983 (beating David Taylor), but his outstanding performance was in last season's Lada Classic in which he beat John Virgo, Silvino Francisco and Eddie Charlton to reach the semi-finals when he lost 5-3 to Tony Meo. He also qualified for the televised phase of the Embassy World Championship in 1983 and extended Terry Griffiths to 10-8 in their first round match.

Cliff Wilson

(Wales)

BORN: 10.5.34
HOME: CALDICOT
WORLD RANKING: 22

Cliff Wilson was born ahead of his time: in his teens he was every bit as fast, fearless and brilliant a potter as Alex Higgins or Jimmy White have ever been. Unfortunately, his prime coincided with a time when there was no future in professional snooker and the game was comprehensively ignored by Fleet Street.

Wilson grew up in Tredegar at the same time as Ray Reardon. He was based in the local billiard hall, Reardon in the Miners Institute. The town divided into two factions, each prepared to back its hero for money.

In the Welsh Amateur Championship, Reardon always won and it was not until he left South Wales for Stoke — thus robbing Wilson of one of his keenest incentives — that Wilson won that title in 1956. In the Welsh qualifying section of the English Championship, though, Wilson always won and in 1954 — after winning the British Junior Championship the two previous years — he reached the final of the English Amateur Championship.

A loss of interest, followed by severe problems with his eyesight, resulted in his retiring for 15 years. He returned to the game when asked to organise his works team to compete in a lowly division of the Newport League. His vision problems led him to develop an unusual sighting system with his cue running underneath his right and only effective eye. In spite of this apparent handicap he won his second Welsh Amateur title in 1977, twenty-one years after his first, so earning the trip to Malta from which he returned world amateur champion the following year.

He won the Welsh Amateur Championship for a third time in 1979 and turned professional, not the player that he was in his youth but still good enough, on his day, to shake the best.

From 1981 he qualified for the final televised stage of the Embassy World Championship three years in succession and in the 1982 Jameson International beat Doug Mountjoy and Jimmy White to reach the last eight, a performance which accounts for two of his four ranking points. He also beat Mountjoy to reach the final of the Woodpecker Welsh Professional Championship in 1981 and was again runner-up in 1984, after beating his old adversary Reardon in the semi-finals.

Dean Reynolds
(England)

BORN: 11.1.63
HOME: GRIMSBY
WORLD RANKING: 23

British Junior champion in 1981 and the inaugural winner of *Junior Pot Black* the same year, Dean Reynolds was only 18 when he turned professional with a relatively slim amateur record behind him.

Nevertheless, he reached the last 16 of the Embassy World Championship at his first attempt in 1982, by beating Fred Davis. Accumulating one ranking point for reaching the last 16 of the Jameson International (beating Willie Thorne) and two for making the quarter-finals of the 1982 Professional Players Tournament (beating Cliff Wilson), he rose to nineteenth in the world rankings. But a disappointing 1983-84 season, in which he accumulated no further ranking points, saw him slide to twenty-third.

Perrie Mans
(South Africa)

BORN: 15.10.40
HOME: JOHANNESBURG
WORLD RANKING: 24

Perrie Mans won the South African Amateur Championship at his first and only attempt in 1960 and became South African Professional champion in 1965, a title he has held ever since except for a one year gap in 1979 when Derek Mienie won the title.

He first entered the World Championship in 1970, but his first notable success did not come until 1974 when he scored a victory over John Spencer to reach the quarter-finals, thus equalling the achievement of his father, Peter, who reached the world quarter-finals in 1950.

In 1976, wins over Graham Miles and Jim Meadowcroft took him to the Embassy World Championship semi-final; in 1978 he beat John Spencer, then the defending champion, Graham Miles and Fred Davis on his way to becoming the first South African and the first left-hander to reach the world final.

With his outstanding long potting and awkward, but highly competitive, style, he extended Ray Reardon to 25-18 in that final and the following year won the Benson and Hedges Masters by beating Cliff Thorburn, Reardon and Alex Higgins. The Masters also provided him with a notable victory over Steve Davis in 1981 when Davis, who had just won the Coral UK title for the first time, was the red-hot favourite.

In the last few years, however, Mans has slipped steadily down the ranking list, travelling to Britain only for selected tournaments and not receiving quite the quality and regularity of domestic competition necessary to maintain his best form.

Mike Hallett
(England)

BORN: 6.7.59
HOME: GRIMSBY
WORLD RANKING: 25

Mike Hallett's 5-2 victory over Steve Davis in the Professional Players Tournament in October 1983 was probably the most surprising result recorded in the whole of last season, not because the snooker world does not recognise the young Humbersider's fluency and potential, but because he has so often failed to produce the goods when he has most needed to.

He has qualified for the tournament proper in the last three Embassy World Championships but has never won a match at the Crucible.

However, his 5-4 defeat of Dennis Taylor in the Lada Classic gave him a place in the last 16 of that event and, by increasing his total ranking points to two, enabled him to rise from thirty-second to his present twenty-fifth position in the world rankings.

Dave Martin
(England)

BORN: 9.5.48
HOME: CHESTERFIELD
WORLD RANKING: 26

Second prize in the Yamaha International Masters was the highlight of Dave Martin's 1983-84 season, even if it did not affect his world ranking of twenty-sixth.

Derby Assembly Rooms, the venue for the Yamaha, had previously been a happy hunting ground for him in 1981 when he reached the semi-finals of the Jameson International, with wins over Bill Werbeniuk, Eddie Charlton and Graham Miles before he lost to Dennis Taylor.

He reached the last 16 of both the Professional Players Tournament and the Jameson last season to earn his two ranking points but, for the first time since turning professional in 1981, he failed to qualify for the tournament proper of the Embassy World Championship.

Of his total season's earnings of £11,900, £8,000 came from reaching the final three-man group of the Yamaha, scoring wins over both Ray Reardon and Eddie Charlton at the semi-final stage.

Eugene Hughes

(Republic of Ireland)

BORN: 4.11.55
HOME: DUBLIN
WORLD RANKING: 27

After winning the British Junior Championship in both billiards and snooker in 1975, Eugene Hughes won two Republic of Ireland amateur titles at both games before turning professional in January 1981. He twice represented his country in the World Amateur Snooker Championship and in 1980 in Launceston, Tasmania, made a break of 127 which still stands as a World Amateur Championship record.

His best professional performance was in last season's Professional Players Tournament in which he beat Eddie Sinclair, Terry Griffiths and Bill Werbeniuk to reach the last eight, so earning two ranking points. He also reached the tournament proper of the Embassy World Championship in 1983, but lost 10-7 to Ray Reardon in the first round.

John Campbell

(Australia)

BORN: 10.4.53
HOME: SYDNEY
WORLD RANKING: 28

Once winner of, and twice runner-up in, the Australian Amateur Championship, John Campbell was also a quarter-finalist in the 1980 World Amateur Championship before turning professional in 1982.

He reached the tournament proper of the Embassy World Championship at his first attempt in 1983 and later that year achieved his best professional performance, a place in the quarter-finals of the Professional Players Tournament with victories over Doug Mountjoy, Graham Miles and Dave Martin.

Murdo McLeod

(Scotland)

BORN: 14.1.47
HOME: LIVINGSTONE
WORLD RANKING: 29

With wins over Willie Thorne in the 1982 Professional Players Tournament and David Taylor in the 1984 Lada Classic, Murdo McLeod earned the two ranking points which gave him twenty-ninth place in the world ranking list.

However, his chief claim to fame is winning the Scottish Professional Championship in September 1983 by beating Eddie Sinclair 11-9 in the final.

Neal Foulds

(England)

BORN: 13.7.63
HOME: PERIVALE
WORLD RANKING: 30

An advertisement in *Snooker Scene* offers the services of 'Geoff and Neal Foulds — snooker's strongest father and son combination' for exhibition games. The strength of that unique combination — the first father and son to be accepted as members of the professional association — was demonstrated during the 1983-84 season, when 20-year-old Neal burst into the limelight. In a highly promising first season as a professional, he survived the battles of the qualifying rounds of three major tournaments and collected the prize scalp of Alex Higgins in a sensational first round upset in the Embassy World Championship.

Foulds junior cannot have failed to impress the millions of armchair viewers who witnessed his 10-9 victory over Higgins in his debut at the Crucible Theatre, the daunting atmosphere of which has 'frozen' many more experienced players.

The key to his cool and level-headed approach is his close relationship with the man who has guided his career from the outset: his father, unofficial manager and, above all, close friend, Geoff Foulds.

The younger Foulds started playing when he was 11. 'I stopped him looking down the cue as if it were a telescope and he won a couple of small events but he was 16 before I thought he would make a player,' said Foulds senior. 'Then I gave him a two-piece cue and he started to

wear contact lenses and in about three months he improved out of all recognition.

'I'm also glad that he worked in an office for a year at Providence Capitol. When he started to play full time it made him appreciate what the alternative was.'

Geoff and Neal Foulds are not merely snooker's strongest father and son combination, they are one of life's most solid and secure father and son pairings.

'I've never called him Dad. It's always been Geoff since I was a little boy,' said Neal. 'We've always been good friends and supported each other's matches wherever we've been playing. He encouraged me from a very early age when I used to go to watch him play. We always talk things over and criticise each other but it's always been constructive criticism.'

Geoff, resident professional at the Ealing Snooker Centre

near the family home in Perivale, Middlesex, had a distinguished amateur career which included eleven England caps and five London amateur titles before turning professional two years ago. But his own game now takes second place as he devotes most of his time and energy to guiding his son through professional snooker – a cut-throat world certainly, if not quite as cut-throat as *Give us a Break*, the BBC drama series about hustlers and stroke-pullers on which Geoff is technical adviser, would have us imagine.

Sunday, 20 November, was an especially proud day for the Foulds family. It was Geoff's 44th birthday and it was the day when he and Neal made history as the first father and son to play alongside each other in a major championship, the Coral UK at Preston.

Both had won through two qualifying rounds and, by coincidence, they lined up at the same time, on either side of a giant black curtain, in their first round matches.

Geoff faced Steve Davis, a very different player to the Davis he had beaten a couple of times in their amateur days five years earlier, and duly lost 9-1. Neal also lost 9-4 to David Taylor, the No 9 seed.

'I was very pleased just to qualify,' said Neal who beat Colin Roscoe and Jim Meadowcroft, both 9-2, to get to Preston. 'I wasn't expecting to win many matches in my first season as a professional. There's a big gap to bridge between being a top amateur and competing against the top professionals.'

John Parrott, whom he beat to win the 1982 British Junior title, was among his victims in the pre-qualifying group of the Yamaha International Masters. He won his qualifying group too but, making his first professional appearance in front of the television cameras at Derby, he lost to Doug French, the Bolton professional, who had also beaten him earlier in the season in the Professional Players Tournament.

The qualifying section of the Embassy World Championship brought Foulds his revenge — he beat French 10-5. He crushed Les Dodd 10-4 and overwhelmed Jim Meadowcroft 10-2 with breaks of 102 and 100 to earn his place in the main event at Sheffield.

What made his results all the more remarkable was that he approached his first round clash with Higgins at the Crucible with the unassuming realism typical of his family. 'I'm really looking forward to playing him,' he reflected. 'My aim is to learn all I can and just to play him at Sheffield will be an education in itself. I'm not saying I'll beat him — that might sound silly — but I'll be trying my hardest. If I can play like I did in the qualifying rounds, I must stand a chance. After all, he can be beaten, John Parrott proved that in the Lada.'

He duly did his stuff with a thrilling 10-9 victory and conducted himself in all the post-match interviews with a fine blend of modesty and common sense. He was clearly enjoying himself but Geoff, pleased as he was, was immediately thinking about the next match as he whisked Neal, his wife Pat, eight-year-old daughter Suzy and Neal's girlfriend, Janet, back to Perivale.

'I wanted to get him home, away from the hectic atmosphere at Sheffield and back among his family and friends in Ealing. We had three days before his next match and we had to get him in the right frame of mind for another important match against another very good player.'

As it turned out, he lost 13-8 to Doug Mountjoy but there was still plenty to be pleased about, not only in Neal's performance but in having earned two ranking points to finish the season in thirtieth place, with the consequent invitation to the next *Pot Black* to look forward to as he dreamt a few summer days away in his favourite manner, watching Middlesex from the Nursery End at Lords.

Alexander Clyde

Rex Williams
(England)

BORN: 20.7.33
HOME: STOURBRIDGE
WORLD RANKING: 31

The record books tend to depict Rex Williams chiefly as a billiards player, for after successfully challenging Clark McConachy for the World Professional Championship in 1968, thus ending the veteran New Zealander's unopposed 17-year tenure of the title, he remained champion until June 1980.

He made four successful title defences in 12 years when the championship was contested on a challenge basis, before it was wrested from him by Fred Davis. He regained it two years later after the event had been restored to a tournament principle, beating Davis in the semi-finals by a mere four points, the closest ever finish in the 109-year history of the championship, and Mark Wildman in the

final. He was also the 1983 champion, beating Davis in the final, but did not defend in 1984. He won the UK title in 1979 and 1981.

However, his playing efforts have been primarily directed towards snooker ever since he won the English Amateur Championship at the age of 17. Unfortunately, his early professional career coincided with a profound slump in the professional game as a whole. Indeed, there had not even been a World Professional Championship for seven years until Williams managed to revive it on a challenge basis in 1964. He twice challenged John Pulman for the title without success, but played a key role in first reviving the defunct Professional Billiards Players Association and then transforming it into the governing body of the professional game, the World Professional Billiards and Snooker Association.

With brief intervals he has remained chairman of the WPBSA ever since, steering it through its transformation from a shoestring organisation in keeping with a tiny membership to an international business turning over several million pounds a year.

He beat Ray Reardon to reach the semi-finals of the 1972 World Professional Championship and was beaten only by the odd frame in 61 by Alex Higgins. He was also a semi-finalist in 1974 but in the last decade has enjoyed only intermittent success.

In 1975 he beat Higgins to reach the semi-finals of the inaugural Benson and Hedges Masters; he won the last seven frames to beat Terry Griffiths 9-8 in the Coral UK qualifying competition in the 1978-79 season, in which the Welshman took the world title at his first attempt; in 1979 he beat Reardon, then world champion, in reaching the semi-finals of the Holsten Lager tournament; and in 1980 he reached the last eight of the Coral UK with wins over Doug Mountjoy and David Taylor.

His sole ranking point was obtained in last year's Lada Classic when he beat Reardon to reach the last 16 before losing to Tony Meo, although his 143 total clearance in that match earned him the tournament's £1,000 highest break prize.

His outstanding strength is the quality of his control which was also evident in the 138 total clearance he compiled in losing to Jimmy White in the first round of the 1984 Embassy World Championship, an effort which gave him the break prize of £4,000. He remains one of four co-world record holders for the 147 maximum he compiled against Mannie Francisco in an exhibition in Cape Town in 1965.

Graham Miles

(England)

BORN: 11.5.41
HOME: BIRMINGHAM
WORLD RANKING: 32

Graham Miles came into the 1973 *Pot Black* tournament as a late substitute: he not only won it, but retained it the following year, by which time he had been the surprise finalist in the 1974 Park Drive World Championship, beating Paddy Morgan, John Dunning and Rex Williams before losing to Ray Reardon.

Without ever winning a major title, he remained among the leading group of players for the rest of the seventies, reaching two world quarter-finals in 1977 and 1978 and the Benson and Hedges Masters final in 1977. His best run in the Coral UK Championship was to the semi-finals in 1978, establishing a record break for the event of 139 which still stands, although Tony Meo has equalled it. In 1979 he beat Alex Higgins in the semi-finals of the Holsten Lager tournament before losing to Spencer in the final, and in 1981 beat Cliff Thorburn to win the Tolly Cobbold Classic.

The one ranking point standing to his name was gained in 1982 and will thus disappear after this season, a fact which illustrates that the 80s have so far brought him very little of the success he enjoyed in the previous decade. He is resident professional at Sandwell Snooker Centre, Birmingham.

Past Masters
Joe Davis

Joe Davis took snooker by the scruff of the neck in the twenties and thirties and by the sheer force of his skill and personality hauled it into position as the premier billiard table game.

Without him, snooker would never have had a World Professional Championship. Without him, it would never have graduated from its early venues — a billiard hall in Birmingham, the backroom of a pub in Nottingham — to Thurston's, the billiards holy of holies in Leicester Square, and from there to larger public venues such as the Horticultural Hall, Westminster, where the fortnight-long final, Joe Davis's last, in 1946 attracted over 20,000 spectators and grossed £12,000.

Without him, indeed, it would have been a different game; it was he who transformed it from a somewhat

crude potting contest — 'The sort of game you play in corduroys and clogs', as Tom Reece acidly put it — into the present sophisticated mixture of break-building techniques and tactical complexities.

Originally, Joe was a billiards player. Born in 1901 in Whitwell, a Derbyshire village, he was 13 when he won the Chesterfield Championship, the only amateur event in which he ever competed; at 25 he reached his first professional billiards final; and the whole of Chesterfield turned out at the station to welcome him when he came home world champion in 1928.

It was, though, in the context of 'scraping and scratching to get a living' that he had approached the Billiards Association in 1926 to sanction a Professional Snooker Championship. He won the event (it rated only three paragraphs in *The Billiard Player* and earned him only £6.10s) and retained it until he abdicated in 1946, by which time snooker had overtaken billiards in popularity.

This was because Joe, the Australian Walter Lindrum, the New Zealander Clark McConachy and another Englishman, Tom Newman, had achieved between them a unique sporting distinction: they had become so good at their game that they had killed it as a public entertainment.

Through their total mastery, notoriously of nursery cannons, they achieved such a degree of perfection in their play that it no longer seemed to bear much resemblance to the game of billiards that amateurs enjoyed in their own clubs. Having exhausted one game, it was time to try another.

Even after his retirement from World Championship play, Joe continued to dominate the snooker scene. He was co-leaseholder of Leicester Square Hall which had succeeded Thurston's as the home of the professional game and he was chairman of the Professional Players Association: what he said, went.

He continued to play brilliantly. He made the game's first official 147 maximum in 1955 and was only beaten three times on level terms, on each occasion by his brother, Fred, in his entire career. He won many tournaments conceding substantial handicaps and was unquestionably accepted as No 1 long after he had ceased to play in the Championship.

During the Second World War, he toured theatres from the Palladium downwards with a variety act of intricate trick shots. Early television snooker revolved round him utterly and he was falling very little short of the incredibly high standards he invariably set himself when he ceased public play altogether in 1964.

It was always his priority to present snooker with a sense of dignity and status and no one took more pleasure than him in seeing the World Professional Championship become established at the Crucible Theatre, Sheffield, as one of sport's great annual spectacles. He died in July 1978, aged 77.

JOE DAVIS
World's Snooker Champion. 1927-28-29-30-31-32-33
1978-29-30-32

Fred Davis

It is in one sense premature to describe Fred Davis as a past master because at the age of 70 he was still good enough to qualify for the tournament proper of the 1984 Embassy World Championship. Even if his standard is two or three blacks worse than when he was in his prime, he enjoys the game as keenly as he ever did.

Still, his opponents find that they are not only playing the master tactician but are battling for the affection of the spectators as well. The warmth with which the audience greets Fred, when he arrives carrying the one cue he has used throughout his 54-year professional career, a twinkle as well as the glint of battle in his eye, makes him not just an opponent but part of a legend.

It is the Davis legend of how his elder brother, Joe, began professional snooker, developed it and, on his retirement, almost ended it; of how Fred was recognised by his peers as being hardly, if at times at all, inferior in skill, although he was unable in the public mind to disturb Joe's aura of invincibility.

Joe's retirement came in two stages. In 1946 he retired undefeated from World Championship play after holding the title for the 20 years since its inception. Fred then won the world professional crown eight times, only to find that the abdicated king was not after all in exile: Joe still ruled.

In his wily way, Joe had continued to play in all the other major tournaments, all of them handicapped, and in most of which he held a promotional interest. Fred, the official champion for the best part of a decade, was the only player who ever played Joe on level terms: he beat him three times. 'This made no impact whatever,' said Fred. 'Whatever I did, I was just Joe's younger brother.'

In 1964 Joe retired altogether, leaving behind only five active professionals. There was no Championship at all between 1957 and 1964 and even when it was revived on a challenge basis it passed virtually unnoticed. 'I didn't play much. One season I didn't play at all. I wasn't interested because there wasn't anything to be interested in,' Fred recalls.

'It's different now. There's so much going on it's exciting just to be part of it.' At 70, pension book and all, he intends to remain part of it as long as he can give 'a reasonable account of myself.'

With snooker re-born through television and sponsorship, Fred is the link with its previous incarnation, the younger brother who has become the game's elder statesman.

In 1980, a boyhood inner certainty that he would win the World Professional Billiards Championship — frustrated when snooker superseded billiards as a public entertainment — became reality when he successfully challenged Rex Williams for the title.

Billiards, on which Fred cut his teeth as a youngster in Chesterfield, calls for a vast knowledge of angles and the greatest delicacy of touch, qualities which Fred uses creatively in snooker in his safety play and close-in work around the reds and black. He dislikes hitting the ball hard and in fact lacks the cue power of younger players brought up solely on snooker. Fencing for openings and manoeuvring for position, rather than power shots and out-and-out potting, have always been his style.

In style and doggedness Walter Donaldson was the Eddie Charlton of his day. An excellent long potter, he limited his range of positional possibilities by his reluctance to use side but nevertheless won two world titles. He left his native Scotland long before the war in order to manage billiard halls in Rotherham and Chesterfield, but made no great impact on the professional game before his five years' war service.

After the war, he immediately embarked on a relentless practice programme, shutting himself away for hours on end in the loft of a friend's house which contained a billiard table. Joe Davis retired in 1946 and to the surprise of most Donaldson succeeded him when he beat Fred Davis in the 1947 world final. He also beat the younger Davis in 1950 and was runner-up to him on six occasions before he retired in 1955.

John Pulman, now chiefly known as a member of the ITV commentary team, was world champion from 1957 until his defeat in the quarter-final of the 1968-69 Championship by John Spencer. His peak years unfortunately coincided with professional snooker's greatest depression: when Pulman won the title in 1957 there were only four entries in the World Championship, and for the next seven years it was not contested because it was not considered a viable commercial proposition. When it was restored on a challenge basis in 1964, he made eight successful defences in four years. After the Championship was re-established with a tournament format, he reached the final in 1970 and the semi-finals in 1977.

The Crucible Theatre, Sheffield, home of the Embassy World Championship since 1977

Embassy World Championship

TOTAL PRIZE MONEY: £200,000
FIRST PRIZE: £44,000
ENTRIES: Open to all professionals
TELEVISION: BBC

Steve Davis became the first champion to make a successful title defence at the Crucible Theatre, Sheffield, home of the Championship since 1977, by beating Jimmy White 18-16 in a final whose incredibly dramatic climax was watched by 13.1m BBC television viewers.

Although Davis survived a tense tactical battle against Terry Griffiths in the quarter-finals 13-10, he never actually appeared in danger of losing his title until the final. White recovered from 4-12 overnight to trail only 11-13 going into the final session. At 16-15 there was only one frame in it; but Davis cleared the colours to win the next frame on the black, going two up with three to play, and clinched the title two frames later.

White's disappointing form on the first day of the final was clearly part of the aftermath of his 16-14 semi-final victory over Kirk Stevens late the previous evening. After the Canadian champion had led 12-10 going into the final session, White won five frames on the reel to lead 15-12 but even then only just managed to win 16-14.

Before the White v Stevens match finished in the evening, Davis concluded his 16-9 semi-final win against Dennis Taylor in the afternoon without needing to expend any of his reserves of mental energy.

The 1984 Championship did not produce quite its usual quota of upsets and close finishes. Silvino Francisco eliminated Tony Meo 10-5 and John Parrott's 10-7 victory over Tony Knowles, the No 4 seed, was also a surprise, notwithstanding Parrott's 5-1 defeat of Knowles in the Lada Classic. The standard of the Parrott/Knowles match was patchy and the match itself was overshadowed by its background, chiefly a tawdry three-part 'Kiss and Tell' series by Knowles in the *Sun,* for which the WPBSA later fined him £5,000 for bringing the game in disrepute.

Two first-round matches went the full 19 frames, Willie Thorne beating John Virgo and, in the biggest coup of the Championship, Neal Foulds ousting Alex Higgins.

Foulds and Parrott in turn fell to Doug Mountjoy and Dennis Taylor respectively, although Parrott only conceded defeat at 13-11, after trailing 7-12. The only other similarly close second-round finish was Cliff Thorburn's 13-11 victory over Thorne, although there was some inspired potting and break-building from White, who won ten of the last twelve frames in putting out Charlton 13-7.

Davis v Griffiths, 13-10, was the closest of the quarter-finals but the least close, Ray Reardon's 13-2 defeat by Stevens, was perhaps the most newsworthy: it was the most comprehensive defeat ever inflicted on the six-times champion in the 15 years he had been competing in the Championship.

Rex Williams took some consolation for his 10-6 first round defeat by White from his break of 138, the highest of the event.

Qualifying

Group 1: John Parrott (England) beat Dennis Hughes (England) 10-3; Parrott beat Clive Everton (Wales) 10-2; Parrott beat Perrie Mans (South Africa) 10-0

Group 2: Bernie Mikkelsen (Canada) beat Paul Medati (England) 10-8; Mikkelsen beat Frank Jonik (Canada) 10-9; Willie Thorne (England) beat Mikkelsen 10-3

Group 3: Mario Morra (Canada) beat Geoff Foulds (England) 10-2; Tommy Murphy (Northern Ireland) beat Jack Fitzmaurice (England) 10-8; Morra beat Murphy 10-5; Morra beat Dean Reynolds (England) 10-7

Group 4: Wayne Sanderson (Canada) beat Paddy Morgan (Australia) 10-8; Paul Mifsud (Malta) beat Eugene Hughes (Rep. of Ireland) 10-5; Mifsud beat Sanderson 10-5; Mifsud beat Cliff Wilson (Wales) 10-8

Group 5: Jimmy van Rensberg (South Africa) beat Vic Harris (England) 10-7; Ray Edmonds (England) beat David Greaves (England) 10-0; van Rensberg beat Edmonds 10-9; Silvino Francisco (South Africa) beat van Rensberg 10-3

Group 6: Ian Williamson (England) beat Pat Houlihan (England) 10-5; Mike Hines (South Africa) beat Ian Black (Scotland) 10-5; Williamson beat Hines 10-6; Graham Miles (England) beat Williamson 10-6

Group 7: Matt Gibson (Scotland) beat Gino Rigitano (Canada) 10-7; Mick Fisher (England) beat Paul Thornley (Canada) 10-8; Gibson beat Fisher 10-7; Joe Johnson (England) beat Gibson 10-3

Group 8: Eddie McLaughlin (Scotland) beat John Hargreaves (England) 10-5; Roy Andrewartha (Wales) w.o. John Bear (Canada) scr; Andrewartha beat McLaughlin 10-8; Andrewartha beat Mark Wildman (England) 10-9

Group 9: Jim Wych (Canada) beat George Ganim Jr (Australia) 10-1; George Scott (England) beat Leon Heywood (Australia) 10-7; Wych beat Scott 10-6; Wych beat Patsy Fagan (Rep. of Ireland) 10-3

Group 10: Paddy Browne (Rep. of Ireland) beat Steve Duggan (England) 10-9; Colin Roscoe (Wales) beat Bert Demarco (Scotland) 10-7; Browne beat Roscoe 10-4; Eddie Sinclair (Scotland) beat Browne 10-1

Group 11: Marcel Gauvreau (Canada) beat John Campbell (Australia) 10-7; Graham Cripsey (England) beat Maurice Parkin (England) 10-4; Gauvreau beat Cripsey 10-1; Gauvreau beat Murdo McLeod (Scotland) 10-6

Group 12: Ian Anderson (Australia) beat Gerry Watson (Canada) 10-4; Jim Donnelly (Scotland) beat Paul Watchorn (Rep. of Ireland) 10-7; Donnelly beat Anderson 10-6; Fred Davis (England) beat Donnelly 10-5

Group 13: Warren King (Australia) beat Tony Jones (England) 10-9; Mike Watterson (England) beat Bernard Bennett (England) 10-5; King beat Watterson 10-8; King beat Dave Martin (England) 10-8

Group 14: Joe Caggianello (Canada) beat Mike Darrington (England) 10-7; Bill Oliver (England) beat John Dunning (England) 10-3; Oliver beat Caggianello 10-7; Rex Williams (England) beat Oliver 10-8

Group 15: Neal Foulds (England) beat Doug French (England) 10-5; Les Dodd (England) beat James Giannaros (Australia) 10-1; Foulds beat Dodd 10-4; Foulds beat Jim Meadowcroft (England) 10-2

Group 16: Bob Harris (England) beat Dessie Sheehan (Rep. of Ireland) 10-3; Pascal Burke (Rep. of Ireland) beat Billy Kelly (Rep. of Ireland) 10-7; Burke beat Harris 10-4; Mike Hallett (England) beat Burke 10-5

Competition Proper

First round: Steve Davis (England) beat King 10-3; John Spencer (England) beat Miles 10-3; Terry Griffiths (Wales) beat Mifsud 10-2; Bill Werbeniuk (Canada) beat F. Davis 10-4; N. Foulds beat Alex Higgins (Northern Ireland) 10-9; Doug Mountjoy (Wales) beat Hallett 10-4; Dennis Taylor (Northern Ireland) beat Johnson 10-1; Parrott beat Tony Knowles (England) 10-7; Cliff Thorburn (Canada) beat Morra 10-3; Thorne beat John Virgo (England) 10-9; Jimmy White (England) beat Williams 10-6; Eddie Charlton (Australia) beat Andrewartha 10-4; Kirk Stevens (Canada) beat Sinclair 10-1; David Taylor (England) beat Gauvreau 10-5; Francisco beat Tony Meo (England) 10-5; Ray Reardon (Wales) beat Wych 10-7

Second round: S. Davis beat Spencer 13-5; Griffiths beat Werbeniuk 13-5; Mountjoy beat N. Foulds 13-6; Dennis Taylor beat Parrott 13-11; Thorburn beat Thorne 13-11; White beat Charlton 13-7; Stevens beat David Taylor 13-10; Reardon beat Francisco 13-8

Quarter-finals: Davis beat Griffiths 13-10; Dennis Taylor beat Mountjoy 13-8; White beat Thorburn 13-8; Stevens beat Reardon 13-2

Semi-finals: Davis beat Dennis Taylor 16-9; White beat Stevens 16-14

Final: Davis beat White 18-16

Previous Years

Snooker's blue riband event could hardly have been less pretentious in its beginnings. The Billiards Association and Control Council (BA & CC), the then-governing body, was sceptical of snooker's public appeal but Joe Davis, who was then world professional billiards champion, and his friend Bill Camkin, a Birmingham billiard trader, both knew that snooker was becoming extremely popular in billiard halls and clubs and between them brought the Championship into being.

The first final, in May 1927, was staged in one of Camkin's public billiard halls in John Bright Street, Birmingham, and attracted little attention. Few of the early Championships, which included one in which the final was played in a back room of a Nottingham public house, were much more prestigious.

In the mid-thirties, snooker started first to share with billiards and later to monopolise the schedule at Thurston's, the showcase venue of the game in Leicester Square.

Whatever the venue, Joe Davis won the Championship annually and with ease. It was not until he beat his younger brother Fred by only 37-36 in the week-long 1940 final that it looked conceivable that he might lose.

After the war, the Championship continued to be played on a season-long basis with each match lasting at least three days. The 1946 final, in which Joe Davis won the fourteenth, and last, of the titles which made up his 20-year reign as world champion, was played over a fortnight at the Horticultural Hall, Westminster, for the very simple and commercial reason that public support, it was calculated, made such a long match the best paying proposition.

For the next few years, all matches in the Championship proper were of a week's duration with the final over a fortnight, usually in the vast arena of Blackpool Tower Circus. Apart from a couple of years when it was sponsored by the now defunct Empire News, the Championship was financed solely by gate money.

What now seems extraordinary is that the public was prepared to watch not only session after session long before a result was in sight, but many sessions after one or other player held a winning lead.

Such long matches were a very reliable test of skill but made relatively little demand on nerve, a supreme quality in modern snooker when matches are frequently no more than the best of nine frames. Even the world final today is only the best of 35.

Fred Davis, with eight wins, and Walter Donaldson with two, monopolised the title in the decade after Joe's last success, but the appeal of the Championship waned with that of professional snooker in general. Despite his retirement from the Championship, Joe continued to play in other events and was universally regarded as No 1, so the Championship itself, without the best player in it, came to be regarded as hollow.

Other professional events, which were contested on a handicap basis partly because the extended length of matches tended to emphasise even small differences of class between players, suffered because the cast did not change often enough.

Fred did not think it worthwhile to enter in 1957 and John Pulman became champion in a field of four. No promoter came forward to stage the Championship for seven years and it required an initiative from Rex Williams to get it going again on a challenge basis in 1964.

Pulman made seven successful title defences and through his exhibition contract with John Player managed to interest them in sponsoring the 1968-69 Championship on the old season-long knock-out formula with eight entries. John Spencer won the title; in 1970 Ray Reardon took it, again with John Player sponsorship.

An offer to stage the Championship six months later in Australia, the first time it had gone overseas, was accepted, so Reardon was champion only for six months before Spencer regained the title.

No sponsor was obtained for the 1971-72 Championship which straggled on for fourteen months before Alex Higgins won the title in February 1972.

The excitement which Higgins generated at a time when sports sponsorships were beginning to be managed in the highly professional way which has now become so familiar led to West Nally, a West End firm specialising in such matters, enlisting the sponsorship of Park Drive. The 1973 Championship was staged, Wimbledon-fashion, on eight tables at the City Exhibition Halls, Manchester, the whole event being streamlined into a fortnight.

Television coverage was obtained for the two Saturdays of the Championship, the first television exposure it had ever received, and it was clear that the new, modern format was more to the public's liking than the discontinuous method of running the Championship which had been standard in the past.

The 1974 Championship at Belle Vue, Manchester, was not quite so successful, particularly as the final was somewhat one-sided. Park Drive also disappeard as sponsors when the World Professional Billiards and Snooker Association, which had taken over from the amateur-based Billiards and Snooker Control Council (formerly the BA & CC) as the professional governing body in 1971, awarded the 1975 Championship to Australia. This multi-venue event provided Reardon with his fourth title.

The first Embassy World Championship was held in 1976, when a new promoter, Maurice Hayes, secured almost out of the blue the sponsorship of W. D. and H. O. Wills. The top half of the draw was played at Middlesborough Town Hall and the bottom half at Wythenshawe Forum, Manchester, where the final was also staged.

Organisational disasters, ranging from imperfect tables to the absence of blackouts for the vast windows and of telephones for the press, did not prevent Reardon retaining the title but it did hasten the departure of Hayes from the sport.

Embassy also had every reason to flee from snooker at high speed but the persuasion of the WPBSA, added to the ideas put forward by a new promoter, Mike Watterson, saw the name not only remain in the sport but go on to be associated with one of the great, modern sporting success stories.

Inspired by his wife's suggestion after she had seen a play there, Watterson booked the Crucible Theatre, Sheffield, for the 1977 Championship. Nick Hunter, who had the previous year managed to distinguish the dramatic quality of the matches from the organisational imperfections with which they were staged, persuaded the BBC to cover the semi-finals and final—the first time a professional tournament, apart from the studio-produced *Pot Black*, had been shown outside the Saturday afternoon *Grandstand* slot.

So successful was the Championship that the 1978 event carried, for the first time, daily BBC coverage of the fortnight's action (then, as now, Nick Hunter was executive producer) as Ray Reardon regained the title from John Spencer to become champion for the sixth time.

Since then, the Championship has remained firmly at the Crucible, with Embassy's sponsorship and BBC's hours of transmission increasing year by year. Spencer, the first champion to be crowned at the Crucible, pocketed a first prize of £6,000 from a total prize fund of £17,000 in 1977. Steve Davis, in winning the title for the third time in 1984, took £44,000 from the total prize money of £200,000.

The Embassy World Championship, which now receives over 100 hours of television coverage during its 17-day Championship proper, has long since transcended the world of snooker to become, like the Cup Final, the Grand National and Wimbledon, one of the nation's great annual sporting occasions. Terry Griffiths took the title at his first attempt in 1979, and was followed in turn by Cliff Thorburn, the first overseas champion, Steve Davis, Higgins and Davis again.

But behind the necessary summary of who won and who lost lies snooker's collective store of memories: Thorburn's 147 maximum in 1983; the 69 clearance in the penultimate frame which helped Higgins beat Jimmy White from two down with three to play in the 1982 semi-final; the emotional scenes after Higgins's victory that year when his wife and baby daughter emerged from backstage to share his moment of triumph; the mixture of pride and incredulity with which Griffiths, then in his first professional season, said to the nation at 1.40a.m.: 'I'm in the final now you know,' after beating Eddie Charlton in their marathon 1979 semi-final.

1927

First round: M. Inman beat T. Newman 8-5; T. Carpenter beat N. Butler 8-3

Second round: T. A. Dennis beat F. Lawrence 8-7; A. Cope beat A. Mann 8-6; J. Davis beat J. Brady 10-5; Carpenter beat Inman 8-3

Semi-finals: J. Davis beat Cope 16-7; Dennis beat Carpenter 12-10.

Final: J. Davis beat Dennis 20-11

1928

First round: T. Newman beat F. Smith 12-6; A. Mann beat A. Cope 14-9

Second round: Newman beat T. A. Dennis 12-5; F. Lawrence beat Mann 12-11

Third round: Lawrence beat Newman 12-7

Final: J. Davis beat Lawrence 16-13

1929

First round: F. Lawrence beat A. Mann 13-12

Semi-finals: J. Davis beat Lawrence 13-10; T. A. Dennis beat K. Prince 14-6

Final: J. Davis beat Dennis 19-14

1930

First round: F. Lawrence beat A. Mann 13-11; N. Butler beat T. Newman 13-11

Semi-finals: J. Davis beat Lawrence 13-2; T. A. Dennis beat Butler 13-11

Final: J. Davis beat Dennis 25-12

1931

Final: J. Davis beat T. A. Dennis 25-21

1932

First round: C. McConachy beat T. A. Dennis 13-11

Final: J. Davis beat McConachy 30-19

1933

First round: W. Donaldson beat W. Leigh 13-11

Semi-finals: J. Davis beat Donaldson 13-1; W. Smith beat T.A. Dennis 16-9

Final: J. Davis beat Smith 25-18

1934

Final: J. Davis beat T. Newman 25-23

1935

First round: W. Smith beat C. Stanbury 13-12

Semi-finals: Smith beat A. Mann 13-4; J. Davis beat T. Newman 15-10

Final: J. Davis beat Smith 25-20

1936

First round: C. O'Donnell beat S. Lee 16-15; H. Lindrum beat H. Terry 20-11; J. Davis beat T. Newman 29-2; W. Smith beat S. Smith 16-15; C. Stanbury beat A. Mann 22-9

Second round: Alec Brown beat Stanbury 16-15; Lindrum beat O'Donnell 19-6 (retired); J. Davis beat W. Smith 22-9; S. Newman w.o.

Semi-finals: J. Davis beat Alec Brown 21-10; Lindrum beat S. Newman 29-2

Final: J. Davis beat Lindrum 34-27

1937

First round: W.A. Withers beat F. Davis 17-14

Second round: J. Davis beat Withers 30-1; H. Lindrum beat S. Lee 20-11; W. Smith beat T. Newman 16-15; S. Smith beat Alec Brown 18-13

Semi-finals: Lindrum beat W. Smith 20-11; J. Davis beat S. Smith 18-13.

Final: J. Davis beat Lindrum 32-29

1938
Qualifying

First round: H. Holt beat C.W. Read 21-10

Second round: F. Davis beat Holt 23-8

Competition Proper

First round: F. Davis beat Alec Brown 14-6 (retired ill); S. Smith beat C. Stanbury 27-4; J. Davis beat S. Lee 24-7; W. Smith beat T. Newman 16-15

Semi-finals: J. Davis beat W. Smith (n.r.s.); S. Smith beat F. Davis (n.r.s.)

Final: J. Davis beat S. Smith 37-24

1939
Qualifying

First round: W. Donaldson beat H. Holt 18-13; H.W. Laws beat S. Newman 19-12

Second round: Donaldson beat Laws 18-13

Competition Proper

First round: S. Smith beat S. Lee 21-10; W. Donaldson beat C. Falkiner 21-10; T. Newman beat A. Mann 19-12; F. Davis beat C. Stanbury 19-12

Second round: J. Davis beat W. Smith 19-12; F. Davis beat T. Newman 20-11; Alec Brown beat H. Lindrum 17-14; S. Smith beat Donaldson 16-15

Semi-finals: J. Davis beat F. Davis 17-14; S. Smith beat Alec Brown 20-11

Final: J. Davis beat S. Smith 43-30

1940
Qualifying

H. Holt beat C. Stanbury 18-13

Competition Proper

First round: W. Donaldson beat Holt 24-7; J. Davis beat Alec Brown 20-11; F. Davis beat S. Lee 20-11; S. Smith beat T. Newman 22-9

Semi-finals: J. Davis beat Donaldson 22-9; F. Davis beat S. Smith 17-14

Final: J. Davis beat F. Davis 37-36

1946
Qualifying

First round: K. Kennerley beat F. Lawrence 22-9; C. Stanbury beat J. Barrie 18-13; S. Newman beat W. Leigh 16-15

Second round: Kennerley beat T. Reece 8-2 (retired); S. Newman beat Stanbury 17-14

Third round: S. Newman beat Kennerley 21-10

Competition Proper

First round: J. Davis beat W. Donaldson 21-10; S. Newman beat S. Lee 19-12; F. Davis beat Alec Brown 24-7; H. Lindrum beat H. Holt 17-14

Semi-finals: J. Davis beat S. Newman 21-10; Lindrum beat F. Davis 16-12

Final: J. Davis beat Lindrum 78-67

1947
Qualifying

First round: Albert Brown beat J. Pulman 21-14; W. Leigh beat H.F. Francis 19-16; S. Lee beat J. Lees 19-16; K. Kennerley beat C. Stanbury 23-12; E. Newman w.o. H. Holt

Second round: J. Barrie beat F. Lawrence 25-10; Albert Brown beat Newman 28-7; Kennerley beat A. Mann 23-12; Leigh beat Lee 25-10

Third round: Albert Brown beat Barrie 24-11; Kennerley beat Leigh 21-14

Fourth round: Albert Brown beat Kennerley 21-14

Competition Proper

First round: H. Lindrum beat Albert Brown 39-34; S. Smith beat Alec Brown 43-28; W. Donaldson beat S. Newman 46-25; F. Davis beat C. McConachy 53-20

Semi-finals: Donaldson beat Lindrum 39-32; F. Davis beat Smith 39-32

Final: Donaldson beat F. Davis 82-63

1948
Qualifying

First round: C. Stanbury beat E. Newman 26-9; W. Leigh beat H. Holt 18-17; J. Barrie beat H.F. Francis 19-16; J. Pulman w.o. S. Lee.

Second round: Leigh beat Barrie 21-14; Pulman beat Stanbury 19-16

Third round: Pulman beat Leigh 18-17

Competition Proper

First round: F. Davis beat Alec Brown 43-28; C. McConachy beat J. Pulman 42-29; Albert Brown beat S. Smith 36-35; W. Donaldson beat K. Kennerley 46-25

Semi-finals: F. Davis beat McConachy 43-28; Donaldson beat Alec Brown 40-31

Final: F. Davis beat Donaldson 84-61

1949
Qualifying

First round: C. Stanbury beat H.F. Francis 18-17

Second round: Stanbury beat J. Rea 18-17

Third round: Stanbury beat H. Holt 18-17

Competition Proper

First round: W. Donaldson beat Stanbury 58-13; J. Pulman beat Albert Brown 42-29; S. Smith beat Alec Brown 41-30; F. Davis beat K. Kennerley 50-21

Semi-finals: Donaldson beat Pulman 49-22; F. Davis beat Smith 42-29

Final: F. Davis beat Donaldson 80-65

1950
Qualifying

First round: W. Smith beat W.A. Withers 28-7; H. Holt beat H.W. Laws 26-9; S. Lee beat C. Stanbury 20-15; K. Kennerley beat J. Barrie 21-14

Second round: Kennerley beat Smith 22-13; Lee beat Holt 16-8 (retired ill)

Third round: Kennerley beat Lee 21-14

Competition Proper

First round: Albert Brown beat J. Pulman 37-34; W. Donaldson beat K. Kennerley 42-29; G. Chenier beat P. Mans 37-34; F. Davis beat Alec Brown 44-27

Semi-finals: Donaldson beat Albert Brown 37-34; F. Davis beat Chenier 43-28

Final: Donaldson beat F. Davis 51-46

1951
Qualifying

First round: J. Barrie beat S. Lee 23-12

Second round: Barrie beat H.W. Laws 28-7

Competition Proper

First round: F. Davis beat Barrie 42-29; H. Lindrum beat Albert Brown 43-28; W. Donaldson beat K. Kennerley 41-30; J. Pulman beat S. Smith 38-33

Semi-finals: Donaldson beat Lindrum 41-30; F. Davis beat Pulman 22-14 (retired ill)

Final: F. Davis beat Donaldson 58-39

1952

First round: Alec Brown beat R. Williams 39-22; J. Rea beat J. Lees 38-32; Albert Brown beat J. Pulman 32-27 (records incomplete)

Semi-finals: W. Donaldson beat Albert Brown 31-30

Final: F. Davis beat Donaldson 38-35

1953
Qualifying

First round: W. Smith beat J. Lees 21-14; K. Kennerley beat R. Williams 25-12

Second round: Kennerley beat Smith 42-29

Competition Proper

First round: Albert Brown beat Alec Brown 35-26; J. Pulman beat J. Rea 36-25; W. Donaldson beat Kennerley 42-19; F. Davis beat J. Barrie 32-29

Semi-finals: Donaldson beat Brown (n.r.s.); F. Davis beat Pulman 36-25

Final: F. Davis beat Donaldson 37-34

1954

First round: J. Pulman beat J. Rea 31-30

Semi-finals: W. Donaldson beat Alec Brown 36-25; F. Davis beat Pulman 32-29

Final: F. Davis beat Donaldson 39-21

1955

First round: J. Pulman beat R. Williams 22-15; J. Rea beat H. Stokes (n.r.s.)

Semi-finals: F. Davis beat Rea 36-25; Pulman beat Alec Brown (n.r.s.)

Final: F. Davis beat Pulman 37-34

1956

Semi-finals: J. Pulman beat J. Rea 36-25; F. Davis beat R. Williams 35-26

Final: F.Davis beat Pulman 38-35

1957

Semi-finals: J. Pulman beat R. Williams 21-16; J. Rea beat K. Kennerley 25-12

Final: Pulman beat Rea 39-34.

Through lack of public support no Championship was organised between 1957 and 1964. After a truce with the BA & CC a new system was adopted whereby the champion defended his title against a series of single challengers. These matches resulted as follows:

1964

J. Pulman beat F. Davis 19-16
J. Pulman beat R. Williams 40-33

1965

J. Pulman beat F. Davis 37-36
J. Pulman beat R. Williams 25-22 (matches)
J. Pulman beat F. van Rensburg 39-12

1966

John Pulman beat Fred Davis 5-2 (matches)

1968

John Pulman beat Eddie Charlton 39-34

1969

First round: John Spencer (England) beat John Pulman (England) 25-18; Rex Williams (England) beat Bernard Bennett (England) 25-4; Gary Owen (England) beat Jack Rea (Northern Ireland) 25-17; Fred Davis (England) beat Ray Reardon (Wales) 25-24

Semi-finals: Spencer beat Williams 37-12; Owen beat Davis 37-24

Final: Spencer beat Owen 37-24

1970 (April)

First round: David Taylor (England) beat Bernard Bennett (England) 11-8

Quarter-finals: John Pulman (England) beat Taylor 31-20; Gary Owen (England) beat Rex Williams (England) 31-11; Ray Reardon (Wales) beat Fred Davis (England) 31-26; John Spencer (England) beat Jack Rea (Northern Ireland) 31-15

Semi-finals: Pulman beat Owen 37-12; Reardon beat Spencer 37-33

Final: Reardon beat Pulman 37-33

1970 (November)

Round robin: John Spencer (England) beat Perrie Mans (South Africa) 20-17; beat Norman Squire (Australia) 27-10; beat John Pulman (England) 23-14
Ray Reardon (Wales) beat Mans 22-15; beat Eddie Charlton (Australia) 21-16; beat Spencer 21-16
Warren Simpson (Australia) beat Gary Owen (England) 19-18; beat Pulman 21-16; beat Mans 19-18
Charlton beat Squire 27-10; beat Mans 26-11; beat Owen 23-14
Owen beat Paddy Morgan (Australia) 26-11; beat Squire 26-11; Morgan beat Simpson 21-16

Semi-finals: Spencer beat Reardon 34-15; Simpson beat Charlton 27-22

Final: Spencer beat Simpson 37-29

1972
Qualifying

First round: Alex Higgins (Northern Ireland) beat Ron Gross (England) 15-6; Maurice Parkin (England) beat Geoffrey Thompson (England) 11-10; Graham Miles (England) beat Bernard Bennett (England) 15-6; John Dunning (England) beat Pat Houlihan (England) 11-10

Second round: Higgins beat Parkin 11-3; Dunning beat Miles 11-5

Competition Proper

First round: John Pulman (England) beat Dunning 19-7; Higgins beat Jack Rea (Northern Ireland) 19-11

Quarter-finals: John Spencer (England) beat Fred Davis (England) 31-21; Eddie Charlton (Australia) beat David Taylor (England) 31-25; Higgins beat Pulman 31-23; Rex Williams (England) beat Ray Reardon (Wales) 25-23

Semi-finals: Higgins beat Williams 31-30; Spencer beat Charlton 37-32

Final: Higgins beat Spencer 37-32

1973

First round: Pat Houlihan (England) beat Jack Rea (Northern Ireland) 9-2; David Greaves (England) beat Bernard Bennett (England) 9-8; Graham Miles (England) beat Geoffrey Thompson (England) 9-5; Perrie Mans (South Africa) beat Ron Gross (England) 9-2; Warren Simpson (Australia) beat Maurice Parkin (England) 9-3; Cliff Thorburn (Canada) beat Dennis Taylor (Northern Ireland) 9-8; David Taylor (England) beat John Dunning (England) 9-4

Second round: Fred Davis (England) beat Greaves 16-1; Miles beat John Pulman (England) 16-10; Eddie Charlton (Australia) beat Mans 16-8; Gary Owen (Australia) beat Simpson 16-14; Ray Reardon (Wales) beat Jim Meadowcroft (England) 16-10; Rex Williams (England) beat Thorburn 16-15; John Spencer (England) beat David Taylor 16-5; Alex Higgins (Northern Ireland) beat Houlihan 16-3

Quarter-finals: Higgins beat Davis 16-14; Spencer beat Williams 16-7; Charlton beat Miles 16-6; Reardon beat Owen 16-6

Semi-finals: Charlton beat Higgins 23-9; Reardon beat Spencer 23-2

Final: Reardon beat Charlton 38-32

1974

Qualifying: John Dunning (England) beat David Greaves (England) 8-2; Warren Simpson (Australia) beat Jack Rea (Northern Ireland) 8-3; Jim Meadowcroft (England) beat Pat Houlihan (England) 8-5; Cliff Thorburn (Canada) beat Alan McDonald (Australia) 8-3; John Pulman (England) beat Jack Karnehm (England) 8-0; David Taylor (England) beat Ron Gross (England) 8-7; Marcus Owen (Wales) beat Dennis Taylor (Northern Ireland) 8-1

First round: Bernard Bennett (England) beat Simpson 8-2; Bill Werbeniuk (Canada) beat Geoffrey Thompson (England) 8-3; Meadowcroft beat Kingsley Kennerley (England) 8-5; M. Owen beat Maurice Parkin (England) 8-5; Perrie Mans (South Africa) beat Ian Anderson (Australia) 8-1; Pulman beat Sydney Lee (England) 8-0; Dunning beat David Taylor 8-6; Paddy Morgan (Australia) beat Thorburn 8-4

Second round: Mans beat John Spencer (England) 15-13; Dunning beat Eddie Charlton (Australia) 15-13; M. Owen beat Gary Owen (Australia) 15-8; Alex Higgins (Northern Ireland) beat Bennett 15-4; Graham Miles (England) beat Morgan 15-7; Rex Williams (England) beat Pulman 15-12; Fred Davis (England) beat Werbeniuk 15-5; Ray Reardon (Wales) beat Meadowcroft 15-3

Quarter-finals: Williams beat Mans 15-4; Miles beat Dunning 15-13; F. Davis beat Higgins 15-14; Reardon beat M. Owen 15-11

Semi-finals: Miles beat Williams 15-7; Reardon beat F. Davis 15-3

Final: Reardon beat Miles 22-12

1975

Qualifying: Phil Tarrant (Australia) beat Bernard Bennett (England) 15-8; Lou Condo (Australia) beat Maurice Parkin (England) 15-8; David Greaves (England) beat Jim Charlton (Australia) 15-14

First round: Warren Simpson (Australia) beat Ron Mares (Australia) 15-5; John Pulman (England) beat Tarrant 15-5; David Taylor (England) beat Rex King (Australia) 15-8; Ian Anderson (Australia) beat Condo 15-8; Dennis Taylor (Northern Ireland) beat Perrie Mans (South Africa) 15-12; Gary Owen (Australia) beat Greaves 15-3; Bill Werbeniuk (Canada) beat Jim Meadowcroft (England) 15-9; Cliff Thorburn (Canada) beat Paddy Morgan (Australia) 15-6

Second round: Ray Reardon (Wales) beat Simpson 15-11; John Spencer (England) beat Pulman 15-10; Alex Higgins (Northern Ireland) beat David Taylor 15-2; Rex Williams (England) beat

John Spencer, world champion three times

Anderson 15-4; Dennis Taylor beat Fred Davis (England) 15-14; Owen beat John Dunning (England) 15-8; Eddie Charlton (Australia) beat Werbeniuk 15-11; Thorburn beat Graham Miles (England) 15-2

Quarter-finals: Reardon beat Spencer 19-17; Higgins beat Williams 19-12; Dennis Taylor beat Owen 19-9; Charlton beat Thorburn 19-12

Semi-finals: Charlton beat Dennis Taylor 19-12; Reardon beat Higgins 19-14

Final: Reardon beat Charlton 31-30

1976
Qualifying

First round: Jack Rea (Northern Ireland) beat Ian Anderson (Australia) 8-5; David Greaves (England) beat Jim Charlton (Australia) 8-5; Jim Meadowcroft (England) beat Dennis Wheelwright (Australia) 8-1; Ron Gross (England) beat Maurice Parkin (England) 8-5; Lou Condo (Australia) beat Marcus Owen (Wales) 8-6

Second round: Rea beat Bernard Bennett (England) 8-5; David Taylor (England) beat Greaves 8-1; Meadowcroft beat Gross 8-4; Willie Thorne (England) beat Condo 8-3

Competition Proper

First round: Ray Reardon (Wales) beat John Dunning (England) 15-7; Dennis Taylor (Northern Ireland) beat Gary Owen (Australia) 15-9; Perrie Mans (South Africa) beat Graham Miles (England) 15-10; Meadowcroft beat Rex Williams (England) 15-7; Eddie Charlton (Australia) beat John Pulman (England) 15-9; Fred Davis

(England) beat Bill Werbeniuk (Canada) 15-12; Alex Higgins (Northern Ireland) beat Cliff Thorburn (Canada) 15-14; John Spencer (England) beat David Taylor (England) 15-5

Quarter-finals: Reardon beat Dennis Taylor 15-2; Mans beat Meadowcroft 15-8; Charlton beat F. Davis 15-13; Higgins beat Spencer 15-14

Semi-finals: Reardon beat Mans 20-10; Higgins beat Charlton 20-18

Final: Reardon beat Higgins 27-16

1977
Qualifying

First round: John Virgo (England) beat Roy Andrewartha (Wales) 11-1

Second round: Patsy Fagan (Rep. of Ireland) beat Jim Meadowcroft (England) 11-9; Virgo beat John Dunning (England) 11-6; Willie Thorne (England) beat Bernard Bennett (England) 11-4; John Pulman (England) w.o.; David Taylor (England) beat David Greaves (England) 11-0; Cliff Thorburn (Canada) beat Chris Ross (Scotland) 11-0; Dennis Taylor (Northern Ireland) beat Jack Karnehm (England) 11-0; Doug Mountjoy (Wales) beat Jack Rea (Northern Ireland) 11-9

Competition Proper

First round: Ray Reardon (Wales) beat Fagan 13-7; John Spencer (England) beat Virgo 13-9; Graham Miles (England) beat Thorne 13-4; Pulman beat Fred Davis (England) 13-12; Eddie Charlton (Australia) beat David Taylor (England) 13-5; Thorburn beat Rex Williams (England) 13-6; Dennis Taylor beat Perrie Mans (South Africa) 13-11; Mountjoy beat Alex Higgins (Northern Ireland) 13-12

Quarter-finals: Spencer beat Reardon 13-6; Pulman beat Miles 13-10; Thorburn beat Charlton 13-12; Dennis Taylor beat Mountjoy 13-11

Semi-finals: Spencer beat Pulman 18–16; Thorburn beat Dennis Taylor 18-16

Final: Spencer beat Thorburn 25-21

1978
Qualifying

First round: Maurice Parkin (England) beat Bernard Bennett (England) 9-4; Roy Andrewartha (Wales) beat Jack Karnehm (England) 9-0; John Barrie (England) beat David Greaves (England) 9-3; Pat Houlihan (England) beat Chris Ross (Scotland) 9-1

Second round: Doug Mountjoy (Wales) beat Andrewartha 9-3; Patsy Fagan (Rep. of Ireland) beat John Dunning (England) 9-5; Willie Thorne (England) beat Rex Williams (England) 9-3; Bill Werbeniuk (Canada) beat Maurice Parkin (England) 9-2; Perrie Mans (South Africa) beat Barrie 9-6; David Taylor (England) beat Paddy Morgan (Australia) 9-7; Houlihan beat Jim Meadowcroft 9-6; Fred Davis (England) beat John Virgo (England) 9-8

Competition Proper

First round: Mans beat John Spencer (England) 13-8; Graham Miles (England) beat David Taylor (England) 13-10; Fagan beat Alex Higgins (Northern Ireland) 13-12; Davis beat Dennis Taylor (Northern Ireland) 13-9; Eddie Charlton (Australia) beat Thorne 13-12; Cliff Thorburn (Canada) beat Houlihan 13-8; Werbeniuk beat John Pulman (England) 13-4; Ray Reardon (Wales) beat Mountjoy 13-9

Quarter-finals: Mans beat Miles 13-7; Davis beat Fagan 13-10; Charlton beat Thorburn 13-12; Reardon beat Werbeniuk 13-6

Semi-finals: Mans beat Davis 18-16; Reardon beat Charlton 18-14

Final: Reardon beat Mans 25-18

1979
Qualifying

First round: Doug Mountjoy (Wales) beat Derek Mienie (South Africa) 9-1; Terry Griffiths (Wales) beat Bernard Bennett (England) 9-2; Pat Houlihan (England) beat John Barrie (England) 9-5; Willie Thorne (England) beat Jim Charlton (Australia) 9-3; John Virgo (England) beat Maurice Parkin (England) 9-0; John Dunning (England) beat Jack Rea (Northern Ireland) 9-5; Rex Williams (England) beat David Greaves (England) 9-2; Jim Meadowcroft (England) beat Jimmy van Rensberg (South Africa) 9-7; Roy Andrewartha (Wales) beat Ray Edmonds (England) 9-8; Steve Davis (England) beat Ian Anderson (Australia) 9-1; Kirk Stevens (Canada) beat Roy Amdor (South Africa) 9-1

Second round: Virgo beat Thorne 9-8; Bill Werbeniuk (Canada) beat Andrewartha 9-2; David Taylor (England) beat Dunning 9-8; Mountjoy beat Houlihan 9-6; S. Davis beat P. Fagan (Rep. of Ireland) 9-2; Griffiths beat Meadowcroft 9-6; Stevens beat John Pulman (England) 9-0; Graham Miles (England) beat Williams 9-5

Competition Proper

First round: Eddie Charlton (Australia) beat Mountjoy 13-6; Werbeniuk beat John Spencer (England) 13-11; Virgo beat Cliff Thorburn 13-10; F. Davis beat Stevens 13-8; Dennis Taylor (Northern Ireland) beat S. Davis 13-11; Alex Higgins (Northern Ireland) beat David Taylor 13-5; Griffiths beat Perrie Mans (South Africa) 13-8; Ray Reardon (Wales) beat Miles 13-8

Quarter-finals: Charlton beat F. Davis 13-4; Dennis Taylor beat Reardon 13-8; Virgo beat Werbeniuk 13-9; Griffiths beat Higgins 13-12

Semi-finals: Griffiths beat Charlton 19-17; Dennis Taylor beat Virgo 19-12

Final: Griffiths beat Dennis Taylor 24-16

1980
Qualifying

Group 1: Jack Rea (Northern Ireland) beat Bernard Bennett (England) 9-1; Willie Thorne (England) beat Kevin Robitaille (Canada) 9-4; Thorne beat Rea 9-1

Group 2: Steve Davis (England) beat Chris Ross (Scotland) 9-3; Paddy Morgan (Australia) beat Paul Thornley (Canada) 9-4; S. Davis beat Morgan 9-0

Group 3: Mike Hallett (England) beat Kingsley Kennerley (England) 9-2; Kirk Stevens (Canada) beat David Greaves (England) 9-3; Stevens beat Hallett 9-3·

Group 4: Joe Johnson (England) beat Roy Andrewartha (Wales) 9-5; Pat Houlihan (England) beat Johnson 9-6; Tony Meo (England) beat Jimmy van Rensberg (South Africa) 9-1; Meo beat Houlihan 9-1

Group 5: Roy Amdor (South Africa) beat Bernie Mikkelsen (Canada) 9-7; Rex Williams (England) beat Amdor 9-4; Jim Wych (Canada) beat John Bear (Canada) 9-5; Wych beat Williams 9-7

Group 6: Frank Jonik (Canada) beat Mark Wildman (England) 9-7; Cliff Wilson (Wales) beat Jonik 9-6

Group 7: Ray Edmonds (England) beat Maurice Parkin (England) 9-2; Sid Hood (England) beat John Dunning (England) 16-7; Edmonds beat Hood 9-6

Group 8: Eddie Sinclair (Scotland) beat Mario Morra (Canada) 9-5; Sinclair beat Derek Mienie (South Africa) 9-7; Jim Meadowcroft (England) beat Sinclair 9-1

Competition Proper

First round: S. Davis beat Patsy Fagan (Rep. of Ireland) 10-6; Alex Higgins (Northern Ireland) beat Meo 10-9; Doug Mountjoy (Wales) beat Wilson 10-6; Wych beat John Pulman (England) 10-5; John Virgo (England) beat Meadowcroft 10-2; Stevens beat Graham Miles (England) 10-3; David Taylor (England) beat Edmonds 10-3; Bill Werbeniuk (Canada) beat Thorne 10-9

Second round: S. Davis beat Terry Griffiths (Wales) 13-10; Higgins beat Perrie Mans (South Africa) 13-6; Stevens beat John Spencer (England) 13-8; Eddie Charlton (Australia) beat Virgo 13-12; Cliff Thorburn (Canada) beat Mountjoy 13-10; Wych beat Dennis Taylor (Northern Ireland) 13-10; Ray Reardon (Wales) beat Werbeniuk 13-6; David Taylor beat Fred Davis (England) 13-5

Quarter-finals: David Taylor beat Reardon 13-11; Thorburn beat Wych 13-6; Stevens beat Charlton 13-7; Higgins beat S. Davis 13-9

Semi-finals: Thorburn beat David Taylor 16-7; Higgins beat Stevens 16-13

Final: Thorburn beat Higgins 18-16

1981
Qualifying

Group 1: Willie Thorne (England) beat Mario Morra (Canada) 9-5; David Greaves (England) beat Maurice Parkin (England) 9-5; Thorne beat Greaves 9-3

Group 2: Jimmy White (England) beat Bernie Mikkelsen (Canada) 9-4; White beat Jim Meadowcroft (England) 9-8

Group 3: Ray Edmonds (England) beat Mark Wildman (England) 9-3; Rex Williams (England) beat Sid Hood (England) 9-4; Edmonds beat Williams 9-7

Group 4: Tony Meo (England) beat Joe Johnson (England) 9-8; Mike Hallett (England) beat Frank Jonik (Canada) 9-1; Meo beat Hallett 9-4

Group 5: John Dunning (England) beat Bernard Bennett (England) 9-6; Dunning beat Patsy Fagan (Rep. of Ireland) 9-7

Group 6: Dave Martin (England) beat Ian Anderson (Australia) 9-3; Martin beat John Pulman (England) 9-2

Group 7: Cliff Wilson (Wales) beat Roy Andrewartha (Wales) 9-4; Eddie Sinclair (Scotland) beat Paddy Morgan (Australia) 9-8; Wilson beat Sinclair 9-4

Group 8: Tony Knowles (England) beat Chris Ross (Scotland) 7-0 (retired); Knowles beat Jim Wych (Canada) 9-3

Competition Proper

First round: Graham Miles (England) beat Knowles 10-8; David Taylor (England) beat Wilson 10-6; Doug Mountjoy (Wales) beat Thorne 10-6; Kirk Stevens (Canada) beat Dunning 10-4; Meo beat John Virgo (England) 10-6; Steve Davis (England) beat White 10-8; Bill Werbeniuk (Canada) beat Martin 10-4; John Spencer (England) beat Edmonds 10-9

Second round: Cliff Thorburn (Canada) beat Miles 13-2; David Taylor beat Fred Davis (England) 13-3; Terry Griffiths (Wales) beat Meo 13-6; S. Davis beat Alex Higgins (Northern Ireland) 13-8; Mountjoy beat Eddie Charlton (Australia) 13-7; Dennis Taylor (Northern Ireland) beat Stevens 13-11; Werbeniuk beat Perrie Mans (South Africa) 13-5; Ray Reardon (Wales) beat Spencer 13-11

Quarter-finals: Thorburn beat David Taylor 13-6; S. Davis beat Griffiths 13-9; Mountjoy beat Dennis Taylor 13-8; Reardon beat Werbeniuk 13-10

Semi-finals: Davis beat Thorburn 16-10; Mountjoy beat Reardon 16-10

Final: Davis beat Mountjoy 18-22

1982
Qualifying

Group 1: John Bear (Canada) beat Frank Jonik (Canada) 9-4; Bear beat Jim Wych (Canada) 9-4

Group 2: Dennis Hughes (England) beat Clive Everton (Wales) 9-4; Tony Meo (England) beat Hughes 9-4

Group 3: Dean Reynolds (England) beat Dessie Sheehand (Rep. of Ireland) 9-5; Reynolds beat Ray Edmonds (England) 9-6

Group 4: Eugene Hughes (Rep. of Ireland) w.o. Derek Mienie (South Africa) scr; Tony Knowles (England) beat Hughes 9-7

Group 5: Mark Wildman (England) beat Geoff Foulds (England) 9-8; Jimmy White (England) beat Wildman 9-4

Group 6: Colin Roscoe (Wales) beat Bernie Mikkelsen (Canada) 9-6; Willie Thorne (England) beat Roscoe 9-1

Group 7: Paul Medati (England) beat John Phillips (Scotland) 9-3; Cliff Wilson (Wales) beat Medati 9-5

Group 8: Pat Houlihan (England) beat Ian Anderson (Australia) 9-5; Dave Martin (England) beat Houlihan 9-3

Group 9: Murdo McLeod (Scotland) beat Eddie McLaughlin (Scotland) 9-8; John Dunning (England) beat McLeod 9-4

Group 10: Mike Watterson (England) beat Bert Demarco (Scotland) 9-6; Jim Meadowcroft (England) beat Watterson 9-7

Group 11: Doug French (England) beat Bernard Bennett (England) 9-3; Patsy Fagan (Rep. of Ireland) beat French 9-6

Group 12: Ian Black (Scotland) beat Maurice Parkin (England) 9-6; Rex Williams (England) beat Black 9-2

Group 13: Joe Johnson (England) beat Vic Harris (England) 9-4; Mike Hallett (England) beat Johnson 9-8

Group 14: Jim Donnelly (Scotland) beat Matt Gibson (Scotland) 9-8; Eddie Sinclair (Scotland) beat Billy Kelly (Rep. of Ireland) 9-8; Donnelly beat Sinclair 9-8

Group 15: Paddy Morgan (Australia) beat David Greaves (England) 9-2; Silvino Francisco (South Africa) beat Chris Ross (Scotland) 9-0; Francisco beat Morgan 9-1

Group 16: Mario Morra (Canada) beat Tommy Murphy (Northern Ireland) 9-5; Jack Fitzmaurice (England) w.o. John Pulman (England) scr; Fitzmaurice beat Morra 9-7

Competition Proper

First round: Knowles beat S. Davis (England) 10-1; Graham Miles (England) beat Martin 10-5; Bill Werbeniuk (Canada) beat Bear 10-7; Eddie Charlton (Australia) beat Wilson 10-5; Francisco beat Dennis Taylor (Northern Ireland) 10-7; Reynolds beat Fred Davis (England) 10-7; John Virgo (England) beat Hallett 10-4; Ray Reardon (Wales) beat Donnelly 10-5; Thorne beat Griffiths 10-6; John Spencer (England) beat Dunning 10-4; Alex Higgins (Northern Ireland) beat Meadowcroft 10-5; Doug Mountjoy (Wales) beat Williams 10-3; Fagan beat David Taylor (England) 10-9; Kirk Stevens (Canada) beat Fitzmaurice 10-4; Perrie Mans (South Africa) beat Meo 10-8; White beat Cliff Thorburn (Canada) 10-4

Second round: Knowles beat Miles 13-7; Charlton beat Werbeniuk 13-5; Francisco beat Reynolds 13-8; Reardon beat Virgo 13-8; Thorne beat Spencer 13-5; Higgins beat Mountjoy 13-12; Stevens beat Fagan 13-7; White beat Mans 13-6

Quarter-finals: Charlton beat Knowles 13-11; Reardon beat Francisco 13-8; Higgins beat Thorne 13-10; White beat Stevens 13-9

Semi-finals: Reardon beat Charlton 16-11; Higgins beat White 16-15

Final: Higgins beat Reardon 18-15

Jimmy White, during his first-round match against Tony Meo in the 1983 Embassy World Championship

1983
Qualifying

Group 1: Billy Kelly (Rep. of Ireland) beat Bert Demarco (Scotland) 10-4; Silvino Francisco (South Africa) beat Kelly 10-5

Group 2: Paddy Morgan (Australia) beat Pascal Burke (Rep. of Ireland) 10-9; Graham Miles (England) beat Morgan 10-6

Group 3: Tommy Murphy (Northern Ireland) beat Pat Houlihan (England) 10-9; John Virgo (England) beat Murphy 10-8

Group 4: Rex Williams (England) beat Mike Darrington (England) 10-0; Williams beat Fred Davis (England) 10-1

Group 5: Mark Wildman (England) beat Bob Harris (England) 10-7; Wildman w.o. Jim Wych (Canada) scr

Group 6: Ray Edmonds (England) beat Frank Jonik (Canada) 10-4; Dean Reynolds (England) beat Edmonds 10-6

Group 7: Mick Fisher (England) beat Patsy Fagan (Rep. of Ireland) 10-8; Eddie McLaughlin (Scotland) beat David Greaves (England) 10-7; Fisher beat McLaughlin 10-9

Group 8: Tony Meo (England) beat Vic Harris (England) 10-0; Geoff Foulds (England) beat Matt Gibson (Scotland) 10-6; Meo beat Foulds 10-4

Group 9: Ian Black (Scotland) beat Mario Morra (Canada) 10-9; Paul Medati (England) beat John Bear (Canada) 10-7; Black beat Medati 10-4

Group 10: Cliff Wilson (Wales) beat Clive Everton (Wales) 10-1; Joe Johnson (England) beat Paul Watchorn (Rep. of Ireland) 10-0; Wilson beat Johnson 10-8

Group 11: Murdo McLeod (Scotland) beat Marcus Owen (Wales) 10-5; Dave Martin (England) beat Maurice Parkin (England) 10-1; Martin beat McLeod 10-7

Group 12: Jim Meadowcroft (England) beat Bernard Bennett (England) 10-3; Graham Cripsey (England) beat Dennis Hughes (England) 10-2; Meadowcroft beat Cripsey 10-6

Group 13: Jim Donnelly (Scotland) beat Dessie Sheehan (Rep. of Ireland) 10-6; John Campbell (Australia) beat Mike Watterson (England) 10-6; Campbell beat Donnelly 10-2

Group 14: Les Dodd (England) w.o. John Dunning (England) scr; Ian Williamson (England) beat Doug French (England) 10-8; Dodd beat Williamson 10-9

Group 15: Mike Hallett (England) beat Roy Andrewartha (Wales) 10-7; Warren King (Australia) beat Ian Anderson (Australia) 10-6; Hallett beat King 10-6

Group 16: Eugene Hughes (Rep. of Ireland) beat Jack Fitzmaurice (England) 10-7; Eddie Sinclair (Scotland) beat Colin Roscoe (Wales) 10-2; Hughes beat Sinclair 10-8

Competition Proper

First round: Alex Higgins (Northern Ireland) beat Reynolds 10-4; Willie Thorne (England) beat Virgo 10-3; Bill Werbeniuk (Canada) beat Martin 10-4; David Taylor (England) beat Meadowcroft 10-2; Eddie Charlton (Australia) beat Dodd 10-7; John Spencer (England) beat Hallett 10-7; Dennis Taylor (Northern Ireland) beat Francisco 10-9; Steve Davis (England) beat Williams 10-4; Cliff Thorburn (Canada) beat Campbell 10-5; Terry Griffiths (Wales) beat Wildman 10-8; Perrie Mans (South Africa) beat Black 10-3; Kirk Stevens (Canada) beat Fisher 10-2; Doug Mountjoy (Wales) beat Wilson 10-2; Meo beat Jimmy White (England) 10-8; Tony Knowles (England) beat Miles 10-3; Ray Reardon (Wales) beat Hughes 10-7

Second round: Higgins beat Thorne 13-8; Werbeniuk beat David Taylor 13-10; Charlton beat Spencer 13-11; Davis beat Dennis Taylor 13-11; Thorburn beat Griffiths 13-12; Meo beat Mountjoy 13-11; Knowles beat Reardon 13-12; Stevens beat Mans 13-3

Quarter-finals: Higgins beat Werbeniuk 13-11; Davis beat Charlton 13-5; Thorburn beat Stevens 13-12; Knowles beat Meo 13-9

Semi-finals: Thorburn beat Knowles 16-15; Davis beat Higgins 16-5

Final: Davis beat Thorburn 18-6

World Championship Prize Money

Year (Sponsor)	No. of Entries	Total Prize Money £	First Prize £
1969 (Players No 6)	8	3,500	1,300
1970 (Players No 6)	9	not known	1,225
1971 (not sponsored)	9	not known	2,333
1972 (not sponsored)	16	not known	not known
1973 (Park Drive)	23	8,000	1,500
1974 (Park Drive)	31	10,000	2,000
1975 (not sponsored)	27	18,900	not known
1976 (Embassy)	27	15,300	6,000
1977 (Embassy)	24	17,000	6,000
1978 (Embassy)	28	24,000	7,500
1979 (Embassy)	35	35,000	10,000
1980 (Embassy)	49	60,000	15,000
1981 (Embassy)	46	75,000	20,000
1982 (Embassy)	67	110,000	25,000
1983 (Embassy)	74	130,000	30,000
1984 (Embassy)	84	200,000	44,000

Professional Snooker League

Amidst all snooker's success stories, there is one resounding commercial failure: the Professional Snooker League, which eventually staggered to a close with debts approaching £100,000.

This was not a reflection of poor attendances. Indeed, on the whole, audiences were sizeable and in many cases as large as the venue could hold. In this respect, at least, the calculation that the public would respond better to a genuinely competitive structure, rather than to an unrelated series of meaningless exhibitions, was proved sound. However, with no television coverage, and none of the sponsorship that this would have engendered, sufficient income could not be generated at the gate.

Originally 12 players were involved – the world's top 16 except for the three Barry Hearn management clients, Steve Davis, Terry Griffiths and Tony Meo, and the Canadian Cliff Thorburn. Another Canadian, Kirk Stevens, withdrew halfway through and his matches were deleted from the record.

It was anticipated that 31 venues would be used in completing the scheduled 66 matches but changes of date and venue, escalating costs and administrative problems saw Professional Snooker League Ltd facing a huge loss long before the final match.

The players themselves valued the chance to mop up

spare dates between major tournaments with extra match-play, a factor which was certainly instrumental in Dennis Taylor and Doug Mountjoy, for instance, finishing the season in great deal better form than they had started it in. Many of the matches were of very high quality and the battle for top place ended in dramatic circumstances.

Eventually, John Virgo needed a win and a draw from his last two matches to finish first. He won the last frame to draw 5-5 with Mountjoy, and then won the first five frames against Tony Knowles, only to lose the next four before a 79 break gave him the 6-4 win which made him the first – and probably last – league champion.

At Richard Dunn Sports Centre, Bradford: John Spencer (England) drew with Jimmy White (England) 5-5; Tony Knowles (England) beat Bill Werbeniuk (Canada) 7-3

At Queensway Hall, Dunstable: Werbeniuk drew with Charlton 5-5; Knowles beat David Taylor 6 (114,106)-4

At Rushcliffe Leisure Centre, Nottingham: Werbeniuk beat David Taylor 6 (131)-4 (102)

At St Andrew's Hall, Norwich: Dennis Taylor (Northern Ireland) beat Doug Mountjoy (Wales) 6-4; John Virgo (England) beat David Taylor (England) 6-4

At Perdiswell Leisure Centre, Worcester: Ray Reardon (Wales) drew with David Taylor 5-5

At Cwmbran Stadium, Gwent: Reardon drew with Spencer 5-5; Eddie Charlton (Australia) beat Mountjoy 6-4 (130)

At St David's Hall, Cardiff: Alex Higgins (Northern Ireland) beat Mountjoy 6-4; Knowles drew with Reardon 5-5 (100)

At Horwich Leisure Centre, Bolton: Spencer beat Higgins 6-4 (113)

At Macclesfield Leisure Centre: David Taylor beat Spencer 6-4; Dennis Taylor beat Charlton 8 (104,125)-2

At Howebridge Leisure Centre, Wigan: Knowles drew with Higgins 5-5 (114); Dennis Taylor beat David Taylor 7-3 (125,108)

At Mansfield Leisure Centre: Spencer beat Werbeniuk 7-3; White beat David Taylor 6-4

At Hexagon, Reading: Dennis Taylor drew with Knowles 5(104)-5; Werbeniuk beat White 6-4; Charlton beat Spencer 7-3; Virgo beat Higgins 6-4 (108)

At Southwold Leisure Centre, Bristol: Virgo beat White 6-4 (114); Spencer beat Mountjoy 8-2

At Stoke Rochford Hall, Grantham: Virgo beat Reardon 6-4; Charlton beat Reardon 6 (115,114)-4 (101)

At Cornwall Coliseum, St Austell: Dennis Taylor beat Werbeniuk 6 (101)-4 (136); Reardon drew with Mountjoy 5 (112)-5

At Woodford Sports Centre, Hull: Charlton beat White 6-4

At Arts Centre, Warwick University: Charlton beat Virgo 7-3; Charlton beat David Taylor 6-4

At Gateshead Leisure Centre: Charlton beat Knowles 8-2; Spencer drew with Virgo 5-5

At Central Hall, York: Mountjoy beat Werbeniuk 7 (123)-3; Virgo beat Dennis Taylor 6 (107,121)-4 (123,139)

At Huddersfield Sports Centre: Higgins drew with Taylor 5-5; Virgo beat Werbeniuk 8(102)-2

At Derngate Centre, Northampton: White beat Reardon 6(119)-4 (105); Mountjoy beat David Taylor 9 (101)-1; White beat Higgins 6-4

At Richard Dunn Sports Centre, Bradford: Higgins beat Dennis Taylor 6 (117,106)-4

At Marco's Leisure, Edinburgh: Mountjoy beat White 7 (109)-3

At Eden Court Theatre, Inverness: White drew with Knowles 5 (105)-5 (104)

At Spectrum Arena, Warrington: Dennis Taylor beat Spencer 7-3; Higgins beat Werbeniuk 7 (136,112)-3; Mountjoy beat Knowles 7(116,110)-3

At Horwich Leisure Centre, Bolton: Dennis Taylor beat White 7-3; Knowles beat Spencer 6-4

At Bath Sports and Leisure Centre: Reardon beat Werbeniuk 6-4

At Fairfield Hall, Croydon: Dennis Taylor beat Reardon 7 (108)-3; Higgins beat Charlton 7-3

At Oasis Leisure Centre, Swindon: Virgo drew with Mountjoy 5-5

At Kelham Hall, Newark: Virgo beat Knowles 6 (106)-4

At Mountbatten Sports Centre, Portsmouth: Higgins drew with Reardon 5-5

Final table

	Won	Drawn	Lost	Frames For	Frames Agst	Pts
John Virgo (Guildford)	7	2	1	57	43	16
Dennis Taylor (Blackburn)	7	1	2	62	38	15
Eddie Charlton (Australia)	7	1	2	56	44	15
Alex Higgins (Manchester)	4	3	3	53	47	11
Doug Mountjoy (Ebbw Vale)	4	2	4	54	46	10
Tony Knowles (Bolton)	3	4	3	48	52	10
John Spencer (Radcliffe)	3	3	4	49	51	9
Jimmy White (Tooting)	3	2	5	46	54	8
Ray Reardon (Stoke)	1	5	4	46	54	7
Bill Werbeniuk (Canada)	2	1	7	39	61	5
David Taylor (Manchester)	1	2	7	40	60	4

David Taylor

National Professional Championships

The WPBSA's decision to give grants to national professional championships has ensured that this type of event will be played on a much more regular and better remunerated basis than in the past.

Starting with the 1984-85 season, the WPBSA is to contribute to each prize fund £1,000 multiplied by the number of entries. In the case of the English Professional Championship, dormant since 1981 when it was held under the sponsorship of John Courage and was won by Steve Davis, the grant is expected to be in the order of £50,000

Since leading professionals have come to expect amounts of prize money that can only be generated by the sponsorship attendant upon television coverage, it became impossible, after the 1981 event, to set up the English Championship in such a way that the leading players could realistically be expected to enter.

However, the WPBSA's contribution, added to sponsorship from Tolly Cobbold, who transferred their support from an annual eight-man invitation event, made the tournament a reasonably attractive proposition, particularly as Anglia Television undertook to cover it (for transmission in their area only) as they had the Tolly Cobbold Classic in the past.

Since England has always supplied more professionals than any other country, it is perhaps a little surprising that the 1981 event is the only time there has ever been an English Championship.

The Welsh Championship has a much longer history, going back to 1922 when J.S. Nicholls beat W. Davies 1032-777 (the aggregate score of 18 frames) for the title.

There were a few other title matches, though none officially recognised, before the championship was revived in 1977 when Ray Reardon beat Doug Mountjoy (at the time the only other Welsh professional) 12-8 for the title, under the sponsorship of William Hill, the bookmakers, at the Club Double Diamond, Caerphilly.

Coverage of that match by BBC Wales provided the precedent for coverage of the four-man Welsh Professional Championship, which was inaugurated under the sponsorship of Woodpecker at Ebbw Vale Leisure Centre in 1980.

Guaranteed television coverage made the Welsh the most secure of the national championships and it has been contested annually at Ebbw Vale ever since, with Doug Mountjoy winning the title three times and Ray Reardon twice.

The Irish Professional Championship was not held in the

Willie Thorne, semi-finalist in the English Professional Championship

1983-84 season. In the absence of television coverage, no promoter was able to assemble a package guaranteeing appropriate prize money.

Jack Rea held the title from 1947 until he was successfully challenged by Alex Higgins in 1972. Higgins made four successful defences, two against Dennis Taylor and two against Patsy Fagan, before losing the title to Taylor in 1980.

Taylor made one successful defence against Fagan and in 1982, when the championship was staged for the first time on a tournament basis, he beat Higgins in the final. Higgins regained the title in 1983.

Although official records no longer remain, the Scottish Professional Championship was played fairly regularly before the war when the most illustrious winner was Walter Donaldson, who went on to win the World Professional Championship twice.

The championship was revived in modern times in 1980 when Eddie Sinclair beat Chris Ross, then the only other Scottish professional, for the title. The following year, there were seven more Scottish professionals and the event has since been staged annually on a tournament basis with Ian Black, Sinclair and Murdo McLeod winning the title in turn.

The Australian Championship has been held since 1964 by Eddie Charlton, except for the year following his 1968 defeat by Warren Simpson. However, no championship had been organised for six years, until the WPBSA's grant enabled it to be revived in August 1984.

Various unofficial Canadian Championships have been staged. The first generally accepted championship was held in September 1983 when Kirk Stevens beat Frank Jonik for the title after Jonik had elminated Cliff Thorburn.

The South African Professional Championship has been intermittently staged, usually on a challenge basis. Perrie Mans won the title from Freddie van Rensberg in 1965 and retained it until defeated by Derek Mienie in 1979. He regained the title the following year and has held it ever since (the event has now been in abeyance for three years).

ENGLISH PROFESSIONAL CHAMPIONSHIP

1981 (sponsored by John Courage)

Qualifying: Edmonds beat Mike Hallet 9-3; Joe Johnson beat Tony Knowles 9-2; Mark Wildman beat Bernard Bennett 9-3; John

Kirk Stevens beat Frank Jonik for the 1983 Canadian Championship

Dunning beat David Greaves 9-4; Jim Meadowcroft beat John Barrie 9-3

First round: Edmonds beat Fred Davis 9-5; Tony Meo beat John Virgo 9-6; Graham Miles beat Sid Hood 9-1; Steve Davis beat Meadowcroft 9-2; John Spencer beat Pat Houlihan 9-1; Willie Thorne beat Wildman 9-2; Johnson w.o.; Dunning beat David Taylor 9-8

Quarter-finals: Davis beat Spencer 9-7; Meo beat Miles 9-7; Thorne beat Dunning 9-0; Edmonds beat Johnson 9-5

Semi-finals: Davis beat Edmonds 9-0; Meo beat Thorne 9-8

Final: Davis beat Meo 9-3

STRONGBOW WELSH PROFESSIONAL CHAMPIONSHIP

1980

First round: Doug Mountjoy beat Terry Griffiths 9-6; Ray Reardon beat Cliff Wilson 9-3

Final: Mountjoy beat Reardon 9-6

1981

Preliminary: Cliff Wilson beat Roy Andrewartha 6-5

First round: Wilson beat Doug Mountjoy 9-6; Ray Reardon beat Terry Griffiths 9-6

Final: Reardon beat Wilson 9-6

1982

First round: Cliff Wilson beat Marcus Owen 6-0; Terry Griffiths beat Colin Roscoe 6-2; Ray Reardon beat Clive Everton 6-1; Doug Mountjoy beat Roy Andrewartha 6-3

Semi-finals: Griffiths beat Wilson 9-6; Mountjoy beat Reardon 9-7

Final: Mountjoy beat Griffiths 9-8

1983

First round: Terry Griffiths beat Clive Everton 6-1; Ray Reardon beat Roy Andrewartha 6-2; Cliff Wilson beat Colin Roscoe 6-4; Doug Mountjoy beat Marcus Owen 6-0

Semi-finals: Reardon beat Griffiths 9-4; Mountjoy beat Wilson 9-3

Final: Reardon beat Mountjoy 9-1

1984

First round: Doug Mountjoy beat Clive Everton 6-1; Terry Griffiths beat Roy Andrewartha 6-1; Ray Reardon beat Marcus Owen 6-1; Cliff Wilson beat Colin Roscoe 6-2

Semi-finals: Mountjoy beat Griffiths 9-5; Wilson beat Reardon 9-4

Final: Mountjoy beat Wilson 9-3

IRISH PROFESSIONAL CHAMPIONSHIP

1982

First round: Eugene Hughes beat Dessie Sheehan 6-1

Quarter-finals: Hughes beat Jack Rea 6-0; Tommy Murphy beat Patsy Fagan 6-2

Semi-finals: Dennis Taylor beat Murphy 6-0; Alex Higgins beat Hughes 6-2

Final: Taylor beat Higgins 16-13

1983

First round: Dennis Taylor beat Billy Kelly 6-0; Patsy Fagan beat Tommy Murphy 6-4; Alex Higgins beat Jack Rea 6-3; Eugene Hughes beat Pascal Burke 6-2

Semi-finals: Higgins beat Hughes 6-2; Taylor beat Fagan 6-1

Final: Higgins beat Taylor 16-11

SCOTTISH PROFESSIONAL CHAMPIONSHIP

1981

First round: Matt Gibson beat Bert Demarco 5-3; Jim Donnelly beat Eddie Sinclair 5-0; Eddie McLaughlin beat Chris Ross 5-3; Ian Black beat Murdo McLeod 5-4

Semi-finals: Gibson beat Donnelly 6-4; Black beat McLaughlin 6-3

Final: Black beat Gibson 11-7

1982

First round: Murdo McLeod beat Jim Donnelly 6-5

Quarter-finals: Chris Ross beat Bert Demarco 6-5; Matt Gibson beat Eddie McLaughlin 6-3; Ian Black beat McLeod 6-0; Eddie Sinclair beat John Phillips 6-3

Semi-finals: Black beat Ross 6-4; Sinclair beat Gibson 6-2

Final: Sinclair beat Black 11-7

1983

First round: Jim Donnelly beat Bert Demarco 6-4; Ian Black beat Eddie McLaughlin 6-4; Murdo McLeod beat Matt Gibson 6-5

Semi-finals: Eddie Sinclair beat Donnelly 6-5; McLeod beat Black 6-2

Final: McLeod beat Sinclair 11-9

PONTINS

Various untelevised invitation tournaments have taken place from time to time but only one has survived on an annual basis, the eight-man Pontins Professional tournament which is run in the same week as the Pontins Spring Open at Prestatyn. Pontins also staged one-offs at Camber Sands in 1980 and Brean Sands in 1983.

	Winner	Runner-up	
1974	Ray Reardon	John Spencer	10-9
1975	Ray Reardon	John Spencer	10-4
1976	Ray Reardon	Fred Davis	10-9
1977	John Spencer	John Pulman	7-5
1978	Ray Reardon	John Spencer	7-2
1979	Doug Mountjoy	Graham Miles	8-4
1980	John Virgo	Ray Reardon	9-6
1980*	Alex Higgins	Dennis Taylor	9-7
1981	Terry Griffiths	Willie Thorne	9-8
1982	Steve Davis	Ray Reardon	9-4
1983	Doug Mountjoy	Ray Reardon	9-7
1983**	Tony Meo	Silvino Francisco	9-7
1984	Willie Thorne	John Spencer	9-7

* held at Camber Sands
** held at Brean Sands

Doug Mountjoy

John Spencer

POT BLACK

Pot Black introduced the game to a non-snooker public who quickly acquired a taste for its civilised combat between pleasant, well-dressed combatants. In this respect, it was the pathfinder in snooker's success as a television sport.

There had been no snooker on television for several years until BBC 2, searching for low-budget programmes which would exploit the use of colour, then available only on that channel, experimented in 1969 with Pot Black.

The format of one-frame matches fitted neatly into a 25-minute slot and immediately attracted some of the channel's highest viewing figures. Pot Black is still going strong on a similar principle 15 years later.

As there is now so much other snooker on television, Pot Black does not receive quite the attention within the snooker world that it used to. And everyone in snooker is well aware that a one-frame match is not a credible test of ability.

Nevertheless, it provides acceptable entertainment and certainly fulfilled its role as snooker's shop window at a time when the game desperately needed one. Sales of the programme have taken the game to parts of the world top-class snooker might otherwise not have reached.

Pot Black Winners

Year	Winner	Year	Winner
1969	Ray Reardon	1977	Perrie Mans
1970	John Spencer	1978	Doug Mountjoy
1971	John Spencer	1979	Ray Reardon
1972	Eddie Charlton	1980	Eddie Charlton
1973	Eddie Charlton	1981	Cliff Thorburn
1974	Graham Miles	1982	Steve Davis
1975	Graham Miles	1983	Steve Davis
1976	John Spencer	1984	Terry Griffiths

Terry Griffiths

Overseas Circuit

The challenge which confronts the WPBSA in the next five years is to reproduce overseas professional snooker's outstanding domestic success story.

Since BBC and ITV are now committed to as much coverage as the market can reasonably bear, there is little if any scope for more major events in Britain.

Without television, there is unlikely to be the kind of sponsorship to which the leading competitors are now accustomed and there is a very severe limit on how much money can be attracted purely at the gate.

The WPBSA has therefore been devoting a greater part of its attention to overseas matters, particularly in building relationships and agreements with sponsors and television companies – the dual foundation stones on which to establish a genuinely worldwide circuit.

It is specially anxious to avoid the situation which existed in Britain right up to the end of the seventies, when promoters could negotiate direct with television companies, often on behalf of sponsors. Snooker itself was in danger of being carried along by commercial interests, instead of being the paramount element in the relationship.

The longest established overseas professional tournament is the Winfield Australian Masters which has taken place in Sydney annually since 1979. It began with a sprint-style *Pot Black* format, but in 1983 and 1984 changed to longer matches ranging from best of five to best of thirteen.

However, all the 1983 event and the latter half of the

1984 were played in the studios of Channel 10, an arrangement which still marks it as a television event rather than a public one which television covers.

In Britain, studio tournaments or productions may not be sponsored (which is why *Pot Black* is not) nor may sponsors control television packages, although these arrangements are permitted in Australia and certain other countries.

Enough snooker is played in Australia to support at least one more major tournament but their domestic professional scene has suffered from the dominance, on and off the

Steve Davis, (left), Terry Griffths (above) and Tony Meo (opposite), the three Barry Hearn management clients who are taking snooker to the Far East

table, of Eddie Charlton, though the recent emergence of other Australians like John Campbell and Warren King is likely to help create a livelier domestic scene.

The Winfield New Zealand Masters, so far only a sprint-style event, has been staged for the last two years immediately after the Australian tournament.

From the mid-seventies until 1980, the Canadian Open was held each year during the Canadian National Exhibition in Toronto in late August/early September. Despite the high summer heat, the noise of other attractions at the exhibition and relatively low prize money, the event always attracted a good quality field. However, the British circuit was tending to start earlier and earlier and the Canadian Open was abandoned because a field of high enough

quality could not be obtained for the 1981 season.

The 1980 final was covered by CBC for later transmission, but snooker's image as a pool hall gambling activity proved even harder to live down in Canada than it had been decades previously in Britain.

No one could obtain sponsorship from blue chip companies outside the game and the television/sponsorship equation, on which the creation of big money tournaments tends to depend, remained unsolved. Even when the WPBSA voted funds to help set up a Canadian Masters in November 1984, no outside sponsorship could be obtained and the project was deferred.

But for the political situation, South Africa would certainly have proved a more productive snooker area than it has. Some players have nevertheless made private visits to South Africa and have been put on Sanroc's blacklist for doing so. There has been some television coverage but the WPBSA is unlikely to be involved in any South African promotion in the foreseeable future.

Probably the largest growth area in the game in the next few years will be the Far East. Barry Hearn has co-ordinated events in Thailand, Hong Kong and Singapore, largely featuring his three management clients, Steve Davis, Terry Griffiths and Tony Meo. Camus have been the major sponsors involved and there has been extensive television coverage. Riley's have used the tours as a focus of interest through which to sell tables. Indeed, as the British domestic market reaches saturation point all British table companies are increasingly looking overseas to maintain sales volume.

Table sales are also becoming increasingly brisk on the European mainland, particularly in Holland, Belgium and Spain. The fact that many Dutch viewers have been able to pick up British television snooker transmissions has stimulated interest. Several overseas countries (particularly Thailand) regularly purchase British tournament coverage.

Perhaps the best guide to the progress snooker has made towards becoming a genuinely worldwide game has been the increase in numbers of countries competing in the World Amateur Championship.

The inaugural World Amateur Championship took place in 1963 with five competitors from four countries: England, Australia, India and Sri Lanka. Since then, Wales, Scotland, Northern Ireland, Republic of Ireland, Isle of Man, Pakistan, New Zealand, Canada, Malta, Singapore, Fiji, Hong Kong, Zimbabwe, Egypt, Sudan and Mauritius have all been internationally represented, most of them regularly.

History
of
Snooker

THE RILEY
RAYLITE SHADE.

ool Tower Circus: Walter Donaldson and Fred Davis await the start of a session in one of their great finals of the forties and fifties

In 1875 Colonel Sir Neville Chamberlain was a young subaltern with the Devonshire Regiment stationed at Jubbulpore. During the rainy season the officers' long afternoons were spent at the mess billiards table where the parent game was less popular than various round games which were better suited to more than two players and to which it was easier to add a modest gambling element.

'Pyramids', perhaps snooker's most obvious forerunner, was a game played with fifteen reds, initially placed in a triangle, with the apex red on what is now the pink spot but which was then known as the pyramid spot. Each time a player potted a red, all his opponents paid across the agreed stake money per ball.

In 'life pool', each player was given a cue-ball and an object-ball (e.g. white on red, red on yellow), the second player's object-ball being the first player's cue-ball and so on. The object was to pot one's specified object-ball three times. Each time a player's ball was potted, he lost a life and had to pay an agreed stake. When he had lost three 'lives' he paid an extra sum for a 'star' (or extra life) and when that was gone he was 'dead'. When only one player remained he scooped the kitty.

'Black pool' was a development of pool in that a black ball was added. When a player had potted his allocated ball, he could attempt the black. If he was successful, each of his opponents paid across an additional sum and he could then attempt the nearest ball. Joe Davis spent many of his youthful hours playing a similar game, 'pink pool'.

Black pool was the preferred game among the Devonshire officers but it was Chamberlain's inspiration gradually to add other coloured balls so that snooker came to be played with fifteen reds, yellow, green, pink and black. Blue and brown were added some years later.

These new colours produced a game whose variety (and variety of monetary forfeits) immediately caught on. The concept of break-building was much in the future and even the point values of the balls were not established until a little later; but it was in these casual and almost chance beginnings that the game undoubtedly had its origin.

When Compton MacKenzie, the novelist, interviewed him in 1938, Chamberlain recalled that the Devons one afternoon received a visit from a young subaltern who had been trained at the Royal Military Academy, Woolwich. In the course of conversation, the latter happened to remark that a first year cadet at Woolwich was referred to as a 'snooker' with the implication that this was the status of the lowest of the low. The original word for a cadet had been the French 'neux' which had been corrupted to 'snooker'.

Chamberlain said: 'The term was a new one to me but I soon had the opportunity of exploiting it when one of our party failed to hole a coloured ball which was close to a corner pocket. I called out to him: 'Why, you're a regular snooker!'

'I had to explain to the company the definition of the word and to soothe the feelings of the culprit I added that we were all, so to speak, snookers at the game so it would be very appropriate to call the game snooker. The suggestion was adopted with enthusiasm and the game has been called snooker ever since.'

Thurston's, Leicester Square, home of championship billiards and snooker before the war

The Basic Rules of Snooker

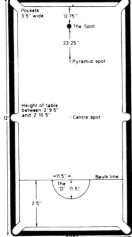

Snooker is played with 22 balls which are positioned at the start of the frame (or game) as shown in the diagram. The cue-ball, which is used alternately by both players, can be placed anywhere in the 'D' for the first stroke but must thereafter be played from where it comes to rest, except after an in-off or if it is forced off the table, in which cases the next player must again play from the 'D'.

'The non-striker may, in case of his enforced absence from the room appoint a substitute to watch his interests and claim a foul if necessary.' (general rule 10)

Points are scored by potting and by receiving penalties from foul strokes. Each player must first attempt to strike a red (value 1). When he pots a red he must then play at a colour, the values of which are: black (7), pink (6), blue (5), brown (4), green (3), yellow (2).

The player should nominate the colour he is attempting, although the letter of this rule is not enforced in cases where this is obvious.

If a colour is potted, it is replaced on its own spot, another red is then attempted and so on until all the reds have been potted.

The colours are then taken in ascending order of value until only the cue-ball remains on the table.

Failure to strike a red incurs a penalty of four points (the minimum penalty for any foul) but the penalty is increased to 5, 6 or 7 if, instead of a red, the cue-ball strikes blue, pink or black. An in-off is a foul carrying a penalty of four points, or more if the ball which the cue-ball initially strikes before entering a pocket is of higher value.

Failure to strike a nominated colour also carries a four point penalty, or more if the ball involved is of higher value.

'If the referee considers that a player is taking an abnormal amount of time over his stroke with the intention of upsetting his opponent the referee should warn him that he runs the risk of being disqualified if he pursues these tactics.' (official decisions)

If, for example, green is nominated but pink is struck, the penalty is 6. If pink is nominated and green is struck the penalty is also 6.

Penalties often result, not from incompetence or chance, but from snookers. A snooker occurs when the balls are so placed that a player cannot strike the ball he is due to play without hitting a cushion or making the cue-ball swerve.

If a player is snookered on the reds after a foul shot by his opponent he may nominate any coloured ball as a red. This is known as a free ball. If he pots it he scores one and can then nominate a colour in the usual way.

If no red remains, a free ball is valued at a number of points equal to that of the lowest value colour remaining and the colours are then taken in sequence.

'The referee should not give any indication that a player is about to make a foul stroke.' (official decisions)

FOUL SHOTS

After any foul shot, whether he is entitled to a free ball or not, a player can ask his opponent to play again. A foul is committed in both billiards and snooker if:

(a) a player's cue-tip strikes the cue-ball more than once in the same stroke
(b) a ball is forced off the table
(c) a player plays with both feet off the floor
(d) a player plays before all the balls have come to rest
(e) a player strikes or touches a ball other than with the tip of the cue
(f) the cue-ball jumps over an intervening ball
(g) the balls are wrongly spotted when the player takes his shot.

'It is a foul to play with both feet off the floor.' (snooker rule 13)

For the purpose of this rule, a player is deemed to be snookered if he cannot directly hit both extremities of the object-ball he is due to play. (The exception to this rule is when one or more reds are preventing a player striking a particular red.)

'For refusing to continue the game when called upon by the referee to do so or for conduct which in the opinion of the referee is wilfully or consistently unfair a player shall lose the game.' (general rule 15)

'The non-striker shall, when the striker is playing, avoid standing or moving in the line of sight; he should sit or stand at a fair distance from the table.' (general rule 10)

If at the end of a frame the scores are level, the black is replaced on its spot and the player winning the toss of a coin has the choice of whether he or his opponent takes first shot at it from anywhere within the 'D'.

Amateur Game

The original concept of amateurism has disappeared from modern snooker, and with it many of the old hypocrises

It used to be the case that anyone, man or woman, who so much as served a cup of tea in a snooker hall was designated a professional, regardless of playing ability.

The moneyed, ruling classes enforced gentlemen and players categorisation in snooker, as they did in most sports. This distinction was gradually eroded by a mixture of commercial pressures and changes in social thinking.

For a while, 'shamateurism' ruled – a system of indirect or even illicit payments, sometimes in the form of sinecures. The governing classes still governed and appearances were preserved.

Official definitions of amateurism were modified, but the façade remained until 1971 when the Billiards and Snooker Control Council, who had been recognised as the official governing body for both the professional and amateur sides of the game, abolished the term 'amateur'.

This, though, was a little too late in the day, for earlier that year the World Professional Billiards and Snooker Association had dissociated itself from the B & SCC and declared itself the sole governing body for the professional game. In effect, this meant that as the WPBSA designated all its members professionals, everyone else was automatically regarded as an amateur.

The International Billiards and Snooker Federation (IBSF), the one-nation, one-vote body for regulating the World Amateur Championships that had come into being in 1971, recognised that 'player' or 'non-professional' were terms either too vague or too negative to be in the title of their events so the term 'amateur' remained.

The definition of amateurism adopted by the IBSF in 1972 defined professionals simply as members of the WPBSA, those who 'declare themselves professional' or those who endorse products connected with the game. All limitations on amateurs receiving prize money or exhibition fees were abolished.

Since 1972, therefore, snooker and billiards have effectively been professional through and through, save that one group of players acknowledges the WPBSA as their controlling and governing body, while the rest acknowledged their own, domestic amateur associations and the IBSF.

Quite openly and properly, many amateurs therefore play full-time as they attempt to accumulate a list of achievements which would further any application for professional status they might wish to make to the WPBSA. Many others welcome any prize money they can earn in amateur tournaments as a supplement to the income they derive from their regular occupations. As things stand, it often happens that a top-class amateur earns more from snooker than a middle-ranked professional.

WORLD AMATEUR CHAMPIONSHIPS

The pinnacle of amateur snooker is the World Amateur Championship which in 1985 will become an annual event, instead of alternating with the World Amateur Billiards Championship. The latter will still be held every two years.

The World Amateur Billiards Championship, originally the British Empire Championship, was grudgingly instituted by the B & SCC (then the Billiards Association and Control Council) under pressure from overseas countries. The BA & CC thought that the Amateur Championship – essentially an English event though its title did not reflect that – was quite sufficient.

It was held eight times before the war and was revived in 1951 as the World Amateur Championship, the Empire having by then diminished, although the same countries, by and large, were represented. The World Amateur Snooker Championship, first mooted in 1952, was instituted in 1963.

Entry to these Championships is made through official national associations. Host nations determine whether one or two competitors per country are accepted. In addition, the defending champion's country is entitled to nominate him; the host country is also entitled to an extra representative and to fill any late vacancies.

The 1984 World Amateur Snooker Championship was played in Dublin in October. The 1985 event will be staged in England and the 1986 in New Zealand.

The 1983 World Amateur Billiards Championship at the De La Salle Gymnasium, Cospicua, Malta, was won by Michael Ferreira, who defeated Subash Agrawal in an all-Indian final, to take the title for the third time.

In the semi-finals, Ferreira made an astonishing recovery to beat England's Norman Dagley, twice champion, by a mere 64 points after trailing by 735 with only one two-hour session to play.

WORLD AMATEUR SNOOKER CHAMPIONSHIP

1963	Calcutta	G. Owen (England)	F. Harris (Australia)
1966	Karachi	G. Owen (England)	J. Spencer (England)
1968	Melbourne	D. Taylor (England)	M. Williams (Australia)
1970	Edinburgh	J. Barron (England)	S. Hood (England)
1972	Cardiff	R. Edmonds (England)	M. Francisco (South Africa)
1974	Dublin	R. Edmonds (England)	G. Thomas (Wales)
1976	Johannesburg	D. Mountjoy (Wales)	P. Mifsud (Malta)
1978	Malta	C. Wilson (Wales)	J. Johnson (England)

| 1980 Launceston | J. White (England) | R. Atkins (Australia) |
| 1982 Calgary | T. Parsons (Wales) | Jim Bear (Canada) |

WORLD AMATEUR BILLIARDS CHAMPIONSHIP

1926 London	J. Earlam (England)	G. Shailer (Australia)
1927 London	A. Prior (South Africa)	H. Coles (Wales)
1929 Johannesburg	L. Hayes (Australia)	A. Prior (South Africa)
1931 Sydney	L. Steeples (England)	S. Lee (England)
1933 London	S. Lee (England)	T. Jones (Wales)
1935 London	H. Coles (Wales)	J. McGhee (Scotland)
1936 Johannesburg	R. Marshall (Australia)	A. Prior (South Africa)
1938 Melbourne	R. Marshall (Australia)	K. Kennerley (England)
1951 London	R. Marshall (Australia)	F. Edwards (England)
1952 Calcutta	L. Driffield (England)	R. Marshall (Australia)
1954 Sydney	T. Cleary (Australia)	R. Marshall (Australia)
1958 Calcutta	W. Jones (India)	L. Driffield (England)
1960 Edinburgh	J. H. Beetham (England)	J. Long (Australia)
1962 Perth	R. Marshall (Australia)	W. Jones (India)
1964 Pukekohe	W. Jones (India)	L. Driffield (England)
1967 Colombo	L. Driffield (England)	M. J. M. Lafir (Sri Lanka)
1969 London	J. Karnehm (England)	M. Ferreira (India) M. Francisco (South Africa) M. J. M. Lafir (Sri Lanka)
1971 Malta	N. Dagley (England)	M. Francisco (South Africa)
1973 Bombay	M. J. M. Lafir (Sri Lanka)	S. Mohan (India)
1975 Auckland	N. Dagley (England)	M. Ferreira (India)
1977 Melbourne	M. Ferreira (India)	R. Close (England)
1979 Colombo	P. Mifsud (Malta)	N. Dagley (England)
1981 Delhi	M. Ferreira (India)	N. Dagley (England)
1983 Malta	M. Ferreira (India)	S. Agrawal (India)

NATIONAL AMATEUR CHAMPIONSHIPS

The English Amateur Billiards Championship, instituted in 1888, and the English Amateur Snooker Championship, in 1916, are the two senior national amateur championships. Indeed, the latter is the oldest snooker championship,

amateur or professional. 'The English' has enjoyed a slightly higher status than other national championships, partly through its seniority and partly because it accepts entries from players qualified to represent other countries, a legacy of the days when the event was known simply as 'The Amateur Championship'.

In the modern game, this has created confusion and possibly injustice as several Welshmen and a few Irishmen have figured prominently in the championships, eliminating players qualified to represent England in the process.

National associations ordinarily use their national championships to select their representatives for the World Amateur Championship, but the open nature of the English Championship has left the B & SCC, which represents the English game, without quite the clearcut method of selection enjoyed by other countries.

ENGLISH AMATEUR SNOOKER CHAMPIONSHIP

1916	C. N. Jacques
1917	C. N. Jacques
1918	T. N. Palmer
1919	S. H. Fry
1920	A. R. Wisdom
1921	M. J. Vaughan
1922	J. McGlynn
1923	W. Coupe
1924	W. Coupe
1925	J. McGlynn
1926	W. Nash
1927	O. T. Jackson
1928	P. H. Matthews
1929	L. Steeples
1930	L. Steeples
1931	P. H. Matthews
1932	W. E. Bach
1933	E. Bedford
1934	C. H. Beavis
1935	C. H. Beavis
1936	P. H. Matthews
1937	K. Kennerley
1938	P. H. Matthews
1939	P. Bendon
1940	K. Kennerley
1941–45	No contests
1946	H. J. Pulman
1947	H. Morris
1948	S. Battye
1949	T. C. Gordon
1950	A. Nolan
1951	R. Williams
1952	C. Downey
1953	T. C. Gordon
1954	G. Thompson
1955	M. Parkin
1956	T. C. Gordon
1957	R. Gross
1958	M. Owen
1959	M. Owen
1960	R. Gross
1961	A. Barnett
1962	R. Gross
1963	G. Owen
1964	R. Reardon
1965	P. Houlihan
1966	J. Spencer
1967	M. Owen
1968	D. Taylor
1969	R. Edmonds
1970	J. Barron
1971	J. Barron
1972	J. Barron
1973	M. Owen
1974	R. Edmonds

1975	S. Hood
1976	C. Ross
1977	T. Griffiths
1978	T. Griffiths
1979	J. White
1980	J. O'Boye
1981	V. Harris
1982	D. Chalmers
1983	T. Jones
1984	S. Longworth

ENGLISH AMATEUR BILLIARDS CHAMPIONSHIP

1888	H. A. O. Lonsdale A. P. Gaskell
1889	A. P. Gaskell A. P. Gaskell
1890	A. P. Gaskell A. P. Gaskell W. D. Courtney
1891	W. D. Courtney A. P. Gaskell
1892	A. R. Wisdom S. S. Christey
1893	A. R. Wisdom S. H. Fry A. H. Vahid
1894	H. Mitchell W. T. Maughan
1896	S. H. Fry
1899	A. R. Wisdom
1900	S. H. Fry
1901	S. S. Christey
1902	A. W. T. Good A. W. T. Good
1903	A. R. Wisdom S. S. Christey
1904	W. A. Lovejoy
1905	A. W. T. Good
1906	E. C. Breed
1907	H. C. Virr
1908	H. C. Virr
1909	Major Fleming
1910	H. A. O. Lonsdale
1911	H. C. Virr
1912	H. C. Virr
1913	H. C. Virr
1914	H. C. Virr
1915	A. W. T. Good
1916	S. H. Fry
1917	J. Graham-Symes
1918	J. Graham-Symes
1919	S. H. Fry
1920	S. H. Fry
1921	S. H. Fry

Year	Winner
1922	J. Graham-Symes
1923	W. P. McLeod
1924	W. P. McLeod
1925	S. H. Fry
1926	J. Earlam
1927	L. Steeples
1928	A. Wardle
1929	H. F. E. Coles
1930	L. Steeples
1931	S. Lee
1932	S. Lee
1933	S. Lee
1934	S. Lee
1935	H. F. E. Coles
1936	J. Thompson
1937	K. Kennerley
1938	K. Kennerley
1939	K. Kennerley
1940	K. Kennerley
1941–45	No contests
1946	M. Showman
1947	J. Thompson
1948	J. Thompson
1949	F. Edwards
1950	F. Edwards
1951	F. Edwards
1952	A. L. Driffield
1953	A. L. Driffield
1954	A. L. Driffield
1955	F. Edwards
1956	F. Edwards
1957	A. L. Driffield
1958	A. L. Driffield
1959	A. L. Driffield
1960	J. H. Beetham
1961	J. H. Beetham
1962	A. L. Driffield
1963	J. H. Beetham
1964	A. Nolan
1965	N. Dagley
1966	N. Dagley
1967	A. L. Driffield
1968	M. Wildman
1969	J. Karnehm
1970	N. Dagley
1971	N. Dagley
1972	N. Dagley
1973	N. Dagley
1974	N. Dagley
1975	N. Dagley
1976	R. Close
1977	R. Close
1978	N. Dagley
1979	N. Dagley
1980	N. Dagley
1981	N. Dagley
1982	N. Dagley
1983	N. Dagley
1984	N. Dagley

NORTHERN IRELAND
SNOOKER

Year	Winner
1927	G. Barron
1928	J. Perry
1929	W. Lyttle
1930	J. Luney
1931	J. McNally
1932	Capt. J. Ross
1933	J. French
1934	Capt. J. Ross
1935	W. Agnew
1936	W. Lowe
1937	J. Chambers
1938	J. McNally
1939	J. McNally
1941	J. McNally
1945	J. McNally
1946	J. McNally
1947	J. Rea

Year	Winner
1948	J. Bates
1949	J. Bates
1950	J. Bates
1951	J. Stevenson
1952	J. Stevenson
1953	J. Stevenson
1954	W. Seeds
1955	J. Stevenson
1956	S. Brooks
1957	M. Gill
1958	W. Agnew
1959	W. Hanna
1960	M. Gill
1961	D. Anderson
1962	S. McMahon
1963	D. Anderson
1964	P. Morgan
1965	M. Gill
1966	S. Crothers
1967	D. Anderson
1968	A. Higgins
1969	D. Anderson
1970	J. Clint
1971	S. Crothers
1972	P. Donnelly
1973	J. Clint
1974	P. Donnelly
1975	J. Clint
1976	E. Swaffield
1977	D. McVeigh
1978	D. McVeigh
1979	R. Burke
1980	S. Clarke
1981	T. Murphy
1982	S. Pavis
1983	J. McLaughlin Jr
1984	J. McLaughlin Jr

BILLIARDS

Year	Winner
1925	T. McCluney
1926	T. McCluney
1927	J. Sloan
1928	A. Davison
1929	J. Blackburn
1930	J. Blackburn
1931	J. Blackburn
1932	W. Lowe
1933	W. Mills
1934	W. Lowe
1935	W. Morrison
1936	J. Blackburn
1937	J. Blackburn
1938	W. Lowe
1939	W. Lowe
1940	No contest
1941	E. Haslem
1942–44	No contests
1945	E. Haslem
1946	J. Holness
1947	J. Bates
1948	J. Bates
1949	J. Bates
1950	J. Bates
1951	E. Haslem
1952	R. Taylor
1953	W. Scanlon
1954	W. Scanlon
1955	D. Turley
1956	J. Stevenson
1957	W. Scanlon
1958	W. Hanna
1959	W. Hanna
1960	W. Dennison
1961	R. Hanna
1962	N. McQuay
1963	W. Hanna
1964	D. Anderson / D. Turley } joint
1965	W. Ashe
1966	D. Anderson

Year	Winner
1967	W. Loughan
1968	D. Anderson
1969	W. Loughan
1970	S. Crothers
1971	J. Bates
1972–73	No contests
1974	P. Donnelly
1975	P. Donnelly
1976	P. Donnelly
1977	T. Taylor
1978	W. Loughan
1979	J. Bates
1980	S. Clarke
1981	W. Loughan
1982	P. Donnelly

REPUBLIC OF IRELAND
SNOOKER

Year	Winner
1931	J. Ayres
1933	S. Fenning
1935	S. Fenning
1937	P. J. O'Connor
1940	P. Merrigan
1942	P. J. O'Connor
1944	S. Fenning
1947	C. Downey
1948	P. Merrigan
1949	S. Fenning
1952	W. Brown
1953	S. Brooks
1954	S. Fenning
1955	S. Fenning
1956	W. Brown
1957	J. Connolly
1958	G. Gibson
1959–60	No contests
1961	W. Brown
1962	J. Weber
1963	J. Rogers
1964	J. Rogers
1965	W. Fields
1966	G. Hanway
1967	P. Morgan
1968	G. Hanway
1969	D. Dally
1970	D. Sheehan
1971	D. Sheehan
1972	J. Rogers
1973	F. Murphy
1974	P. Burke
1975	F. Nathan
1976	P. Burke
1977	J. Clusker
1978	E. Hughes
1979	E. Hughes
1980	D. Sheehan
1981	A. Kearney
1982	P. Browne
1983	J. Long
1984	P. Ennis

BILLIARDS

Year	Winner
1931	J. Ayres
1933	J. Ayres
1934	S. Fenning
1935	S. Fenning
1936	S. Fenning
1937	T. O'Brien
1938–41	No contests
1942	S. Fenning
1943	No contest
1944	S. Fenning
1945–47	No contests
1948	W. Brown
1949	S. Fenning
1950–1	No contests
1952	M. Nolan

Year	Winner
1953	D. Turley
1954	M. Nolan
1955	M. Nolan
1956	M. Nolan
1957	M. Nolan
1958	W. Dennison
1959–60	No contests
1961	K. Smyth
1962	K. Smyth
1963	J. Bates
1964	J. Bates
1965	L. Codd
1966	L. Codd
1967	P. Morgan
1968	P. Morgan
1969	J. Rogers
1970	L. Drennan
1971	L. Codd
1972	L. Codd
1973	T. Martin
1974	T. Doyle
1975	P. Fenelon
1976	J. Rogers
1977	E. Hughes
1978	E. Hughes
1979	L. Drennan
1980	P. Burke
1981	P. Burke
1982	D. Elliott
1984	A. Murphy

SCOTLAND
SNOOKER

Year	Winner
1931	G. Brown
1946	J. Levey
1947	J. Levey
1948	I. Wexelstein
1949	W. Ramage
1950	W. Ramage
1951	A. Wilson
1952	D. Emerson
1953	P. Spence
1954	D. Edmond
1955	L. U. Demarco
1956	W. Barrie
1957	T. Paul
1958	J. Phillips
1959	J. Phillips
1960	E. Sinclair
1961	J. Phillips
1962	A. Kennedy
1963	E. Sinclair
1964	J. Phillips
1965	L. U. Demarco
1966	L. U. Demarco
1967	E. Sinclair
1968	E. Sinclair
1969	A. Kennedy
1970	D. Sneddon
1971	J. Phillips
1972	D. Sneddon
1973	E. Sinclair
1974	D. Sneddon
1975	E. Sinclair
1976	E. Sinclair
1977	R. Miller
1978	J. Donnelly
1979	S. Nivison
1980	M. Gibson
1981	R. Lane
1982	P. Kippie
1983	G. Carnegie
1984	S. Hendry

AMATEUR BILLIARDS CHAMPIONSHIP

Year	Winner
1913	Captain Croneen
1914–21	No contests
1922	H. L. Fleming

1923	M. Smith
1924	No contest
1925	W. D. Greenlees
1926	M. Smith
1927	M. Smith
1928	M. Smith
1929	J. McGhee
1930	M. Smith
1933	A. Ramage
1934	N. Canney
1935	H. King
1936	N. Canney
1937	J. McGhee
1938	J. McGhee
1939	No contest
1940	W. McCann
1941–45	No contests
1946	J. Levey
1947	A. Ramage
1948	W. Ramage
1949	W. Ramage
1950	A. Ramage
1951	W. Ramage
1952	J. Murray
1953	J. Bates
1954	J. Bates
1955	W. Ramage
1956	W. Ramage
1957	W. Ramage
1958	W. Ramage
1959	W. Ramage
1960	A. Ramage
1961	P. Spence
1962	W. Ramage
1963	W. Ramage
1964	W. Ramage
1965	W. Ramage
1966	W. Ramage
1967	W. Ramage
1968	A. Kennedy
1969	A. Kennedy
1970	D. Sneddon
1971	D. Sneddon
1972	L. U. Demarco
1973	D. Sneddon
1974	D. Sneddon
1975	D. Sneddon
1976	D. Sneddon
1977	J. Nugent
1978	D. Sneddon
1979	H. Nimmo
1980	D. Sneddon
1981	D. Sneddon
1982	W. Kelly
1983	H. Nimmo

WALES
SNOOKER

1930	T. Jones
1931	T. Jones
1932	T. Jones
1933	T. Jones
1934	T. Jones
1935	T. Jones
1936	T. Jones
1937	G. Howells
1938	B. Gravenor
1939	W. E. James
1947	T. Jones
1948	R. Smith
1949	A. J. Ford
1950	R. Reardon
1951	R. Reardon
1952	R. Reardon
1953	R. Reardon
1954	R. Reardon
1955	R. Reardon
1956	C. Wilson
1957	R. D. Meredith
1958	A. Kemp

1959	J. R. Price
1960	L. Luker
1961	T. Parsons
1962	A. J. Ford
1963	R. D. Meredith
1964	M. L. Berni
1965	T. Parsons
1966	L. L. O'Neill
1967	L. L. O'Neill
1968	D. Mountjoy
1969	T. Parsons
1970	D. T. May
1971	D. T. May
1972	G. Thomas
1973	A. Lloyd
1974	A. Lloyd
1975	T. Griffiths
1976	D. Mountjoy
1977	C. Wilson
1978	A. Lloyd
1979	C. Wilson
1980	S. Newbury
1981	C. Roscoe
1982	T. Parsons
1983	W. Jones
1984	T. Parsons

BILLIARDS

1920	H. F. E. Coles
1921	H. F. E. Coles
1922	H. F. E. Coles
1923	H. F. E. Coles
1924	H. F. E. Coles
1925	Unknown
1926	Unknown
1927	Unknown
1928	G. Moore
1929	J. Tregoning
1930	Unknown
1931	L. Prosser
1932	T. Jones
1933	T. Jones
1934	Unknown
1935	I. Edwards
1936	J. Tregoning
1937	B. Gravenor
1938	J. Tregoning
1939	B. Gravenor
1940–46	No contests
1946	T. G. Rees
1947	T. C. Morse
1948	J. Tregoning
1949	I. Edwards
1950	W. Pierce
1951	W. Pierce
1952	J. Tregoning
1953	B. Sainsbury
1954	R. Smith
1955	J. Tregoning
1956	A. J. Ford
1957	R. Smith
1958	R. W. Oriel
1959	A. J. Ford
1960	C. Everton
1961	R. W. Oriel
1962	R. W. Oriel
1963	R. W. Oriel
1964	R. W. Oriel
1965	R. W. Oriel
1966	R. W. Oriel
1967	R. W. Oriel
1968	D. E. Edwards
1969	R. W. Oriel
1970	R. W. Oriel
1971	R. W. Oriel
1972	C. Everton
1973	C. Everton
1974	R. W. Oriel
1975	R. W. Oriel
1976	C. Everton
1977	C. Everton

1978	R. W. Oriel
1979	R. W. Oriel
	No further contests

AUSTRALIA
SNOOKER

1953	W. Simpson
1954	W. Simpson
1955	E. Pickett
1956	R. Marshall
1957	W. Simpson
1958	F. Harris
1959	K. Burles
1960	K. Burles
1961	M. Williams
1962	W. Barrie
1963	F. Harris
1964	W. Barrie
1965	W. Barrie
1966	M. Williams
1967	M. Williams
1968	M. Williams
1969	W. Barrie
1970	M. Williams
1971	M. Williams
1972	M. Williams
1973	M. Williams
1974	L. Condo
1975	R. Atkins
1976	R. Atkins
1977	R. Atkins
1978	K. Burles
1979	J. Campbell
1980	W. King
1981	W. King
1982	J. Giannaros
1983	G. Lackenby
1984	G. Wilkinson

BILLIARDS

1913	G. B. Shailer
1914–19	No contests
1920	J. R. Hooper
1921	G. B. Shailer
1922	G. B. Shailer
1923	G. B. Shailer
1924	E. Eccles
1925	G. B. Shailer
1926	L. W. Hayes
1927	L. W. Hayes
1928	L. W. Hayes
1929	A. H. Hearndon
1930	S. Ryan
1931	H. L. Goldsmith
1932	A. Sakzewski
1933	L. W. Hayes
1934	L. W. Hayes
1935	L. W. Hayes
1936	R. Marshall
1937	R. Marshall
1938	R. Marshall
1939	R. Marshall
1940–45	No contests
1946	R. Marshall
1947	T. Cleary
1948	R. Marshall
1949	R. Marshall
1950	T. Cleary
1951	R. Marshall
1952	R. Marshall
1953	R. Marshall
1954	R. Marshall
1955	R. Marshall
1956	J. Long
1957	R. Marshall
1958	T. Cleary
1959	R. Marshall
1960	J. Long

1961	R. Marshall
1962	R. Marshall
1963	R. Marshall
1964	J. Long
1965	T. Cleary
1966	T. Cleary
1967	J. Long
1968	J. Long
1969	R. Marshall
1970	R. Marshall
1971	M. Williams
1972	P. Tarrant
1973	P. Tarrant
1974	J. Reece
1975	J. Long
1976	G. Ganim Jr
1977	G. Ganim Jr
1978	G. Ganim Jr
1979	G. Ganim Jr
1980	G. Ganim Jr
1981	G. Ganim Jr
1982	R. Foldvari
1983	R. Foldvari

CANADA
SNOOKER

1979	J. Wych
1980	Jim Bear
1981	R. Chaperon
1983	A. Robidoux
1984	T. Finstad

BILLIARDS

1979	E. Fisher
1980	S. Holden
1981	R. Chaperon
1982	R. Chaperon

INDIA
SNOOKER

1939	P. K. Deb
1940	P. K. Deb
1941	V. R. Freer
1942	P. K. Deb
1943–45	No contests
1946	T. A. Selvaraj
1947	T. Sadler
1948	W. Jones
1949	T. A. Selvaraj
1950	F. Edwards (Eng)
1951	T. A. Selvaraj
1952	W. Jones
1953	A. L. Driffield (Eng)
1954	W. Jones
1955	T. A. Selvaraj
1956	M. J. M. Lafir
1957	M. J. M. Lafir
1958	W. Jones
1959	M. J. M. Lafir
1960	W. Jones
1961	M. J. M. Lafir
1962	R. Marshall (Aust)
1963	M. J. M. Lafir
1964	S. Shroff
1965	S. Shroff
1966	T. Monteiro
1967	S. Shroff
1968	S. Mohan
1969	S. Shroff
1970	S. Shroff
1971	T. Monteiro
1972	S. Shroff
1973	S. Shroff
1974	M. J. M. Lafir
1975	M. J. M. Lafir
1976	A. Savur

1977	M. J. M. Lafir
1978	A. Savur
1979	A. Savur
1980	J. White (Eng)
1981	G. Parikh

BILLIARDS

1931	M. M. Begg
1932	P. K. Deb
1933	Major Meade
1934	Mg Ba Sin
1935	P. K. Deb
1936	P. K. Deb
1937	M. M. Begg
1938	P. K. Deb
1939	P. K. Deb
1940	S. H. Lyth
1941	V. R. Freer
1942	V. R. Freer
1943–45	No contests
1946	C. Hirjee
1947	C. Hirjee
1948	V. R. Freer
1949	T. A. Selvaraj
1950	W. Jones
1951	W. Jones
1952	W. Jones
1953	L. Driffield (Eng)
1954	W. Jones
1955	W. Jones
1956	C. Hirjee
1957	W. Jones
1958	C. Hirjee
1959	T. Cleary (Aust)
1960	W. Jones
1961	W. Jones
1962	R. Marshall (Aust)
1963	W. Jones
1964	W. Jones
1965	W. Jones
1966	W. Jones
1967	A. Savur
1968	S. Mohan
1969	M. Ferreira
1970	S. Mohan
1971	S. Mohan
1972	S. Mohan
1973	S. Mohan
1974	M. Ferreira
1975	G. C. Parikh
1976	M. Ferreira
1977	M. J. M. Lafir
1978	M. Ferreira
1979	M. Ferreira
1980	M. Ferreira
1981	G. Sethi

MALTA
SNOOKER

1947	L. Galea
1948	T. B. Oliver
1949	L. Galea
1950	W. Asciak
1951	W. Asciak
1952	A. Borg
1953	A. Borg
1954	W. Asciak
1955	A. Borg
1956	W. Asciak
1957	W. Asciak
1958	W. Asciak
1959	A. Borg
1960	A. Borg
1961	A. Borg
1962	A. Borg
1963	M. Tonna
1964	A. Borg
1965	A. Borg
1966	A. Borg
1967	A. Borg
1968	P. Mifsud
1969	P. Mifsud
1970	P. Mifsud
1971	P. Mifsud
1972	P. Mifsud
1973	A. Borg
1974	A. Borg
1975	P. Mifsud
1976	P. Mifsud
1977	A. Borg
1978	P. Mifsud
1979	P. Mifsud
1980	J. Grech
1981	J. Grech
1982	P. Mifsud
1983	P. Mifsud
1984	T. Drago

BILLIARDS

1947	V. Micallef
1948	No contest
1949	E. Bartolo
1950	W. Asciak
1951	W. Asciak
1952	W. Asciak
1953	W. Asciak
1954	W. Asciak
1955	W. Asciak
1956	A. Asciak
1957	A. Asciak
1958	A. Asciak
1959	A. Asciak
1960	A. Asciak
1961	A. Borg
1962	J. Bartolo
1963	J. Bartolo
1964	W. Asciak
1965	A. Asciak
1966	A. Asciak
1967	A. Asciak

Michael Ferreira, three times world amateur billiards champion

1969	P. Mifsud
1970	W. Asciak
1971	P. Mifsud
1972	W. Asciak
1973	P. Mifsud
1974	P. Mifsud
1975	P. Mifsud
1976	P. Mifsud
1977	P. Mifsud
1978	J. Grech
1979	P. Mifsud
1980	J. Grech
1981	No contest
1982	V. Ellul
1983	J. Grech

NEW ZEALAND
SNOOKER

1945	S. Moses
1946	J. Munro
1947	W. Thompson
1948	L. Stout
1949	L. Stout
1950	L. Stout
1951	N. Lewis
1952	L. Stout
1953	L. Stout
1954	R. Franks
1955	L. Stout
1956	L. Stout
1957	W. Harcourt
1958	W. Harcourt
1959	W. Thomas
1960	T. Yesberg
1961	F. Franks
1962	K. Murphy
1963	W. Harcourt
1964	T. Yesberg
1965	L. Napper
1966	L. Napper
1967	R. Flutey
1968	L. Napper
1969	L. Glozier
1970	K. Tristram
1971	B. J. Bennett
1972	N. Stockman
1973	W. Hill
1974	K. Tristram
1975	K. Tristram
1976	D. Kwok
1977	D. Meredith
1978	D. Meredith
1979	D. Meredith
1980	D. O'Kane
1981	G. Kwok
1982	D. Kwok
1983	D. Kwok

BILLIARDS

1908	J. Ryan
1909	No contest
1910	F. Lovelock
1911	F. Lovelock
1912	H. Valentine
1913	H. Valentine
1914	N. Lynch
1915	W. E. Warren
1916	H. Siedeberg
1917	H. Siedeberg
1918	W. E. Warren
1919	H. Siedeberg
1920	W. E. Warren
1921	H. Siedeberg
1922	E. V. Roberts
1923	E. V. Roberts
1924	R. Fredotovich
1925	C. Mason
1926	E. V. Roberts
1927	E. V. Roberts
1928	A. Bowie
1929	L. Stout
1930	W. E. Hackett
1931	A. Duncan
1932	C. Mason
1933	A. Albertson
1934	H. McLean
1935	L. Holdsworth
1936	S. Moses
1937	S. Moses
1938	L. Holdsworth
1939	R. Carrick
1940	S. Moses
1941	R. Carrick
1942	R. Carrick
1943	A. Albertson
1944	S. Moses
1945	J. Shepherd
1946	R. Carrick
1947	C. Peek
1948	R. Carrick
1949	R. Carrick
1950	R. Carrick
1951	R. Carrick
1952	L. Stout
1953	A. Twohill
1954	A. Twohill
1955	A. Twohill
1956	A. Twohill
1957	A. Twohill
1958	A. Albertson
1959	A. Twohill
1960	W. Harcourt
1961	A. Albertson
1962	W. Harcourt
1963	H. C. Robinson
1964	T. Yesberg
1965	L. Napper
1966	A. Twohill
1967	A. Twohill
1968	A. Twohill
1969	E. Simmons
1970	L. Napper
1971	W. Harcourt
1972	B. Kirkness
1973	H. C. Robinson
1974	H. C. Robinson
1975	T. Yesberg
1976	H. C. Robinson
1977	B. Kirkness
1978	B. Kirkness
1979	R. Adams
1980	D. Meredith
1981	D. Meredith
1982	D. Meredith
1983	D. Meredith

SOUTH AFRICA
SNOOKER

1937	A. Prior
1938	A. H. Ashby
1939	A. Prior
1940–45	No contests
1946	F. Walker
1947	No contest
1948	F. Walker
1949	E. Kerr
1950	T. G. Rees
1951	T. G. Rees
1952	T. G. Rees
1953	J. van Rensburg
1954	J. van Rensburg
1955	J. van Rensburg
1956	F. Walker
1957	J. van Rensburg
1958	R. Walker
1959	M. Francisco
1960	P. Mans Jr.
1961	J. van Rensburg
1962	J. van Rensburg
1963	J. van Rensburg

1964	M. Francisco
1965	M. Francisco
1966	M. Francisco
1967	J. van Rensburg
1968	S. Francisco
1969	S. Francisco
1970	J. van Rensburg
1971	M. Francisco
1972	J. van Rensberg
1973	J. van Rensburg
1974	S. Francisco
1975	M. Francisco
1976	No contest
1977	S. Francisco
1978	J. van Niekerk
1979	F. Ellis
1980	F. Ellis

BILLIARDS

1920	Sgt. Bruyns
1921	A. Prior
1922	A. Prior
1923	No contest
1924	A. Prior
1925	P. Rutledge
1926	A. Prior
1927	A. Percival
1928	P. Rutledge
1929-30	No contests
1931	A. Prior
1932-36	No contests
1937	A. M. Burke
1938	A. Prior
1939	A. Prior
1940-45	No contests
1946	P. G. Kempen
1947	No contest
1948	P. G. Kempen
1949	T. G. Rees
1950	T. G. Rees
1951	I. Drapin
1952	T. G. Rees
1953	T. G. Rees
1954	F. Walker
1955	F. Walker
1956	G. Povall
1957	F. Walker
1958	F. Walker
1959	M. Francisco
1960	R. Walker
1961	M. Francisco
1962	M. Francisco
1963	M. Francisco
1964	M. Francisco
1965	M. Francisco
1966	M. Francisco
1967	J. van Rensburg
1968	M. Francisco
1969	M. Francisco
1970	M. Francisco
1971	M. Francisco
1972	S. Francisco
1973	S. Francisco
1974	M. Francisco
1975	S. Francisco
1976	No contest
1977	M. Francisco
1978	C. van Dijk
1979	C. van Dijk
1980	C. van Dijk
1981	P. Spence

SRI LANKA
SNOOKER

1948	M. J. M. Lafir
1949	M. M. Faiz
1950	M. J. M. Lafir
1951	M. S. A. Hassan
1952	M. J. M. Lafir
1953	M. J. M. Lafir
1954	M. J. M. Lafir
1955	M. J. M. Lafir
1956	M. J. M. Lafir
1957	M. J. M. Lafir
1958	M. J. M. Lafir
1959	M. J. M. Lafir
1960	M. J. M. Lafir
1961	M. J. M. Lafir
1962	M. J. M. Lafir
1963	M. J. M. Izzath
1964	M. J. M. Lafir
1965	M. J. M. Lafir
1966	M. J. M. Lafir
1967	N. J. Rahim
1968	No contest
1969	N. J. Rahim
1970	N. J. Rahim
1971	No contest
1972	N. J. Rahim
1973	M. J. M. Lafir
1974	Abandoned
1975	N. A. Rahim
1976	M. S. U. Mohideen
1977	M. S. U. Mohideen
1978	N. A. Rahim
1981	J. W. H. Boteju
1982	J. A. Wahid

BILLIARDS

1948	A. C. Cambal
1949	M. J. M. Lafir
1950	M. J. M. Lafir
1951	M. J. M. Lafir
1952	M. J. M. Lafir
1953	M. J. M. Lafir
1954	A. C. Cambal
1955	T. A. Selvaraj
1956	T. A. Selvaraj
1957	M. J. M. Lafir
1959	M. J. M. Lafir
1960	M. J. M. Lafir
1961	M. J. M. Lafir
1962	M. J. M. Lafir
1963	M. H. M. Mujahid
1964	M. J. M. Lafir
1966	M. J. M. Lafir
1967	J. K. Bakshani
1969	M. J. M. Lafir
1970	M. J. M. Lafir
1972	M. J. M. Lafir
1973	M. J. M. Lafir
1974	S. Shaharwardi
1975	M. S. U. Mohideen
1976	W. Weerasinghe
1977	W. Weerasinghe
1978	J. W. H. Boteju
1979	W. Weerasinghe
1981	J. W. H. Boteju

ZIMBABWE
SNOOKER

1981	A. Thomson
1982	A. Thomson
1983	J. Daly

BRITISH JUNIOR CHAMPIONSHIPS
SNOOKER (under 16)

1944	G. Owen
1945	R. Baker
1946	D. Thomas
1947	M. Knapp
1948	R. Williams
1949	R. Williams
	D. Lewis
1950	M. Owen
1951	M. Owen
1952	M. Wildman
1953	J. Board
1954	D. Bond
1955	P. Shelley
1956	A. Hart
1957	P. Shelley
1958	D. Bend
1959	J. Doyle
1960	N. Cripps
1961	No contest
1962	J. Virgo
1963	P. Hollis
1964	D. Clinton
1965	No contest
1966	J. Terry
1967	No contest
1968	E. Stone
1969	P. Hughes
1970	W. Thorne
1971	J. Mills
1972	J. Mills
1973	P. Bardsley
1974	S. Holroyd
1975	M. Hallett
1976	W. Jones
1977	J. White
1978	D. Adds
1979	A. Pyle
1980	T. Whitthread
1981	C. Hamson
1982	S. Ventham
1983	S. Hendry

SNOOKER (under 19)

1949	A. Kemp
1950	J. Carney
1951	R. Williams
1952	C. Wilson
1953	C. Wilson
1954	M. Wildman
1955	W. McGivern
1956	E. Sinclair
1957	H. Burns
1958	W. West
1959	D. Root
1960	D. Bend
1961	I. Rees
1962	A. Matthews
1963	A. Matthews
1964	J. Fisher
1965	J. Virgo
1966	J. Hollis
1967	No contest
1968	J. Maughan
1969	J. Terry
1970	J. Terry
1971	J. Johnson
1972	A. Knowles
1973	W. Thorne
1974	A. Knowles
1975	E. Hughes
1976	I. Williamson
1977	I. Williamson
1978	T. Meo
1979	J. O'Boye
1980	T. Murphy
1981	D. Reynolds
1982	N. Foulds
1983	M. Thompson

BILLIARDS (under 16)

1922	W. Donaldson
1923	W. Leigh
1924	L. Steeples
1925	S. Lee
1926	R. Gartland
1927	R. Gartland
1928	R. L. Bennett
1929	F. Davis
1930	H. J. Bennett
1931	C. Desbottes
1932	D. Hawkes
1933	Unknown
1934	W. Swinhoe
1935	D. Cruikshank
1936	D. Cruikshank
1937	D. Curson
1938	J. Hamilton
1939	R. Smith
1940	B. Smith
1941-47	No contests
1948	R. Williams
1949	R. Williams
1950	M. Owen
1951	E. Parry
1952	M. Wildman
1953	C. Everton
1954	H. Burns
1955	D. Deakes
1956	C. Dean
1957	P. Shelley
1958	P. Morgan
1959	P. Morgan
1960	A. Matthews
1961	B. Whitehead
1962-67	No contests
1968	C. Williamson
1969	P. Bardsley
1970	W. Thorne
1971	P. Bardsley
1972	P. Bardsley
1973	T. Wells
1974	P. Allan
1975	S. McNamara
1976	D. Bonney
1977	D. Bonney
1978	K. Walsh
1979	A. Pyle
1980	K. Walsh
1981	D. Presgrave
1982	S. Naisby
1983	S. Naisby
1984	C. Rowntree

BILLIARDS (under 19)

1949	G. Toner
1950	R. Williams
1951	R. Williams
1952	J. Sinclair
1953	M. Wildman
1954	M. Wildman
1955	D. Scott
1956	C. Everton
1957	C. Myers
1958	C. Marks
1959	P. Morgan
1960	D. Bend
1961	P. Morgan
1962	A. Matthews
1963	A. Matthews
1964-67	No contests
1968	D. Taylor
1969	D. Burgess
1970	J. Terry
1971	W. Thorne
1972	W. Thorne
1973	W. Thorne
1974	T. Wells
1975	E. Hughes
1976	S. Davis
1977	I. Williamson
1978	I. Williamson
1979	M. Garvey
1980	G. Charville
1981	S. Hawkins
1982	R. Marshall
1983	P. Gilchrist
1984	S. Naisby

Amateur Home International Championship

The first official amateur home international, a challenge match between Wales and England, was staged at the Afan Lido, Port Talbot, in 1969. In 1970, the Republic of Ireland joined to make a triangular series and Scotland made it quadrangular in 1971.

Matches were played either home or away until 1978 when Pontins offered to sponsor the event at its annual Autumn Festival of Snooker at Prestyn. The Isle of Man joined the competition that year and Northern Ireland competed for the first time in 1979.

Only England (seven wins) and Wales (six) have won the series, within which each match consists of six three-frame contests.

Home International Snooker Championships

1969

England beat Wales *Port Talbot*	10-8

1970-1

England beat Wales *Harringay*	14-4
England beat Rep. of Ireland *Dublin*	14-4
Wales beat Rep. of Ireland *Port Talbot*	17-1

	W	D	L	For	Agst	Pts
England	2	0	0	28	8	4
Wales	1	0	1	21	15	2
Rep. of Ireland	0	0	2	5	31	0

Friendly:

Wales beat Scotland *Neath*	10-8

1971-2

England beat Scotland *Newcastle*	10-8
England beat Rep. of Ireland *Harringay*	14-4
England drew with Wales *Neath*	9-9
Scotland drew with Wales *Edinburgh*	9-9
Scotland beat Rep. of Ireland *Dublin*	12-6
Wales beat Rep. of Ireland *Dublin*	13-5

	W	D	L	For	Agst	Pts
England	2	1	0	33	21	5
Wales	1	2	0	31	23	4
Scotland	1	1	1	29	25	3
Rep. of Ireland	0	0	3	15	39	0

1972-3

England beat Scotland *Edinburgh*	16-2
England beat Rep. of Ireland *Dublin*	13-5
England drew with Wales *Hull*	9-9
Wales beat Rep. of Ireland *Pontygwaith*	15-3
Wales beat Scotland *Llay*	10-8
Scotland beat Rep. of Ireland *Dublin*	13-5

	W	D	L	For	Agst	Pts
England	2	1	0	38	16	5
Wales	2	1	0	32	22	5
Scotland	1	0	2	23	31	2
Rep. of Ireland	0	0	3	15	41	0

1973-4

England beat Wales *Garnant*	14-4
England beat Scotland *Carlisle*	11-7
England drew with Rep. of Ireland *Bolton*	9-9
Wales beat Rep. of Ireland *Dublin*	11-7
Wales beat Scotland *Dublin*	9-9

	W	D	L	For	Agst	Pts
England	2	1	0	34	20	5
Wales	2	0	1	29	25	4
Rep. of Ireland	0	2	1	25	29	2
Scotland	0	1	2	20	34	1

1974-5

Wales beat Rep. of Ireland *Neath*	12-6
Wales beat Scotland *Maerdy*	14-4
Wales beat England *Exeter*	10-8
England beat Scotland *Edinburgh*	12-6
England beat Rep. of Ireland *Glasnevin*	11-7
Scotland beat Rep. of Ireland *Dundee*	12-6

	W	D	L	For	Agst	Pts
Wales	3	0	0	36	18	6
England	2	0	1	31	23	4
Scotland	1	0	2	22	32	2
Rep. of Ireland	0	0	3	19	35	0

1975-6

Wales beat Rep. of Ireland *Dublin*	13-5
Wales beat Scotland *Edinburgh*	11-7
Wales beat England *Merthyr*	11-7
England beat Rep. of Ireland *Grimsby*	13-5
England beat Scotland *Southport*	12-6
Scotland beat Rep. of Ireland *Dunloaghaire*	12-6

	W	D	L	For	Agst	Pts
Wales	3	0	0	35	19	6
England	2	0	1	32	22	4
Scotland	1	0	2	25	29	2
Rep. of Ireland	0	0	3	16	38	0

1976-7

England beat Rep. of Ireland *Dublin*	13-5
England beat Wales *Doncaster*	12-6
England beat Scotland *Glasgow*	11-7
Wales beat Scotland *Trealaw*	14-4
Wales beat Rep. of Ireland *Cardiff*	13-5
Scotland beat Rep. of Ireland *Edinburgh*	12-6

	W	D	L	For	Agst	Pts
England	3	0	0	36	18	6
Wales	2	0	1	33	21	4
Scotland	1	0	2	23	31	2
Rep. of Ireland	0	0	3	16	38	0

1977-8

Wales beat England *Caerphilly*	10-8
Wales beat Scotland *Dublin*	12-6
Wales beat Rep. of Ireland *Dublin*	15-3
England beat Scotland *Doncaster*	10-8
England beat Rep. of Ireland *Portsmouth*	11-7
Scotland beat Rep. of Ireland *Dublin*	12-6

	W	D	L	For	Agst	Pts
Wales	3	0	0	37	17	6
England	2	0	1	29	25	4
Scotland	1	0	2	26	28	2
Rep. of Ireland	0	0	3	16	38	0

1978

England beat Isle of Man *Prestatyn*	15-3
England beat Rep. of Ireland	14-4
England beat Scotland	16-2
England beat Wales	10-7
Wales beat Isle of Man	16-2
Wales beat Rep. of Ireland	11-7
Wales drew with Scotland	9-9
Scotland beat Isle of Man	15-3
Scotland drew with Rep. of Ireland	9-9
Rep. of Ireland beat Isle of Man	15-3

	W	D	L	For	Agst	Pts
England	4	0	0	55	16	8
Wales	2	1	1	43	28	5
Scotland	1	2	1	35	37	4
Rep. of Ireland	1	1	2	34	38	3
Isle of Man	0	0	4	12	60	0

1979

England beat Northern Ireland *Prestatyn*	16-2
England beat Isle of Man	16-2
England beat Rep. of Ireland	11-7
England beat Scotland	10-8
England beat Wales	10-7
Wales beat Northern Ireland	12-6
Wales beat Isle of Man	16-2
Wales beat Scotland	11-7
Wales drew with Rep. of Ireland	9-9
Rep. of Ireland beat Scotland	10-8
Rep. of Ireland drew with Northern Ireland	9-9
Rep. of Ireland drew with Wales	9-9
Rep. of Ireland beat Isle of Man	12-6
Scotland beat Isle of Man	13-5
Scotland beat Northern Ireland	10-8
Northern Ireland drew with Rep. of Ireland	9-9
Northern Ireland beat Isle of Man	14-4

	W	D	L	For	Agst	Pts
England	5	0	0	63	26	10
Wales	3	1	1	55	34	7
Rep. of Ireland	2	2	1	47	43	6
Scotland	2	0	3	46	44	4
Northern Ireland	1	1	3	39	51	3
Isle of Man	0	0	5	19	71	0

1980

England beat Northern Ireland *Prestatyn*	15-3
Scotland beat Isle of Man	14-4
Wales beat Northern Ireland	10-8
England beat Isle of Man	15-3
Wales beat Scotland	12-6
Rep. of Ireland beat Northern Ireland	11-7
Northern Ireland beat Isle of Man	12-6
Wales beat Rep. of Ireland	14-4
Rep. of Ireland drew with Scotland	9-9
Wales beat Isle of Man	15-3
England beat Rep. of Ireland	12-6
Scotland drew with Northern Ireland	9-9
England beat Scotland	14-4
Wales beat England	10-7

	W	D	L	For	Agst	Pts
Wales	5	0	0	61	28	10
England	4	0	1	63	26	8
Rep. of Ireland	2	1	2	43	47	5
Scotland	1	2	2	42	48	4
Northern Ireland	1	1	3	39	51	3
Isle of Man	0	0	5	21	69	0

1981

Northern Ireland drew with Rep. of Ireland *Prestatyn*	9-9
Scotland beat Isle of Man	13-5
England beat Isle of Man	17-1
Wales beat Northern Ireland	11-7
England beat Rep. of Ireland	11-7
Wales beat Scotland	13-5
Wales beat Rep. of Ireland	12-6
England beat Northern Ireland	10-8
Rep. of Ireland drew with Isle of Man	9-9
Scotland beat Northern Ireland	19-8
Wales beat Isle of Man	15-3
Rep. of Ireland beat Scotland	10-8
Scotland beat England	10-8
Northern Ireland beat Isle of Man	10-8
England led Wales 9-7 (match abandoned)	

	W	D	L	A	For	Agst
Wales	4	–	–	1	58	29
England	3	–	1	1	54	33
Scotland	3	–	2	–	46	44
Rep. of Ireland	1	2	2	–	41	49
Northern Ireland	1	1	3	–	42	48
Isle of Man	–	1	4	–	26	64

The Wales v England match was abandoned at the point when Wales was assured of retaining the championship

1982

Wales beat Isle of Man *Prestatyn*	16-2
England drew with Scotland	9-9
Rep. of Ireland drew with Northern Ireland	9-9
Isle of Man drew with Scotland	9-9
England beat Isle of Man	12-6
Wales beat Northern Ireland	10-8
Wales beat Scotland	12-6
England beat Rep. of Ireland	11-7
Rep. of Ireland beat Isle of Man	15-3
Northern Ireland beat Scotland	12-6
England beat Northern Ireland	14-4
Wales beat Rep. of Ireland	11-7
Scotland beat Rep. of Ireland	11-7
Northern Ireland beat Isle of Man	15-3
Wales led England 9-8 (match abandoned)	

	W	D	L	For	Agst	Pts
Wales*	4	0	0	49	23	8
England*	3	1	0	46	26	7
Northern Ireland	2	1	2	53	37	5
Scotland	1	2	2	41	49	4
Rep. of Ireland	1	1	3	44	46	3
Isle of Man	0	1	4	26	66	1

* Not including Wales v England match which was curtailed when Wales led 9-8 at which point they could not be overtaken.

1983

Wales beat Scotland *Prestatyn*	13-5
England beat Rep. of Ireland	13-5
Wales beat Northern Ireland	13-5
Scotland beat Isle of Man	11-7
Isle of Man beat Rep. of Ireland	11-7
Scotland drew with Northern Ireland	9-9
Rep. of Ireland beat Northern Ireland	10-8
England beat Isle of Man	14-4
England beat Northern Ireland	13-5
Wales beat Isle of Man	10-8
Wales beat Rep. of Ireland	14-4
England beat Scotland	11-7
Northern Ireland beat Isle of Man	13-5
Scotland beat Rep. of Ireland	10-8
Wales beat England	10-7

	W	D	L	For	Agst	Pts
Wales	5	0	0	60	29	10
England	4	0	1	58	31	8
Scotland	2	1	2	42	48	5
Northern Ireland	1	1	3	40	50	3
Isle of Man	1	0	4	35	55	2
Rep. of Ireland	1	0	4	34	56	2

Individual performances in the home internationals

ENGLAND
R. Andrewartha
1974–5
v Rep. of Ireland *Glasnevin* beat P. Miley	2-1
v Wales *Exeter* lost to M. Berni	1-2
v Scotland *Edinburgh* beat I. Wallace	3-0

1975–6
v Scotland *Southport* beat S. Nivison	3-0
v Wales *Merthyr* lost to T. Parsons	0-3

J. Barron
1969
v Wales *Port Talbot* beat D. Mountjoy	3-0

1970–1
v Wales *Harringay* beat D. May	2-1
v Rep. of Ireland *Dublin* beat J. Weber	2-1

1971–2
v Scotland *Newcastle* beat J. Phillips	2-1
v Rep. of Ireland *Harringay* beat D. Sheehan	3-0
v Wales *Neath* beat D. May	2-1

1972–3
v Scotland *Edinburgh* beat D. Sneddon	3-0
v Wales *Hull* lost to G. Thomas	1-2

M. Bradley
1982
v Isle of Man *Prestatyn* beat P. Reynolds	2-1
v Scotland beat J. Allan	3-0
v Rep. of Ireland beat M. Ralph	3-0
v Wales lost to W. Jones	1-2

1983
v Rep. of Ireland *Prestatyn* beat M. Kane	2-1
v Northern Ireland beat A. Sharpe	3-0
v Scotland lost to G. Carnegie	1-2
v Wales lost to W. Jones	1-2

D. Chalmers
1982
v Isle of Man *Prestatyn* lost to C. Cooper	1-2
v Scotland lost to K. Baird	0-3

1983
v Rep. of Ireland *Prestatyn* lost to M. Ralph	1-2
v Scotland lost to K. Baird	1-2

G. Cripsey
1981
v Isle of Man *Prestatyn* beat P. Reynolds	3-0
v Northern Ireland beat P. Donnelly	2-1
v Scotland lost to R. Lane	0-3

M. Darrington
1980
v Northern Ireland *Prestatyn* beat T. Murphy	2-1
v Isle of Man beat K. Kinrade	3-0
v Rep. of Ireland beat P. Watchorn	2-1

1981
v Isle of Man *Prestatyn* beat J. Kinrade	3-0
v Rep. of Ireland beat G. Sutton	3-0
v Northern Ireland beat D. McVeigh	3-0
v Scotland beat J. Zonfrillo	3-0
v Wales lost to A. Lloyd	1-2

S. Davis
1977–8
v Scotland *Doncaster* beat D. Sneddon	3-0
v Wales *Caerphilly* beat T. Parsons	2-1

L. Dodd
1981
v Rep. of Ireland *Prestatyn* beat M. Kane	2-1
v Northern Ireland lost to E. Swaffield	1-2
v Scotland lost to J. Rankeillor	0-3

S. Duggan
1982
v Isle of Man *Prestatyn* beat R. Crowley	2-1
v Scotland lost to R. Land	0-3
v Northern Ireland beat A. Sharpe	2-1
v Wales lost to T. Parsons	1-2

R. Edmonds
1969
v Wales *Port Talbot* beat T. Parsons	3-0

1970–1
v Wales *Harringay* beat D. Mountjoy	2-1
v Rep. of Ireland *Dublin* beat F. Murphy	2-1

1971–2
v Scotland *Newcastle* lost to D. Sneddon	1-2
v Rep. of Ireland *Harringay* beat J. Weber	3-0
v Wales *Neath* lost to M. Berni	1-2

1972–3
v Scotland *Edinburgh* beat B. Demarco	3-0
v Wales *Hull* lost to D. May	1-2

1973–4
v Wales *Garnant* beat A. Lloyd	3-0
v Rep. of Ireland *Bolton* lost to D. Sheehan	1-2

1974–5
v Rep. of Ireland *Glasnevin* lost to P. Burke	1-2
v Wales *Exeter* beat A. Lloyd	2-1

1975–6
v Rep. of Ireland *Grimsby* beat E. Hughes	2-1
v Scotland *Southport* lost to J. Zonfrillo	1-2
v Wales *Merthyr* beat M. Berni	3-0

1976–7
v Rep. of Ireland *Dublin* beat P. Burke	2-1
v Wales *Doncaster* beat J. Prosser	2-1
v Scotland *Glasgow* beat E. McLaughlin	2-1

1977–8
v Rep. of Ireland *Portsmouth* lost to P. Burke	1-2
v Scotland *Doncaster* lost to E. Sinclair	1-2
v Wales *Caerphilly* beat C. Wilson	2-1

J. Fitzmaurice
1972–3
v Rep. of Ireland *Dublin* beat G. Hanway	3-0

1975–6
v Rep. of Ireland *Grimsby* beat N. Clarke	3-0
v Scotland *Southport* lost to M. McLeod	1-2
v Wales *Merthyr* lost to J. Selby	1-2

1976–7
v Rep. of Ireland *Dublin* lost to G. Sutton	1-2

G. Foulds
1976–7
v Rep. of Ireland *Dublin* lost to R. Brennan	1-2
v Scotland *Glasgow* beat B. Demarco	2-1

1977–8
v Rep. of Ireland *Portsmouth* beat T. Langan	3-0
v Scotland *Doncaster* lost to E.McLaughlin	0-3
v Wales *Caerphilly* beat G. Thomas	2-1

1978
v Isle of Man *Prestatyn* beat P. Reynolds	2-1
v Scotland beat J. Halcrow	3-0
v Wales lost to C. Everton	1-2

1979
v Isle of Man *Prestatyn* beat C. Cooper	3-0
v Scotland lost to J. Halcrow	0-3

N. Foulds
1982
v Isle of Man *Prestatyn* beat M. Colquitt	3-0
v Rep. of Ireland lost to J. Long	0-3
v Northern Ireland beat J. McLaughlin	2-1
v Wales lost to S. Newbury	0-3

D. Fowler
1983
v Rep. of Ireland *Prestatyn* beat G. Gibson	2-1
v Northern Ireland beat J. McLaughlin	3-0
v Scotland beat R. Lane	2-1
v Isle of Man beat T. Wilson	2-1
v Wales lost to T. Parsons	1-2

D. French
1971–2
v Wales *Neath* lost to D. Meredith	1-2

1972–3
v Rep. of Ireland *Dublin* beat F. Nathan	2-1
v Rep. of Ireland *Bolton* lost to D. Lenehan	1-2
v Scotland *Carlisle* beat D. Sneddon	2-1

T. Graham
1972–3
v Rep. of Ireland *Dublin* beat R. Brennan	2-1

1973–4
v Scotland *Carlisle* lost to B. Demarco	1-2

M. Hallett

1978
v Isle of Man *Prestatyn* beat R. Cowley   3-0
v Rep. of Ireland beat J. Rogers   2-1
v Scotland beat D. Sneddon   2-1
v Wales lost to C. Wilson   0-3

J. Hargreaves

1974–5
v Scotland *Edinburgh* beat J. Zonfrillo   2-1
1975–6
v Scotland *Southport* beat E. McLaughlin   3-0
1976–7
v Rep. of Ireland *Dublin* beat J. Clusker   3-0
v Scotland *Glasgow* beat D. Sneddon   2-1
v Wales *Doncaster* beat S. Newbury   2-1
1977–8
v Rep. of Ireland *Portsmouth* beat D. Wilson   2-1
v Scotland *Doncaster* beat R. Cadman   3-0
v Wales *Caerphilly* lost to T. Griffiths   0-3
1978
v Isle of Man *Prestatyn* beat J. Radcliffe   3-0
v Scotland beat M. Gibson   3-0
v Wales beat T. Parsons   2-1
1979
v Northern Ireland *Prestatyn* beat R. Burke   3-0
v Isle of Man beat P. Partington   3-0
v Rep. of Ireland lost to D. Sheehan   1-2
v Scotland lost to M. Gibson   1-2
v Wales beat J. Selby   3-0
1980
v Northern Ireland *Prestatyn* beat D. McVeigh   2-1
v Scotland beat P. Kippie   3-0
v England lost to J. Selby   0-2
1981
v Isle of Man *Prestatyn* beat R. Cowley   2-1
v Rep. of Ireland beat M. Ralph   2-1
v Northern Ireland lost to A. Sharpe   0-3
v Wales beat T. Parsons   2-1
1982
v Scotland *Prestatyn* J. Zonfrillo   2-1
v Rep. of Ireland beat P. Ennis   2-1
v Northern Ireland beat E. Swaffield   2-1
v Wales beat T. Chappel   2-0

B. Harris

1981
v Isle of Man *Prestatyn* beat C. Cooper   3-0
v Rep. of Ireland beat P. Watchorn   2-1
v Scotland beat J. McNellan   2-1
v Wales beat D. May   2-1

V. Harris

1980
v Northern Ireland *Prestatyn* beat S. Clarke   3-0
v Rep. of Ireland beat G. Sutton   3-0
v Scotland beat J. Donnelly   3-0
v Wales lost to D. John   0-3

S. Hood

1969
v Wales *Port Talbot* lost to J. Ford   1-2
1970–1
v Wales *Harringay* beat J. Ford   2-1
v Rep. of Ireland *Dublin* lost to A. Roche   1-2
1971–2
v Scotland *Newcastle* beat E. Sinclair   2-1
v Rep. of Ireland *Harringay* beat F. Byrne   2-1
v Wales *Neath* beat D. John   2-1
1972–3
v Scotland *Edinburgh* beat J. Phillips   2-1
v Wales *Hull* beat D. Mountjoy   2-1
1973–4
v Wales *Garnant* beat D. May   3-0
v Rep. of Ireland *Bolton* lost to P. Miley   1-2
v Scotland *Carlisle* beat J. Phillips   2-1
1974–5
v Wales *Exeter* beat G. Thomas   2-1
v Scotland *Edinburgh* lost to E. Sinclair   1-2
v Rep. of Ireland *Glasnevin* beat N. Clarke   2-1

1975–6
v Rep. of Ireland *Grimsby* beat F. Nathan   3-0
v Scotland *Southport* beat E. Sinclair   2-1
v Wales *Merthyr* lost to T. Griffiths   1-2
1976–7
v Rep. of Ireland *Dublin* beat E. Hughes   3-0
v Scotland *Glasgow* lost to E. Sinclair   1-2
v Wales *Doncaster* beat D. Thomas   2-1
1977–8
v Rep. of Ireland *Portsmouth* lost to J. Clusker   1-2
1978
v Rep. of Ireland *Prestatyn* beat D. Wilson   2-1

P. Houlihan

1969
v Wales *Port Talbot* lost to M. Berni   0-3

D. Hughes

1979
v Northern Ireland *Prestatyn* beat J. Begley   3-0
v Rep. of Ireland lost to G. Sutton   0-3

R. Jarmak

1983
v Northern Ireland *Prestatyn* beat E. Swaffield   2-1
v Isle of Man beat C. Cooper   2-1
v Wales drew with R. Jones   1-1

J. Johnson

1976–7
v Rep. of Ireland *Dublin* beat D. Sheehan   3-0
v Scotland *Glasgow* beat R. Miller   2-1
v Wales *Doncaster* lost to T. Griffiths   1-2
1977–8
v Rep. of Ireland *Portsmouth* beat R. Brennan   2-1
v Scotland *Doncaster* beat R. Miller   2-1
v Wales *Caerphilly* lost to A. Lloyd   1-2
1978
v Isle of Man *Prestatyn* beat C. Cooper   2-1
v Rep. of Ireland beat P. Burke   3-0
v Scotland beat J. Zonfrillo   2-1
v Wales beat J. Selby   3-0

A. Knowles

1978
v Isle of Man *Prestatyn* beat M. Quine   3-0
v Rep. of Ireland beat F. Nathan   2-1
v Scotland beat J. Donnelly   3-0
v Wales beat A. Lloyd   2-0
1979
v Northern Ireland *Prestatyn* beat D. McVeigh   3-0
v Isle of Man beat J. Radcliffe   2-1
v Rep. of Ireland beat T. Langan   3-0
v Scotland beat I. Wallace   3-0
v Wales beat T. Parsons   2-1

S. Longworth

1983
v Rep. of Ireland *Prestatyn* beat J Long   2-1
v Scotland beat J. Rankeillor   3-0
v Isle of Man beat P. Reynolds   2-1
v Wales beat S. Newbury   3-0

D. Martin

1979
v Northern Ireland *Prestatyn* beat S. Pavis   2-1
v Isle of Man beat A. Christian   3-0
v Rep. of Ireland beat P. Miley   3-0
v Scotland lost to M. McLeod   1-2
v Wales lost to A. Lloyd   1-2
1980
v Northern Ireland *Prestatyn* beat P. Donnelly   3-0
v Isle of Man beat P. Reynolds   2-1
v Rep. of Ireland lost to D. Sheehan   1-2
v Wales beat D. May   3-0

T. Meo

1978
v Isle of Man *Prestatyn* beat W. Craig   2-1
v Rep. of Ireland beat E. Hughes   2-1
v Scotland beat E. Sinclair   3-0
v Wales beat S. Newbury   2-1

J. O'Boye

1980
v Northern Ireland *Prestatyn* J. Begley   3-0
v Isle of Man beat C. Cooper   2-1
v Rep. of Ireland lost to P. Burke   1-2
v Scotland beat I. Black   2-1
v Wales beat A. Lloyd   2-1

B. Oliver

1982
v Isle of Man *Prestatyn* lost to T. Wilson   1-2
v Northern Ireland beat S. Pavis   2-1

J. Parrott

1982
v Scotland *Prestatyn* beat J. Rea   2-1
v Rep. of Ireland beat P. Browne   2-1
v Northern Ireland beat F. Cahoon   3-0
v Wales beat A. Lloyd   2-1

C. Ross

1969
v Wales *Port Talbot* beat A. Kemp   2-1
1970–1
v Wales *Harringay* beat E. Richards   3-0
v Rep. of Ireland *Dublin* beat R. Dunne   3-0
1971–2
v Scotland *Newcastle* B. Demarco   2-1
v Rep. of Ireland *Harringay* beat A. Roche   3-0
v Wales *Neath* beat D. Thomas   2-1
1972–3
v Scotland *Edinburgh* beat E. Sinclair   2-1
v Wales *Hull* lost to A. Lloyd   1-2
v Rep. of Ireland *Dublin* lost to J. Rogers   1-2
1973–4
v Wales *Garnant* beat M. Berni   2-1
1974–5
v Rep. of Ireland *Glasnevin* lost to F. Nathan   1-2
v Wales *Exeter* lost to D. Mountjoy   1-2
1975–6
v Rep. of Ireland *Grimsby* beat J. Rogers   2-1
v Wales *Merthyr* lost to A. Lloyd   1-2

G. Scott

1974–5
v Scotland *Edinburgh* beat M. Gibson   3-0
1976–7
v Scotland *Glasgow* beat J. Phillips   2-1
v Wales *Doncaster* beat T. Parsons   2-1
1977–8
v Rep. of Ireland *Portsmouth* beat P. Watchorn   2-1
v Scotland *Doncaster* lost to M. Gibson   1-2
v Wales *Caerphilly* lost to S. Newbury   1-2
1978
v Rep. of Ireland *Prestatyn* beat R. Brennan   3-0
1979
v Isle of Man *Prestatyn* beat R. Cowley   2-1
v Rep. of Ireland beat P. Burke   2-1
v Wales drew with C. Everton   1-1

M. Smith

1983
v Northern Ireland *Prestatyn* lost to W. Walker   0-3

D. Taylor

1971–2
v Wales *Neath* lost to R. Oriel   1-2

G. Thompson

1969
v Wales *Port Talbot* lost to A. Lloyd   1-2

S. Ventham

1983
v Scotland *Prestatyn* beat J. Rea   2-1
v Isle of Man beat R. Cowley   3-0

J. Virgo

1970–1
v Wales *Harringay* beat G. Thomas   3-0
v Rep. of Ireland *Dublin* beat M. Lowth   3-0

1971–2
v Scotland *Newcastle* beat G. Carnegie 2-1
v Rep. of Ireland *Harringay* beat F. Murphy 2-1
1972–3
v Scotland *Edinburgh* beat J. Wilson 3-0
v Wales *Hull* lost to M. Berni 1-2
v Rep. of Ireland *Dublin* beat F. Byrne 3-0
1973–4
v Wales *Garnant* beat G. Thomas 2-1
v Rep. of Ireland *Bolton* beat P. Burke 2-1
v Scotland *Carlisle* beat E. Sinclair 2-1
1974–5
v Rep. of Ireland *Glasnevin* beat D. Sheehan 3-0
v Scotland *Edinburgh* beat J. Phillips 2-1
1975–6
v Rep. of Ireland *Grimsby* beat P. Burke 2-1
v Scotland *Southport* beat D. Sneddon 2-1
v Wales *Merthyr* lost to D. Mountjoy 1-2

W. Thorne

1972–3
v Rep. of Ireland *Dublin* beat F. Murphy 2-1
1973–4
v Wales *Garnant* beat J. Prosser 2-1
v Rep. of Ireland *Bolton* beat F. Byrne 3-0
v Scotland *Carlisle* beat J. Zonfrillo 2-1
1974–5
v Wales *Exeter* beat T. Griffiths 2-1
v Scotland *Edinburgh* lost to W. McKerron 1-2
v Rep. of Ireland *Glasnevin* beat L. Kenna 2-1
1975–6
v Rep. of Ireland *Grimsby* lost to P. Fagan 1-2

M. Watterson

1979
v Northern Ireland *Prestatyn* beat P. Donnelly 2-1
v Scotland beat S. Nevison 3-0
v Wales lost to S. Newbury 0-3
1980
v Isle of Man *Prestatyn* beat J. Radcliffe 3-0
v Scotland beat M. Gibson 3-0
v Wales beat C. Roscoe 2-1

B. West

1981
v Rep. of Ireland *Prestatyn* beat P. Ennis 2-1
v Northern Ireland beat S. Pavis 3-0
v Wales beat D. John 2-1
1982
v Scotland beat *Prestatyn* J. Rankeillor 2-1
v Rep. of Ireland beat R. Brennan 3-0
v Northern Ireland beat K. Erwin 3-0
v Wales beat J. Selby 2-1
1983
v Rep. of Ireland *Prestatyn* beat R. Brennan 3-0
v Northern Ireland beat J. McLaughlin 3-0
v Scotland beat J. Halcrow 2-1
v Isle of Man beat M. Colquitt 3-0
v Wales lost to A. Lloyd 1-2

J. White

1979
v Northern Ireland *Prestatyn* beat E. Swaffield 3-0
v Isle of Man beat P. Reynolds 3-0
v Rep. of Ireland beat E. Hughes 2-1
v Scotland beat E. McLaughlin 2-1
v Wales beat G. Thomas 3-0
1980
v Northern Ireland *Prestatyn* beat S. Pavis 2-1
v Isle of Man beat W. Craig 3-0
v Rep. of Ireland beat M. Kane 2-1
v Scotland beat E. McLaughlin 2-1
v Wales lost to S. Newbury 0-3

M. Wildman

1970–1
v Wales *Harringay* beat M. Berni 2-1
v Rep. of Ireland *Dublin* beat G. Hanway 3-0
1971–2
v Scotland *Newcastle* lost to W. McKerron 1-2
v Rep. of Ireland *Harringay* lost to J. Rogers 1-2
1972–3
v Scotland *Edinburgh* beat W. McKerron 3-0

---

v Wales *Hull* beat T. Parsons 3-0
1973–4
v Wales *Garnant* beat D. Mountjoy 2-1
v Rep. of Ireland *Bolton* lost to J. Weber 1-2
v Scotland *Carlisle* beat R. Eprile 2-1
1974–5
v Wales *Exeter* lost to T. Parsons 0-3

I. Williamson

1981
v Isle of Man *Prestatyn* beat M. Quine 3-0
v Northern Ireland lost to S. Clarke 1-2
v Scotland lost to J. Rea 1-2
v Wales beat J. Selby 1-0

G. Wood

1980
v Isle of Man *Prestatyn* beat M. Quine 2-1
v Rep. of Ireland beat E. Hughes 3-0
v Scotland lost to J. McNellan 1-2
1981
v Isle of Man *Prestatyn* beat J. Radcliffe 3-0
v Rep. of Ireland lost to P. Burke 0-3
v Scotland beat K. Baird 2-1
v Wales lost to S. Newbury 0-2
1982
v Isle of Man *Prestatyn* beat M. Clinton 3-0
v Rep. of Ireland lost to G. Gibson 1-2
1983
v Rep. of Ireland *Prestatyn* beat P. Ennis 3-0
v Northern Ireland beat S. Pavis 2-1
v Isle of Man beat M. Clinton 2-1
v Wales lost to T. Chappel 0-3

ISLE OF MAN
A. Christian

1979
v England *Prestatyn* lost to D. Martin 0-3

M. Clinton

1981
v Rep. of Ireland *Prestatyn* lost to P. Watchorn 1-2
v Wales lost to J. Selby 0-3
1982
v Scotland lost to J. Zonfrillo 1-2
v Wales lost to A. Lloyd 1-2
v England lost to G. Wood 0-3
v Rep. of Ireland lost to P. Browne 1-2
v Northern Ireland lost to F. Cahoon 0-3
1983
v Scotland lost to R. Lane 1-2
v England lost to G. Wood 1-2

M. Colquitt

1982
v Scotland lost to J. Rankeillor 1-2
v Wales lost to S. Newbury 0-3
v England lost to N. Foulds 0-3
v Northern Ireland lost to J. McLaughlin 1-2
1983
v Rep. of Ireland beat R. McCrum 2-1
v Wales lost to J. Selby 1-2
v Scotland lost to J. McNellan 1-2
v England lost B. West 0-3
v Northern Ireland lost to S. Pavis 1-2

C. Cooper

1978
v England *Prestatyn* lost to J. Johnson 1-2
v Wales lost to A. Lloyd 0-3
v Rep. of Ireland lost to P. Burke 0-3
v Scotland lost to J. Zonfrillo 1-2
1979
v Scotland *Prestatyn* lost to S. Nivison 1-2
v England lost to G. Foulds 0-3
v Wales lost to C. Everton 0-3
v Northern Ireland lost to B. Harvey 0-3
v Rep. of Ireland beat J. Long 3-0
1980
v Scotland *Prestatyn* lost to P. Kippie 1-2
v England lost to J. O'Boye 1-2

---

v Northern Ireland lost to J. Begley 1-2
v Wales lost to R. Welch 1-2
v Rep. of Ireland lost to P. Burke 1-2
1981
v Scotland *Prestatyn* lost to K. Baird 1-2
v England lost to B. Harris 0-3
v Rep. of Ireland beat G. Sutton 3-0
v Wales lost to A. Lloyd 0-3
v Northern Ireland lost to S. Pavis 1-2
1982
v Scotland *Prestatyn* beat J. Rea 2-1
v Wales lost to T. Parsons 0-3
v England beat D. Chalmers 2-1
v Rep. of Ireland lost to P. Ennis 0-3
v Northern Ireland lost to S. Pavis 1-2
1983
v Rep. of Ireland *Prestatyn* lost to D. Cranley 1-2
v Wales beat W. Jones 3-0
v Scotland lost to J. Halcrow 1-2
v England lost to R. Jarmak 1-2
v Northern Ireland lost to E. Swaffield 0-3

R. Cowley

1978
v England *Prestatyn* lost to M. Hallett 0-3
v Wales lost to G. Thomas 1-2
v Rep. of Ireland beat J. Rogers 2-1
v Scotland lost to J. Donnelly 0-3
1979
v Scotland *Prestatyn* lost to I. Wallace 0-3
v England lost to G. Scott 1-2
v Wales lost to T. Parsons 1-2
v Northern Ireland lost to J. Begley 1-2
v Rep. of Ireland lost to E. Hughes 0-3
1981
v Scotland *Prestatyn* beat R. Miller 2-1
v England lost to J. Hargreaves 0-3
v Rep. of Ireland lost to M. Ralph 1-2
v Wales lost to D. May 1-2
v Northern Ireland beat J. McLaughlin 2-1
1982
v Scotland *Prestatyn* beat G. Carnegie 3-1
v Wales lost to W. Jones 0-3
v England lost to S. Duggan 1-2
v Rep. of Ireland lost to P. Watchorn 0-3
v Northern Ireland lost to E. Swaffield 0-3
1983
v Rep. of Ireland *Prestatyn* beat M. Kane 3-0
v Wales lost to T. Parsons 0-3
v Scotland beat G. Carnegie 3-0
v England lost to S. Ventham 0-3
v Northern Ireland lost to J. McLaughlin 1-2

W. Craig

1978
v England *Prestatyn* lost to T. Meo 1-2
v Wales lost to J. Selby 1-2
v Rep. of Ireland beat J. Langan 2-1
v Scotland lost to J. Halcrow 1-2
1979
v Scotland *Prestatyn* lost to J. Donnelly 0-3
v Wales lost to V. Rosser 0-3
v Northern Ireland lost to D. McVeigh 0-3
1980
v Scotland *Prestatyn* lost to M. Gibson 0-3
v England lost to J. White 0-3
v Wales lost to C. Roscoe 0-3

J. Kinrade

1978
v Rep. of Ireland *Prestatyn* lost to E. Hughes 0-3
1981
v Scotland *Prestatyn* lost to R. Lane 1-2
v England lost to M. Darrington 3-0
v Rep. of Ireland lost to M. Kane 0-3
v Wales lost to W. Jones 0-3

K. Kinrade

1978
v Wales *Prestatyn* lost to T. Parsons 0-3
1980
v Scotland *Prestatyn* lost to M. McLeod 1-2
v England lost to M. Darrington 0-3

v Northern Ireland lost to T. Murphy 1-2
v Wales lost to A. Lloyd 1-2
v Rep. of Ireland lost to E. Hughes 0-3
1983
v Northern Ireland *Prestatyn* lost to A. Sharpe 0-3

P. Partington
1979
v Scotland *Prestatyn* lost to M. McLeod 1-2
v England lost to J. Hargreaves 0-3
v Rep. of Ireland lost to P. Burke 1-2
1980
v Scotland *Prestatyn* lost to I. Black 0-3
v Northern Ireland lost to G. Sharpe 0-3
v Rep. of Ireland beat G. Sutton 2-1
1981
v Rep. of Ireland *Prestatyn* beat P. Browne 2-1
v Wales lost to T. Parsons 1-2
v Northern Ireland lost to A. Sharpe 1-2
1983
v Rep. of Ireland *Prestatyn* beat P. McNally 2-1
v Wales lost to S. Newbury 0-3

M. Quine
1978
v England *Prestatyn* lost to A. Knowles 0-3
v Wales lost to C. Everton 0-3
v Scotland lost to D. Sneddon 0-3
1979
v Wales *Prestatyn* lost to S. Newbury 0-3
v Northern Ireland lost to D. McVeigh 1-2
v Rep. of Ireland beat T. Langan 2-1
1980
v England *Prestatyn* lost to G. Wood 1-2
v Northern Ireland lost to S. Pavis 1-2
v Wales lost to S. Newbury 0-3
v Rep. of Ireland lost to D. Sheehan 1-2
1981
v Scotland *Prestatyn* lost to J. Zonfrillo 0-3
v England lost to I. Williamson 0-3
v Northern Ireland lost to E. Swaffield 1-2
1982
v Rep. of Ireland *Prestatyn* lost to G. Gibson 1-2

J. Radcliffe
1978
v England *Prestatyn* lost to J. Hargreaves 0-3
v Scotland lost to E. McLaughlin 0-3
1979
v Scotland *Prestatyn* lost to E. McLaughlin 1-2
v England lost to A. Knowles 1-2
v Wales lost to A. Lloyd 0-3
v Northern Ireland lost to S. Pavis 1-2
v Rep. of Ireland lost to G. Sutton 0-3
1980
v Scotland *Prestatyn* lost to E. McLaughlin 0-3
v England lost to M. Watterson 0-3
v Northern Ireland lost to E. Swaffield 1-2
v Wales lost to D. May 0-3
v Rep. of Ireland lost to M. Kane 0-3
1981
v Scotland *Prestatyn* lost to J. Rea 0-3
v England lost to G. Wood 0-3
v Northern Ireland lost to D. McVeigh 1-2

N. Radcliffe
1978
v Rep. of Ireland *Prestatyn* lost to J. Clusker 0-3

P. Reynolds
1978
v England *Prestatyn* lost to G. Foulds 1-2
v Wales lost to C. Wilson 0-3
v Rep. of Ireland lost to G. Sutton 0-3
v Scotland lost to R. Miller 1-2
1979
v Scotland *Prestatyn* beat J. Phillips 2-1
v England lost to J. White 0-3
v Wales lost to J. Selby 1-2
v Northern Ireland lost to P. Donnelly 1-2
v Rep. of Ireland lost to D. Sheehan 0-3

1980
v Scotland *Prestatyn* beat J. Donnelly 2-1
v England lost to D. Martin 1-2
v Northern Ireland beat S. Clarke 2-1
v Wales lost to J. Selby 1-2
v Rep. of Ireland lost to M. Ralph 1-2
1981
v Scotland *Prestatyn* lost to J. Halcrow 1-2
v England lost to G. Cripsey 0-3
v Rep. of Ireland beat A. Kearney 2-1
v Wales lost to M. Bennett 1-2
v Northern Ireland beat P. Donnelly 2-1
1982
v Scotland *Prestatyn* lost to D. Sneddon 1-2
v Wales lost to J. Terry 1-2
v England lost to M. Bradley 1-2
v Rep. of Ireland lost to J. Long 1-2
v Northern Ireland lost to A. Sharpe 1-2
1983
v Rep. of Ireland *Prestatyn* beat J. Long 2-1
v Wales lost to R. Jones 1-2
v Scotland lost to S. Muir 0-3
v England lost to S. Longworth 1-2
v Northern Ireland beat S. McClarey 2-1

T. Wilson
1982
v Scotland *Prestatyn* lost to J. Allan 1-2
v Wales lost to J. Selby 0-3
v England beat B. Oliver 2-1
v Rep. of Ireland lost to M. Kane 0-3
v Northern Ireland lost to S. Clarke 0-3
1983
v Rep. of Ireland *Prestatyn* lost to M. Ralph 1-2
v Wales beat J. Griffiths 3-0
v Scotland lost to K. Baird 1-2
v England lost to D. Fowler 1-2
v Northern Ireland lost to K. Erwin 1-2

NORTHERN IRELAND
J. Begley
1979
v England *Prestatyn* lost to D. Hughes 0-3
v Wales lost to J. Terry 1-2
v Scotland lost to M. Gibson 1-2
v Rep. of Ireland beat E. Hughes 2-1
v Isle of Man beat R. Cowley 2-1
1980
v England *Prestatyn* lost to J. O'Boye 0-3
v Isle of Man beat C. Cooper 2-1

R. Burke
1979
v England *Prestatyn* lost to J. Hargreaves 0-3
v Scotland lost to E. McLaughlin 0-3

F. Cahoon
1982
v England *Prestatyn* lost to J. Parrott 0-3
v Isle of Man beat M. Clinton 3-0

S. Clarke
1980
v England *Prestatyn* lost to V. Harris 0-3
v Rep. of Ireland lost to M. Kane 1-2
v Isle of Man lost to P. Reynolds 1-2
1981
v Rep. of Ireland *Prestatyn* lost to P. Ennis 1-2
v Wales lost to W. Jones 1-2
v England beat I. Williamson 2-1
v Scotland lost to J. Rankeillor 0-3
1982
v Scotland *Prestatyn* lost to J. Rankeillor 1-2
v Isle of Man beat T. Wilson 3-0

F. Connolly
1982
v Rep. of Ireland *Prestatyn* lost to G. Gibson 1-2

P. Donnelly
1979
v England *Prestatyn* lost to M. Watterson 1-2
v Wales beat A. Lloyd 2-1
v Scotland beat J. Phillips 3-0
v Rep. of Ireland beat D. Sheehan 2-1
v Isle of Man beat P. Reynolds 2-1
1980
v England *Prestatyn* lost to J. O'Boye 0-3
v Wales lost to A. Lloyd 1-2
v Rep. of Ireland lost to G. Sutton 1-2
v Scotland lost to E. McLaughlin 1-2
1981
v Rep. of Ireland *Prestatyn* lost to M. Kane 1-2
v Wales lost to S. Newbury 1-2
v England lost to G. Cripsey 1-2
v Isle of Man lost to P. Reynolds 1-2
1982
v Scotland *Prestatyn* beat R. Lane 2-1
v Wales lost to S. Newbury 0-3

K. Erwin
1982
v Wales *Prestatyn* beat J. Griffiths 2-1
v Rep. of Ireland lost to P. Watchorn 1-2
v England lost to B. West 0-3
1983
v Wales *Prestatyn* lost to R. Jones 0-3
v Isle of Man beat T. Wilson 2-1
v Scotland lost to R. Lane 0-3

B. Harvey
1979
v Wales *Prestatyn* lost to J. Terry 1-2
v Isle of Man beat C. Cooper 3-0

S. McClarey
1983
v Rep. of Ireland *Prestatyn* lost to P. Ennis 1-2
v Isle of Man lost to P. Reynolds 1-2
v Scotland lost to J. Rea 1-2

Jim McLaughlin
1983
v England *Prestatyn* lost to D. Fowler 0-3
v Rep. of Ireland lost to M. Kane 0-3

John McLaughlin
1979
v Rep. of Ireland *Prestatyn* lost to T. Langan 0-3
v Isle of Man beat M.Quine 2-1
1981
v Rep. of Ireland *Prestatyn* lost to M. Ralph 1-2
v Scotland lost to J. Rea 1-2
v Isle of Man lost to R. Cowley 1-2
1982
v Scotland *Prestatyn* beat J. Zonfrillo 3-0
v Wales lost to A. Lloyd 1-2
v Rep. of Ireland lost to P. Browne 1-2
v England lost to N. Foulds 1-2
v Isle of Man beat M. Colquitt 2-1
1983
v England *Prestatyn* lost to B. West 0-3
v Wales beat A. Lloyd 3-0
v Rep. of Ireland lost to R. Brennan 1-2
v Isle of Man beat R. Cowley 2-1
v Scotland beat J. Laidlaw 3-0

D. McVeigh
1979
v England *Prestatyn* lost to A. Knowles 0-3
v Wales lost to T. Parsons 0-3
v Scotland beat J. Donnelly 2-1
v Rep. of Ireland beat G. Sutton 3-0
v Isle of Man beat W. Craig 3-0
1980
v England *Prestatyn* lost to J. Hargreaves 1-2
v Wales lost to D. John 1-2
v Rep. of Ireland lost to D. Sheehan 0-3
v Scotland beat J. Halcrow 2-1
1981
v Rep. of Ireland *Prestatyn* lost to G. Sutton 1-2
v Wales lost to A. Lloyd 1-2

v England lost to M. Darrington 0-3
v Scotland lost to J. Zonfrillo 1-2
v Isle of Man beat J. Radcliffe 2-1

T. Murphy
1980
v England *Prestatyn* lost to M. Darrington 1-2
v Wales beat V. Rosser 3-0
v Rep. of Ireland beat P. Burke 2-1
v Isle of Man beat K. Kinrade 2-1
v Scotland beat P. Kippie 2-1

S. Pavis
1979
v England *Prestatyn* lost to D. Martin 1-2
v Wales lost to S. Newbury 0-3
v Scotland lost to S. Nivison 1-2
v Rep. of Ireland lost to P. Burke 1-2
v Isle of Man beat J. Radcliffe 2-1
1980
v England *Prestatyn* lost to J. White 1-2
v Wales lost to D. May 1-2
v Isle of Man beat M. Quine 2-1
v Rep. of Ireland lost to E. Hughes 1-2
v Scotland lost to J. Donnelly 1-2
1981
v Rep. of Ireland *Prestatyn* beat A. Kearney 3-0
v Wales lost to T. Parsons 0-3
v England lost to B. West 0-3
v Scotland beat J. McNellan 2-1
v Isle of Man beat C. Cooper 2-1
1982
v Scotland *Prestatyn* beat D. Sneddon 3-0
v Wales lost to T. Parsons 1-2
v Rep. of Ireland beat M. Kane 3-0
v England lost to B. Oliver 1-2
v Isle of Man beat C. Cooper 2-1
1983
v England *Prestatyn* lost to G. Wood 1-2
v Wales lost to T. Parsons 0-3
v Rep. of Ireland beat R. McCrum 3-0
v Isle of Man beat M. Colquitt 2-1
v Scotland lost to J. Halcrow 1-2

A. Sharpe
1980
v Wales *Prestatyn* lost to S. Newbury 1-2
v Isle of Man beat P. Partington 3-0
v Scotland lost to I. Black 1-2
1981
v Rep. of Ireland *Prestatyn* beat P. Burke 2-1
v Wales beat D. John 2-1
v England beat J. Hargreaves 3-0
v Scotland beat K. Baird 2-1
v Isle of Man beat P. Partington 2-1
1982
v Scotland *Prestatyn* beat J. Rea 2-1
v Wales beat T. Chappel 2-1
v Rep. of Ireland lost to P. Ennis 1-2
v England lost to S. Duggan 1-2
v Isle of Man beat R. Reynolds 2-1
1983
v England *Prestatyn* lost to M. Bradley 0-3
v Wales lost to T. Chappel 1-2
v Rep. of Ireland beat D. Cranley 2-1
v Isle of Man beat K. Kinrade 3-0
v Scotland beat J. McNellan 3-0

E. Swaffield
1979
v England *Prestatyn* lost to J. White 0-3
v Wales beat J. Selby 2-1
v Scotland lost to J. Halcrow 1-2
v Rep. of Ireland lost to P. Miley 1-2
1980
v Wales *Prestatyn* lost to C. Roscoe 1-2
v Rep. of Ireland beat P. Watchorn 2-1
v Isle of Man beat J. Radcliffe 2-1
v Scotland beat M. McLeod 2-1
1981
v Wales *Prestatyn* beat D. May 2-1
v England beat L. Dodd 2-1

v Scotland beat R. Miller 2-1
v Isle of Man beat M. Quine 2-1
1982
v Scotland *Prestatyn* lost to K. Baird 1-2
v Wales beat W. Jones 2-1
v Rep. of Ireland beat A. Kearney 2-1
v England lost to J. Hargreaves 1-2
v Isle of Man beat R. Cowley 3-0
1983
v England *Prestatyn* lost to R. Jarmak 1-2
v Wales lost to S. Newbury 1-2
v Rep. of Ireland lost to M. Ralph 1-2
v Isle of Man beat C. Cooper 3-0
v Scotland lost to G. Carnegie 1-2

W. Walker
1983
v England *Prestatyn* beat M. Smith 3-0
v Wales lost to W. Jones 0-3

REPUBLIC OF IRELAND
R. Brennan
1971–2
v Wales *Dublin* lost to R. Oriel 0-3
1972–3
v England *Dublin* lost to T. Graham 1-2
1976–7
v Wales *Cardiff* lost to T. Griffiths 0-3
v Scotland *Edinburgh* beat R. Cadman 2-1
v England *Dublin* beat G. Foulds 2-1
1977–8
v Scotland *Dublin* beat W. McKerron 3-0
v England *Portsmouth* lost to J. Johnson 1-2
1978
v England *Prestatyn* lost to G. Scott 0-3
v Scotland lost to D. Sneddon 1-2
1982
v England *Prestatyn* lost to B. West 0-3
1983
v England *Prestatyn* lost to B. West 0-3
v Northern Ireland beat J. McLaughlin 2-1
v Scotland beat J. McNellan 2-1

P. Browne
1981
v Isle of Man *Prestatyn* lost to P. Partington 1-2
1982
v Northern Ireland *Prestatyn* beat J. McLaughlin 2-1
v Isle of Man beat M. Clinton 2-1
v Scotland lost to J. Allan 1-2
v England lost to J. Parrott 1-2
v Wales beat W. Jones 2-1

P. Burke
1973–4
v Scotland *Dublin* D. Sneddon 2-1
v England *Bolton* lost to J. Virgo 1-2
v Wales *Dublin* lost to T. Griffiths 1-2
1974–5
v Wales *Neath* lost to D. Mountjoy 1-2
v England *Glasnevin* beat R. Edmonds 2-1
v Scotland *Dundee* beat E. Sinclair 2-1
1975–6
v England *Grimsby* lost to J. Virgo 1-2
v Wales *Dublin* beat G. Thomas 2-1
v Scotland *Dunlaoghaire* lost to E. Sinclair 0-3
1976–7
v Wales *Cardiff* lost to T. Parsons 0-2
v Scotland *Edinburgh* lost to E. Sinclair 0-3
v England *Dublin* lost to R. Edmonds 1-2
1977–8
v Wales *Dublin* lost to T. Parsons 1-2
v Scotland *Dublin* lost to E. Sinclair 1-2
v England *Portsmouth* beat R. Edmonds 2-1
1978
v England *Prestatyn* lost to J. Johnson 0-3
v Isle of Man beat C. Cooper 3-0
v Wales beat A. Lloyd 2-1
v Scotland beat J. Zonfrillo 2-1
1979
v Scotland *Prestatyn* beat J. Donnelly 2-1

v England lost to G. Scott 1-2
v Northern Ireland beat S. Pavis 2-1
v Wales beat J. Terry 2-1
v Isle of Man beat P. Partington 2-1
1980
v Northern Ireland *Prestatyn* lost to T. Murphy 1-2
v Wales lost to A. Lloyd 0-3
v Scotland beat J. McNellan 2-1
v England beat J. O'Boye 2-1
v Isle of Man beat C. Cooper 2-1
1981
v Northern Ireland *Prestatyn* lost to A. Sharpe 1-2
v England beat G. Wood 3-0
v Wales lost to T. Parsons 0-3
v Scotland beat J. Rea 3-0

F. Byrne
1971–2
v England *Harringay* lost to S. Hood 1-2
1972–3
v Wales *Pontygwaith* lost to M. Berni 1-2
v England *Dublin* lost to J. Virgo 0-3
1973–4
v Scotland *Dublin* lost to B. Demarco 1-2
v England *Bolton* lost to W. Thorne 0-3
v Wales *Dublin* lost to J. Selby 1-2
1975–6
v Scotland *Dunlaoghaire* beat B. Demarco 2-1

N. Clarke
1973–4
v Wales *Dublin* lost to M. Berni 0-3
1974–5
v England *Glasnevin* lost to S. Hood 1-2
v Scotland *Dundee* lost to B. Demarco 1-2
v Wales *Neath* lost to M. Berni 0-3
1975–6
v England *Grimsby* lost to J. Fitzmaurice 0-3
1977–8
v Scotland *Dublin* lost to M. Gibson 0-3

J. Clusker
1976–7
v Wales *Cardiff* lost to C. Wilson 1-2
v England *Dublin* lost to J. Hargreaves 0-3
1977–8
v Wales *Dublin* beat C. Wilson 2-1
v Scotland *Dublin* lost to R. Miller 1-2
v England *Portsmouth* beat S. Hood 2-1
1978
v Isle of Man *Prestatyn* beat N. Radcliffe 3-0
v Wales lost to C. Everton 1-2

D. Cranley
1983
v Isle of Man *Prestatyn* beat C. Cooper 2-1
v Wales lost to W. Jones 1-2
v Northern Ireland lost to A. Sharpe 1-2
v Scotland lost to J. Rea 1-2

R. Dunne
1970–1
v England *Dublin* lost to C. Ross 0-3

P. Ennis
1981
v Northern Ireland *Prestatyn* beat S. Clarke 2-1
v England lost to B. West 1-2
v Wales lost to D. John 0-3
v Scotland beat K. Baird 2-1
1982
v Northern Ireland *Prestatyn* beat A. Sharpe 2-1
v Isle of Man beat C. Cooper 3-0
v Scotland beat R. Lane 2-1
v England lost to J. Hargreaves 1-2
v Wales lost to T. Parsons 1-2
1983
v England *Prestatyn* lost to G. Wood 0-3
v Wales lost to T. Parsons 0-3
v Northern Ireland beat S. McClarey 2-1
v Scotland beat S. Muir 3-0

P. Fagan
1975–6
v England *Grimsby* beat W. Thorne	2-1
v Wales *Dublin* lost to D. Mountjoy	1-2
v Scotland *Dunlaoghaire* beat J. Phillips	2-1

G. Gibson
1982
v England *Prestatyn* beat G. Wood	2-1
v Wales lost to J. Terry	0-3
v Scotland lost to J. Rea	1-2

1983
v England *Prestatyn* lost to D. Fowler	1-2
v Wales lost to A. Lloyd	0-3

J. Grace
1970–1
v Wales *Port Talbot* lost to G. Thomas	1-2

1972–3
v Wales *Pontygwaith* lost to D. Mountjoy	0-3

G. Hanway
1970–1
v England *Dublin* lost to M. Wildman	0-3
v Wales *Port Talbot* lost to J. Ford	0-3

1971–2
v Scotland *Dublin* beat C. Brown	2-1

1972–3
v Scotland *Dublin* lost to G. Hadden	1-2
v Wales *Pontygwaith* lost to T. Parsons	1-2
v England *Dublin* lost to J. Fitzmaurice	0-3

1973–4
v England *Dublin* lost to J. Phillips	0-3

E. Hughes
1974–5
v Scotland *Dundee* lost to I. Wallace	1-2

1975–6
v England *Grimsby* lost to R. Edmonds	1-2
v Wales *Dublin* lost to M. Berni	0-3
v Scotland *Dunlaoghaire* lost to M. McLeod	1-2

1976–7
v Scotland *Edinburgh* lost to E. McLaughlin	1-2
v England *Dublin* lost to S. Hood	0-3

1978
v England *Prestatyn* lost to T. Meo	1-2
v Isle of Man beat J. Kinrade	3-0
v Wales beat J. Selby	2-1
v Scotland beat J. Donnelly	2-1

1979
v Scotland *Prestatyn* lost to S. Nivison	1-2
v England lost to J. White	1-2
v Northern Ireland lost to J. Begley	1-2
v Isle of Man beat R. Cowley	3-0
v Wales beat T. Parsons	3-0

1980
v Northern Ireland *Prestatyn* beat S. Pavis	2-1
v Wales lost to D. May	1-2
v Scotland lost to E. McLaughlin	1-2
v England lost to G. Wood	0-3
v Isle of Man beat K. Kinrade	3-0

M. Kane
1977–8
v Scotland *Dublin* lost to D. Sneddon	0-3

1980
v Northern Ireland *Prestatyn* beat S. Clarke	2-1
v Wales beat C. Roscoe	2-1
v Scotland lost to J. Halcrow	1-2
v England lost to J. White	1-2
v Isle of Man beat J. Radcliffe	3-0

1981
v Northern Ireland *Prestatyn* beat P. Donnelly	2-1
v England lost to L. Dodd	1-2
v Wales beat J. Selby	2-1
v Isle of Man beat J. Kinrade	3-0
v Scotland lost to R. Lane	1-2

1982
v Northern Ireland *Prestatyn* lost to S. Pavis	0-3
v Isle of Man beat T. Wilson	3-0
v Scotland lost to G. Carnegie	1-2

v Wales lost to S. Newbury	0-3

1983
v England *Prestatyn* lost to M. Bradley	1-2
v Isle of Man lost to R. Cowley	0-3
v Northern Ireland beat J. McLaughlin	3-0

A. Kearney
1981
v Northern Ireland *Prestatyn* lost to S. Pavis	0-3
v Wales lost to S. Newbury	1-2
v Isle of Man lost to P. Reynolds	1-2
v Scotland lost to J. McNellan	1-2

1982
v Northern Ireland *Prestatyn* lost to E. Swaffield	1-2

L. Kenna
1970–1
v Wales *Port Talbot* lost to D. Mountjoy	0-3

1974–5
v England *Glasnevin* lost to W. Thorne	1-2

1975–6
v Wales *Dublin* lost to J. Selby	0-3

1976–7
v Wales *Cardiff* beat S. Newbury	3-0
v Scotland *Edinburgh* lost to J. Phillips	0-3

1977–8
v Wales *Dublin* lost to S. Newbury	0-3

T. Langan
1977–8
v England *Portsmouth* lost to G. Foulds	0-3

1978
v Isle of Man *Prestatyn* lost to W. Craig	1-2

1979
v Scotland *Prestatyn* lost to M. Gibson	1-2
v England lost to A. Knowles	0-3
v Northern Ireland beat J. McLaughlin	3-0
v Wales lost to S. Newbury	1-2
v Isle of Man lost to M. Quine	1-2

D. Lenehan
1973–4
v Scotland *Dublin* beat E. Sinclair	2-1
v England *Bolton* beat D. French	2-1
v Wales *Dublin* beat C. Wilson	2-1

J. Long
1979
v Isle of Man *Prestatyn* lost to C. Cooper	0-3

1982
v Isle of Man *Prestatyn* beat P. Reynolds	2-1
v Scotland beat J. Rankeillor	2-1
v England beat N. Foulds	3-0
v Wales beat T. Griffiths	2-1

1983
v England *Prestatyn* lost to S. Longworth	1-2
v Isle of Man lost to P. Reynolds	1-2
v Wales lost to S. Newbury	1-2
v Scotland lost to J. Laidlaw	0-3

M. Lowth
1970–1
v England *Dublin* lost to J. Virgo	0-3

P. Miley
1973–4
v England *Bolton* beat S. Hood	2-1
v Wales *Dublin* lost to G. Thomas	0-3

1974–5
v England *Glasnevin* lost to R. Andrewartha	1-2

1979
v Scotland *Prestatyn* lost to J. Halcrow	1-2
v England lost to D. Martin	0-3
v Northern Ireland beat E. Swaffield	2-1
v Wales lost to A. Lloyd	0-3

F. Murphy
1970–1
v England *Dublin* lost to R. Edmonds	1-2

1971–2
v England *Harringay* lost to J. Virgo	1-2

v Scotland *Dublin* lost to W. McKerron	1-2

1972–3
v England *Dublin* lost to W. Thorne	1-2

1976–7
v Wales *Cardiff* lost to A. Lloyd	0-3

R. McCrum
1983
v Isle of Man *Prestatyn* lost to M. Colquitt	1-2
v Northern Ireland lost to S. Pavis	0-3

P. McNally
1983
v Isle of Man *Prestatyn* lost to P. Partington	1-2
v Wales lost to P. Jones	1-2
v Scotland beat K. Baird	2-1

F. Nathan
1972–3
v England *Dublin* lost to D. French	1-2

1974–5
v England *Glasnevin* beat C. Ross	2-1
v Scotland *Dundee* lost to J. Phillips	1-2
v Wales *Neath* lost to A. Lloyd	1-2

1975–6
v England *Grimsby* lost to S. Hood	0-3

1978
v England *Prestatyn* lost to A. Knowles	1-2
v Wales lost to S. Newbury	0-3
v Scotland lost to E. McLaughlin	0-3

M. Ralph
1980
v Isle of Man *Prestatyn* beat P. Reynolds	2-1

1981
v Northern Ireland *Prestatyn* beat J. McLaughlin	2-1
v England lost to J. Hargreaves	1-2
v Wales lost to A. Lloyd	1-2
v Isle of Man beat R. Cowley	2-1
v Scotland lost to J. Rankeillor	1-2

1982
v England *Prestatyn* lost to M. Bradley	0-3

1983
v England *Prestatyn* beat D. Chalmers	2-1
v Isle of Man beat T. Wilson	2-1
v Wales lost to R. Jones	1-2
v Northern Ireland beat E. Swaffield	2-1
v Scotland lost to J. Halcrow	0-3

A. Roche
1970–1
v England *Dublin* beat S. Hood	2-1

1971–2
v England *Harringay* lost to C. Ross	0-3
v Scotland *Dublin* lost to J. Phillips	1-2
v Wales *Dublin* beat M. Berni	2-1

1972–3
v Wales *Pontygwaith* lost to D. May	0-3
v Scotland *Dublin* lost to B. Demarco	1-2

J. Rogers
1970–1
v Wales *Port Talbot* lost to M. Berni	0-3

1971–2
v England *Harringay* beat M. Wildman	2-1
v Scotland *Dublin* lost to D. Sneddon	1-2
v Wales *Dublin* lost to D. May	1-2

1972–3
v Scotland *Dublin* lost to J. Phillips	0-3
v England *Dublin* beat C. Ross	2-1

1974–5
v Wales *Neath* beat G. Thomas	2-1

1975–6
v England *Grimsby* lost to C. Ross	1-2
v Wales *Dublin* lost to T. Griffiths	0-3

1977–8
v Wales *Dublin* lost to T. Griffiths	0-3

1978
v England *Prestatyn* lost to M. Hallett	1-2
v Isle of Man lost to R. Cowley	1-2
v Wales lost to T. Parsons	0-3

D. Sheehan

1970–1
v Wales *Port Talbot* lost to D. May — 0-3
1971–2
v England *Harringay* lost to J. Barron — 0-3
v Wales *Dublin* lost to D. Meredith — 0-3
1973–4
v Scotland *Dublin* beat J. Zonfrillo — 2-1
v England *Bolton* beat R. Edmonds — 2-1
v Wales *Dublin* lost to D. Mountjoy — 0-3
1974–5
v England *Glasnevin* lost to J. Virgo — 0-3
v Scotland *Dundee* lost to D. Sneddon — 0-3
v Wales *Neath* lost to T. Parsons — 1-2
1975–6
v Wales *Dublin* beat J. Prosser — 2-1
v Scotland *Dunlaoghaire* lost to J. Zonfrillo — 1-2
1976–7
v England *Dublin* lost to J. Johnson — 0-3
v Scotland *Edinburgh* lost to D. Sneddon — 1-2
v Wales *Dublin* lost to G. Thomas — 0-3
1979
v Scotland *Prestatyn* beat I. Wallace — 3-0
v England beat J. Hargreaves — 2-1
v Northern Ireland lost to P. Donnelly — 1-2
v Wales beat V. Rosser — 2-1
v Isle of Man beat P. Reynolds — 3-0
1980
v Northern Ireland *Prestatyn* beat D. McVeigh — 3-0
v Wales lost to D. John — 0-3
v Scotland lost to I. Black — 1-2
v England beat D. Martin — 2-1
v Isle of Man beat M. Quine — 2-1

G. Sutton

1976–7
v England *Dublin* beat J. Fitzmaurice — 2-1
v Scotland *Edinburgh* beat J. Zonfrillo — 2-1
v Wales *Cardiff* lost to D. Thomas — 1-2
1977–8
v Wales *Dublin* lost to A. Lloyd — 0-3
v Scotland *Dublin* lost to R. Cadman — 0-3
1978
v Wales *Prestatyn* beat C. Wilson — 2-1
v Isle of Man beat P. Reynolds — 3-0
v Scotland beat M. Gibson — 3-0
1979
v Scotland *Prestatyn* beat E. McLaughlin — 2-1
v England beat D. Hughes — 3-0
v Northern Ireland lost to D. McVeigh — 0-3
v Wales lost to J. Selby — 1-2
v Isle of Man beat J. Radcliffe — 3-0
1980
v Northern Ireland *Prestatyn* beat P. Donnelly — 2-1
v Wales lost to J. Selby — 1-2
v Scotland beat M. McLeod — 2-1
v England lost to V. Harris — 0-3
v Isle of Man lost to P. Partington — 1-2
1981
v Northern Ireland *Prestatyn* beat D. McVeigh — 2-1
v England lost to M. Darrington — 0-3
v Isle of Man lost to C. Cooper — 0-3

P. Thornton

1970–1
v Wales *Port Talbot* lost to E. Richards — 0-3
1971–2
v Scotland *Dublin* lost to E. Sinclair — 0-3
1972–3
v Scotland *Dublin* lost to E. Sinclair — 1-2

P. Watchorn

1977–8
v England *Portsmouth* lost to G. Scott — 1-2
1980
v Northern Ireland *Prestatyn* lost to E. Swaffield — 1-2
v Wales lost to S. Newbury — 0-3
v Scotland beat M. Gibson — 2-1
v England lost to M. Darrington — 1-2
1981
v England *Prestatyn* lost to V. Harris — 1-2
v Wales beat D. May — 2-1
v Isle of Man beat M. Clinton — 2-1

v Scotland beat J. Zonfrillo — 2-1
1982
v Northern Ireland *Prestatyn* beat K. Erwin — 2-1
v Isle of Man beat R. Cowley — 3-0
v Scotland lost to K. Baird — 0-3
v Wales beat A. Lloyd — 2-1

L. Watson

1972–3
v Wales *Pontygwaith* lost to A. Lloyd — 0-3
1975–6
v Scotland *Dunlaoghaire* lost to W. McKerron — 0-3

J. Weber

1970–1
v England *Dublin* lost to J. Barron — 1-2
1971–2
v England *Harringay* lost to R. Edmonds — 0-3
v Scotland *Dublin* lost to B. Demarco — 1-2
v Wales *Dublin* beat D. Mountjoy — 2-1
1972–3
v Scotland *Dublin* lost to D. Sneddon — 1-2
v Wales *Pontygwaith* lost to G. Thomas — 1-2
1973–4
v Scotland *Dublin* beat W. McKerron — 2-1
v England *Bolton* beat M. Wildman — 2-1
1974–5
v Wales *Neath* lost to T. Griffiths — 1-2
v Scotland *Dundee* lost to J. Zonfrillo — 1-2

N. Wills

1971–2
v Wales *Dublin* lost to D. John — 0-3

D. Wilson

1977–8
v England *Portsmouth* lost to J. Hargreaves — 1-2
1978
v England *Prestatyn* lost to S. Hood — 1-2
v Scotland lost to E. Sinclair — 1-2

G. Wilson

1982
v Northern Ireland *Prestatyn* beat F. Connolly — 2-1
v Isle of Man beat M. Quine — 2-1
v Scotland lost to J. Rea — 1-2

SCOTLAND

J. Allan

1982
v England *Prestatyn* lost to M. Bradley — 0-3
v Wales lost to T. Chappel — 1-2
v Isle of Man beat T. Wilson — 2-1
v Rep. of Ireland beat P. Browne — 2-1

K. Baird

1981
v Isle of Man *Prestatyn* beat C. Cooper — 2-1
v Northern Ireland lost to A. Sharpe — 1-2
v Rep. of Ireland lost to P. Ennis — 1-2
v England lost to G. Wood — 1-2
1982
v England *Prestatyn* beat D. Chalmers — 3-0
v Wales lost to W. Jones — 1-2
v Northern Ireland beat E. Swaffield — 2-1
v Rep. of Ireland beat P. Watchorn — 3-0
1983
v Wales *Prestatyn* lost to S. Newbury — 0-3
v England beat D. Chalmers — 2-1
v Isle of Man beat T. Wilson — 2-1
v Rep. of Ireland lost to P. McNally — 1-2

I. Black

1980
v Wales *Prestatyn* lost to A. Lloyd — 0-3
v Isle of Man beat P. Partington — 3-0
v Rep. of Ireland beat D. Sheehan — 2-1
v Northern Ireland beat A. Sharpe — 2-1
v England lost to J. O'Boye — 1-2

C. Brown

1971–2
v Wales *Edinburgh* lost to D. Mountjoy — 0-3
v Rep. of Ireland *Dublin* lost to G. Hanway — 1-2

R. Cadman

1976–7
v Rep. of Ireland *Edinburgh* lost to D. Brennan — 1-2
1977–8
v Rep. of Ireland *Dublin* beat G. Sutton — 3-0
v England *Doncaster* lost to J. Hargreaves — 0-3

G. Carnegie

1971–2
v England *Newcastle* lost to to J. Virgo — 1-2
1982
v Isle of Man *Prestatyn* lost to R. Cowley — 0-3
v Rep. of Ireland beat M. Kane — 2-1
1983
v Wales *Prestatyn* lost to W. Jones — 1-2
v Northern Ireland beat E. Swaffield — 2-1
v England beat M. Bradley — 2-1
v Isle of Man lost to R. Cowley — 0-3

B. Demarco

1971–2
v England *Newcastle* lost to C. Ross — 1-2
v Wales *Edinburgh* beat J. Terry — 3-0
v Rep. of Ireland *Dublin* beat J. Weber — 2-1
1972–3
v Rep. of Ireland *Dublin* beat A. Roche — 2-1
v England *Edinburgh* lost to R. Edmonds — 0-3
v Wales *Llay* beat J. Prosser — 2-1
1973–4
v Rep. of Ireland *Dublin* beat F. Byrne — 2-1
v England *Carlisle* beat T. Graham — 2-1
v Wales *Edinburgh* lost to J. Selby — 1-2
1974–5
v Wales *Maerdy* beat D. Mountjoy — 2-1
v Rep. of Ireland *Dundee* beat N. Clarke — 2-1
1975–6
v Wales *Edinburgh* lost to J. Selby — 1-2
v Rep. of Ireland *Dunlaoghaire* lost to F. Byrne — 1-2
1976–7
v Wales *Trealaw* lost to J. Selby — 1-2
v England *Glasgow* lost to G. Foulds — 1-2
1977–8
v Wales *Dublin* beat T. Parsons — 2-1

J. Donnelly

1978
v Wales *Prestatyn* beat S. Newbury — 3-0
v England lost to A. Knowles — 0-3
v Isle of Man beat R. Cowley — 3-0
v Rep. of Ireland lost to E. Hughes — 1-2
1979
v Isle of Man *Prestatyn* beat W. Craig — 3-0
v Rep. of Ireland lost to P. Burke — 1-2
v Northern Ireland lost to D. McVeigh — 1-2
v Wales lost to S. Newbury — 0-3
1980
v Isle of Man *Prestatyn* lost to P. Reynolds — 1-2
v Wales lost to D. John — 1-2
v Northern Ireland beat S. Pavis — 2-1
v England lost to V. Harris — 0-3

R. Eprile

1973–4
v England *Carlisle* lost to M. Wildman — 1-2

M. Gibson

1974–5
v England *Edinburgh* lost to G. Scott — 0-3
v Wales *Maerdy* lost to T. Parsons — 0-3
1977–8
v Rep. of Ireland *Dublin* beat N. Clarke — 2-1
v England *Doncaster* beat G. Scott — 2-1
1978
v Wales *Prestatyn* lost to A. Lloyd — 1-2
v England lost to J. Hargreaves — 0-3
v Rep. of Ireland lost to G. Sutton — 0-3

1979
v England *Prestatyn* beat J. Hargreaves	2-1
v Rep. of Ireland beat T. Langan	2-1
v Northern Ireland beat J. Begley	2-1
v Wales beat T. Parsons	2-1

1980
v Isle of Man *Prestatyn* beat W. Craig	3-0
v Wales beat J. Selby	2-1
v Rep. of Ireland lost to P. Watchorn	1-2
v England lost to M. Watterson	0-3

G. Hadden

1972–3
v Rep. of Ireland *Dublin* beat G. Hanway	2-1
v Wales *Llay* lost to A. Lloyd	0-3

J. Halcrow

1978
v England *Prestatyn* lost to G. Foulds	0-3
v Isle of Man beat W. Craig	2-1

1979
v England *Prestatyn* beat G. Foulds	3-0
v Rep. of Ireland beat P. Miley	2-1
v Northern Ireland beat E. Swaffield	2-1
v Wales beat J. Terry	2-1

1980
v Rep. of Ireland *Prestatyn* beat M. Kane	2-1
v Northern Ireland lost to D. McVeigh	1-2

1981
v Isle of Man *Prestatyn* beat P. Reynolds	2-1
v Wales lost to S. Newbury	0-3

1983
v Northern Ireland *Prestatyn* beat S. Pavis	2-1
v England lost to B. West	1-2
v Isle of Man beat C. Cooper	2-1
v Rep. of Ireland beat M. Ralph	3-0

P. Kippie

1980
v Isle of Man *Prestatyn* beat C. Cooper	2-1
v Wales lost to S. Newbury	1-2
v Northern Ireland lost to T. Murphy	1-2
v England lost to J. Hargreaves	0-3

J. Laidlaw

1983
v Northern Ireland *Prestatyn* lost to J. McLaughlin	0-3
v Rep. of Ireland beat J. Long	3-0

R. Lane

1981
v Isle of Man *Prestatyn* beat J. Kinrade	2-1
v Wales lost to T. Parsons	1-2
v Rep. of Ireland beat M. Kane	2-1
v England beat G. Cripsey	3-0

1982
v England *Prestatyn* beat S. Duggan	3-0
v Wales lost to A. Lloyd	1-2
v Northern Ireland lost to P. Donnelly	1-2
v Rep. of Ireland lost to P. Ennis	1-2

1983
v Wales *Prestatyn* lost to A. Lloyd	1-2
v Northern Ireland beat K. Erwin	3-0
v England lost to D. Fowler	1-2
v Isle of Man beat M. Clinton	2-1

W. McKerron

1971–2
v England *Newcastle* beat M. Wildman	2-1
v Wales *Edinburgh* lost to R. Oriel	1-2
v Rep. of Ireland *Dublin* beat F. Murphy	2-1

1972–3
v England *Edinburgh* lost to M. Wildman	0-3
v Wales *Llay* lost to R. Oriel	1-2

1973–4
v Rep. of Ireland *Dublin* lost to J. Weber	1-2
v Wales *Edinburgh* lost to C. Wilson	1-2

1974–5
v England *Edinburgh* beat W. Thorne	2-1
v Wales *Maerdy* lost to M. Berni	0-3

1975–6
v Wales *Edinburgh* lost to A. Lloyd	0-3

v Rep. of Ireland *Dunlaoghaire* beat L. Watson	3-0

1976–7
v Wales *Trealaw* lost to S. Newbury	1-2
v Rep. of Ireland *Dublin* lost to R. Brennan	0-3

E. McLaughlin

1975–6
v England *Southport* lost to J. Hargreaves	0-3

1976–7
v Rep. of Ireland *Edinburgh* beat E. Hughes	2-1
v England *Glasgow* lost to R. Edmonds	1-2

1977–8
v Wales *Dublin* beat A. Lloyd	2-1
v England *Doncaster* beat G. Foulds	3-0

1978
v Wales *Prestatyn* lost to C. Wilson	1-2
v Isle of Man beat J. Radcliffe	3-0
v Rep. of Ireland beat F. Nathan	3-0

1979
v England *Prestatyn* lost to J. White	1-2
v Wales beat C. Everton	2-1
v Northern Ireland beat R. Burke	3-0
v Rep. of Ireland lost to G. Sutton	2-1
v Isle of Man beat J. Radcliffe	2-1

1980
v Isle of Man *Prestatyn* beat J. Radcliffe	3-0
v Wales beat R. Welch	2-1
v Rep. of Ireland beat E. Hughes	2-1
v Northern Ireland beat P. Donnelly	2-1
v England lost to J. White	1-2

M. McLeod

1975–6
v Wales *Edinburgh* lost to D. Mountjoy	0-3
v England *Southport* beat J. Fitzmaurice	2-1
v Rep. of Ireland *Dunlaoghaire* beat E. Hughes	2-1

1976–7
v Wales *Trealaw* lost to T. Griffiths	0-3

1979
v Isle of Man *Prestatyn* beat P. Partington	2-1
v Wales lost to G. Thomas	1-2
v England beat D. Martin	2-1

1980
v Isle of Man *Prestatyn* beat K. Kinrade	2-1
v Wales lost to C. Roscoe	0-3
v Rep. of Ireland lost to G. Sutton	1-2
v Northern Ireland lost to E. Swaffield	1-2

J. McNellan

1980
v Rep. of Ireland *Prestatyn* lost to P. Burke	1-2
v England beat G. Wood	2-1

1981
v Wales *Prestatyn* lost to D. May	0-3
v Northern Ireland lost to S. Pavis	1-2
v Rep. of Ireland beat A. Kearney	2-1
v England lost to B. Harris	1-2

1983
v Wales *Prestatyn* beat R. Jones	2-1
v Northern Ireland lost to A. Sharpe	0-3
v Isle of Man beat M. Colquitt	2-1
v Rep. of Ireland lost to R. Brennan	1-2

R. Miller

1976–7
v England *Glasgow* lost to J. Johnson	1-2

1977–8
v Wales *Dublin* lost to C. Wilson	0-3
v Rep. of Ireland *Dublin* beat J. Clusker	2-1
v England *Doncaster* lost to J. Johnson	1-2

1978
v Wales *Prestatyn* beat D. John	2-1
v Isle of Man beat P. Reynolds	2-1

1981
v Isle of Man *Prestatyn* lost to R. Cowley	1-2
v Northern Ireland lost to E. Swaffield	1-2

S. Muir

1983
v Isle of Man *Prestatyn* beat P. Reynolds	3-0
v Rep. of Ireland lost to P. Ennis	0-3

S. Nivison

1975–6
v England *Southport* lost to R. Andrewartha	0-3

1979
v England *Prestatyn* lost to M. Watterson	0-3
v Wales lost to A. Lloyd	0-3
v Northern Ireland beat S. Pavis	2-1
v Rep. of Ireland beat E. Hughes	2-1
v Isle of Man beat C. Cooper	2-1

J. Phillips

1971–2
v England *Newcastle* lost to J. Barron	1-2
v Wales *Edinburgh* beat M. Berni	2-1
v Rep. of Ireland *Dublin* A. Roche	2-1

1972–3
v Rep. of Ireland *Dublin* beat J. Rogers	3-0
v England *Edinburgh* lost to S. Hood	1-2
v Wales *Llay* beat M. Berni	2-1

1973–4
v Rep. of Ireland *Dublin* beat G. Hanway	3-0
v England *Carlisle* lost to S. Hood	1-2
v Wales *Edinburgh* T. Griffiths	0-3

1974–5
v Rep. of Ireland *Dundee* beat F. Nathan	2-1
v Wales *Maerdy* lost to T. Griffiths	0-3
v England *Edinburgh* lost to J. Virgo	1-2

1975–6
v Wales *Edinburgh* lost to T. Parsons	1-2
v Rep. of Ireland *Dunlaoghaire* lost to P. Fagan	1-2

1976–7
v Wales *Trealaw* lost to T. Parsons	0-3
v Rep. of Ireland *Edinburgh* beat L. Kenna	3-0
v England *Glasgow* lost to G. Scott	1-2

1977–8
v Wales *Dublin* lost to G. Thomas	1-2

1979
v Isle of Man *Prestatyn* lost to P. Reynolds	1-2
v Northern Ireland lost to P. Donnelly	0-3

J. Rankeillor

1981
v Wales *Prestatyn* lost to J. Selby	1-2
v Northern Ireland beat S. Clarke	3-0
v Rep. of Ireland beat M. Ralph	2-1
v England beat L. Dodd	3-0

1982
v England *Prestatyn* lost to B. West	1-2
v Wales beat J. Selby	2-1
v Isle of Man beat M. Colquitt	2-1
v Northern Ireland beat S. Clarke	2-1
v Rep. of Ireland lost to J. Long	1-2

1983
v Wales *Prestatyn* lost to T. Chappel	0-3
v England lost to S. Longworth	0-3

J. Rea

1981
v Isle of Man *Prestatyn* beat J. Radcliffe	3-0
v Wales lost to A. Lloyd	1-2
v Northern Ireland beat J. McLaughlin	2-1
v Rep. of Ireland lost to P. Burke	0-3
v England beat I. Williamson	2-1

1982
v England *Prestatyn* lost to J. Parrott	1-2
v Isle of Man lost to C. Cooper	1-2
v Northern Ireland lost to A. Sharpe	1-2
v Rep. of Ireland beat G. Gibson	2-1

1983
v Wales *Prestatyn* lost to T. Parsons	1-2
v Northern Ireland beat S. McClarey	2-1
v England lost to S. Ventham	1-2
v Rep. of Ireland beat D. Cranley	2-1

E. Sinclair

1971–2
v England *Newcastle* lost to S. Hood	1-2
v Wales *Edinburgh* beat G. Thomas	2-1
v Rep. of Ireland *Dublin* beat P. Thornton	3-0

1972–3
v Rep. of Ireland *Dublin* lost to P. Thornton	2-1

v England *Edinburgh* lost to C. Ross   1-2
v Wales *Llay* beat D. May   2-1
1973–4
v Rep. of Ireland *Dublin* lost to D. Lenehan   1-2
v England *Carlisle* lost to J. Virgo   1-2
v Wales *Edinburgh* lost to A. Lloyd   0-3
1974–5
v England *Edinburgh* beat S. Hood   2-1
v Wales *Maerdy* lost to G. Thomas   1-2
v Rep. of Ireland *Dundee* lost to P. Burke   1-2
1975–6
v Wales *Edinburgh* beat T. Griffiths   3-0
v England *Southport* lost to S. Hood   1-2
v Rep. of Ireland *Dunlaoghaire* beat P. Burke   3-0
1976–7
v Wales *Trealaw* lost to A. Lloyd   1-2
v Rep. of Ireland *Edinburgh* beat P. Burke   3-0
v England *Glasgow* beat S. Hood   2-1
1977–8
v Wales *Dublin* lost to T. Griffiths   0-3
v Rep. of Ireland *Dublin* lost to P.Burke   2-1
v England *Doncaster* beat R. Edmonds   2-1
1978
v Wales *Prestatyn* lost to T. Parsons   0-3
v England lost to T. Meo   0-3
v Rep. of Ireland beat D. Wilson   2-1

D.Sneddon
1971–2
v England *Newcastle* beat R. Edmonds   2-1
v Wales *Edinburgh* lost to D. May   1-2
v Rep. of Ireland *Dublin* beat J. Rogers   2-1
1972–3
v Rep. of Ireland *Dublin* beat J. Weber   2-1
v England *Edinburgh* lost to J. Barron   0-3
v Wales *Llay* lost to G. Thomas   1-2
1973–4
v Rep. of Ireland *Dublin* lost to P. Burke   1-2
v England *Carlisle* lost to D. French   1-2
v Wales *Edinburgh* lost to D. Mountjoy   0-3
1974–5
v Rep. of Ireland *Dundee* beat D. Sheehan   3-0
v Wales *Maerdy* lost to A. Lloyd   1-2
1975–6
v Wales *Edinburgh* beat M. Berni   2-1
v England *Southport* lost to J. Virgo   1-2
1976–7
v Wales *Trealaw* lost to J. Prosser   1-2
v Rep. of Ireland *Edinburgh* beat D. Sheehan   2-1
v England *Glasgow* lost to J. Hargreaves   1-2
1977–8
v Wales *Dublin* lost to S. Newbury   1-2
v Rep. of Ireland *Dublin* beat M. Kane   3-0
v England *Doncaster* lost to S. Davis   0-3
1978
v England *Prestatyn* lost to M. Hallett   1-2
v Isle of Man beat M. Quine   3-0
v Rep. of Ireland beat R. Brennan   2-1
1982
v Wales *Prestatyn* lost to T. Parsons   0-3
v Isle of Man beat P. Reynolds   2-1
v Northern Ireland lost to S. Pavis   0-3

I. Wallace
1974–5
v Rep. of Ireland *Dundee* beat E. Hughes   2-1
v England *Edinburgh* lost to R. Andrewartha   0-3
1979
v England *Prestatyn* lost to A. Knowles   0-3
v Rep. of Ireland lost to D. Sheehan   0-3
v Isle of Man beat R. Cowley   3-0

J. Wilson
1972–3
v England *Edinburgh* lost to J. Virgo   0-3

J. Zonfrillo
1973–4
v Rep. of Ireland *Dublin* lost to D. Sheehan   1-2
v England *Carlisle* lost to W. Thorne   1-2
v Wales *Edinburgh* beat G. Thomas   2-1
1974–5
v England *Edinburgh* lost to J. Hargreaves   1-2

v Rep. of Ireland *Dundee* beat J. Weber   2-1
1975–6
v England *Southport* beat R. Edmonds   2-1
v Rep. of Ireland *Dunlaoghaire* lost to D. Sheehan   2-1
1976–7
v Rep. of Ireland *Edinburgh* lost to G. Sutton   1-2
1978
v Wales *Prestatyn* beat J. Selby   2-1
v England lost to J. Johnson   1-2
v Isle of Man beat C. Cooper   2-1
v Rep. of Ireland lost to P. Burke   1-2
1981
v Rep. of Ireland *Prestatyn* beat M. Quine   3-0
v Wales beat D. John   2-1
v Northern Ireland beat D. McVeigh   2-1
v Rep. of Ireland lost to P. Watchorn   1-2
v England lost to M. Darrington   0-3
1982
v England *Prestatyn* lost to J. Hargreaves   1-2
v Wales lost to S. Newbury   1-2
v Isle of Man beat M. Clinton   2-1
v Northern Ireland lost to J. McLaughlin   0-3

WALES

M. Bennett
1981
v Isle of Man *Prestatyn* beat P. Reynolds   2-1

M. Berni
1969
v England *Port Talbot* beat P. Houlihan   3-0
1970–1
v England *Harringay* lost to M. Wildman   1-2
v Rep. of Ireland *Port Talbot* beat J. Rogers   3-0
1971–2
v England *Neath* beat R. Edmonds   2-1
v Scotland *Edinburgh* lost to J. Phillips   1-2
v Rep. of Ireland *Dublin* lost to A. Roche   1-2
1972–3
v Rep. of Ireland *Pontygwaith* beat F. Byrne   2-1
v England *Hull* beat J. Virgo   2-1
v Scotland *Llay* lost to J. Phillips   1-2
1973–4
v England *Garnant* lost to C. Ross   1-2
v Rep. of Ireland *Dublin* lost to N. Clarke   0-3
1974–5
v Scotland *Maerdy* beat W. McKerron   3-0
v England *Exeter* beat R. Andrewartha   2-1
v Rep. of Ireland *Neath* beat N. Clarke   3-0
1975–6
v Scotland *Edinburgh* lost to D. Sneddon   2-1
v Rep. of Ireland *Dublin* beat E. Hughes   3-0
v England *Merthyr* lost to R. Edmonds   0-3

T. Chappel
1982
v Northern Ireland *Prestatyn* lost to A. Sharpe   1-2
v Scotland beat J. Allan   2-1
v England lost to J. Hargreaves   0-2
1983
v Scotland *Prestatyn* beat J. Rankeillor   3-0
v Northern Ireland beat A. Sharpe   2-1
v England beat G. Wood   3-0

C. Everton
1978
v Isle of Man *Prestatyn* beat M. Quine   3-0
v Rep. of Ireland beat J. Clusker   2-1
v England beat G. Foulds   2-1
1979
v Isle of Man *Prestatyn* beat C. Cooper   3-0
v Scotland lost to E. McLaughlin   1-2
v England drew with G. Scott   1-1

J. Ford
1969
v England *Port Talbot* beat S. Hood   2-1
1970–1
v England *Harringay* lost to S. Hood   1-2
v Rep. of Ireland *Port Talbot* beat G. Hanway   3-0

J. Griffiths
1982
v Northern Ireland *Prestatyn* lost to K. Erwin   1-2
v Rep. of Ireland lost to J. Lang   1-2
1983
v Isle of Man *Prestatyn* beat M. Colquitt   2-1

T. Griffiths
1973–4
v Rep. of Ireland *Dublin* beat P. Burke   2-1
v Scotland *Edinburgh* beat J. Phillips   3-0
1974–5
v Scotland *Maerdy* beat J. Phillips   3-0
v England *Exeter* lost to W. Thorne   1-2
v Rep. of Ireland *Neath* beat J. Weber   2-1
1975–6
v Scotland *Edinburgh* lost to E. Sinclair   0-3
v Rep. of Ireland *Dublin* beat J. Rogers   3-0
v England *Merthyr* beat S. Hood   2-1
1976–7
v Scotland *Trealaw* beat M. McLeod   3-0
v England *Doncaster* beat J. Johnson   2-1
v Rep. of Ireland *Cardiff* beat R. Brennan   3-0
1977–8
v Scotland *Dublin* beat E. Sinclair   3-0
v Rep. of Ireland *Dublin* beat J. Rogers   3-0
v England *Caerphilly* beat J. Hargreaves   3-0

D. John
1971–2
v England *Neath* lost to S. Hood   1-2
v Rep. of Ireland *Dublin* beat N. Wills   3-0
1978
v Scotland *Prestatyn* lost to R. Miller   1-2
1980
v Northern Ireland *Prestatyn* beat D. McVeigh   2-1
v Scotland beat J. Donnelly   2-1
v Rep. of Ireland beat D. Sheehan   3-0
v England beat V. Harris   3-0
1981
v Northern Ireland *Prestatyn* lost to A. Sharpe   1-2
v Scotland lost to J. Zonfrillo   1-2
v Rep. of Ireland beat P. Ennis   3-0
v England lost to B. West   1-2

P. Jones
1983
v Rep. of Ireland *Prestatyn* beat P. McNally   2-1

R. Jones
1983
v Scotland *Prestatyn* lost to J. McNellan   1-2
v Isle of Man beat P. Reynolds   2-1
v Rep. of Ireland beat M. Ralph   2-1
v Northern Ireland beat K. Erwin   3-0
v England drew with R. Jarmak   1-1

W. Jones
1981
v Northern Ireland *Prestatyn* beat S. Clarke   2-1
v Isle of Man beat J. Kinrade   3-0
1982
v Isle of Man *Prestatyn* beat R. Cowley   3-0
v Northern Ireland lost to E. Swaffield   1-2
v Scotland beat K. Baird   2-1
v Rep. of Ireland lost to P. Browne   1-2
v England beat M. Bradley   2-1
1983
v Scotland *Prestatyn* beat G. Carnegie   2-1
v Isle of Man lost to C. Cooper   0-3
v Rep. of Ireland beat D. Cranley   2-1
v Northern Ireland beat W. Walker   3-0
v England beat M. Bradley   2-1

A. Kemp
1969
v England *Port Talbot* lost to C. Ross   1-2

A. Lloyd
1969
v England *Port Talbot* beat G. Thompson   2-1

1972–3
v Rep. of Ireland *Pontygwaith* beat L. Watson   3-0
v England *Hull* beat C. Ross   2-1
v Scotland *Llay* beat G. Hatton   3-0
1973–4
v England *Garnant* lost to R. Edmonds   0-3
v Scotland *Edinburgh* beat E. Sinclair   3-0
1974–5
v Scotland *Maerdy* beat D. Sneddon   2-1
v England *Exeter* lost to R. Edmonds   1-2
v Rep. of Ireland *Neath* beat F. Nathan   2-1
1975–6
v Scotland *Edinburgh* beat W. McKerron   3-0
v England *Merthyr* beat C. Ross   2-1
1976–7
v Scotland *Trealaw* beat E. Sinclair   2-1
v Rep. of Ireland *Cardiff* beat F. Murphy   3-0
1977–8
v Scotland *Dublin* lost to E. McLaughlin   1-2
v Rep. of Ireland *Dublin* beat G. Sutton   3-0
v England *Caerphilly* beat J. Johnson   2-1
1978
v Scotland *Prestatyn* beat M. Gibson   2-1
v Isle of Man beat C. Cooper   3-0
v Rep. of Ireland lost to P. Burke   1-2
v England lost to A. Knowles   0-2
1979
v Northern Ireland lost to P. Donnelly   1-2
v Isle of Man beat J. Radcliffe   3-0
v Rep. of Ireland beat P. Miley   3-0
v England beat D. Martin   2-1
1980
v Northern Ireland *Prestatyn* beat P. Donnelly   2-1
v Scotland beat I. Black   3-0
v Rep. of Ireland beat P. Burke   3-0

v Isle of Man beat K. Kinrade   2-1
v England lost to J. O'Boye   1-2
1981
v Northern Ireland *Prestatyn* beat D. McVeigh   2-1
v Scotland beat J. Rea   2-1
v Rep. of Ireland beat M. Ralph   2-1
v Isle of Man beat C. Cooper   3-0
v England beat M. Darrington   2-1
1982
v Isle of Man *Prestatyn* beat M. Clinton   2-1
v Scotland beat R. Lane   2-1
v Northern Ireland beat J. McLaughlin   2-1
v Rep. of Ireland lost to P. Watchorn   1-2
v England beat J. Parrott   1-2
1983
v Scotland *Prestatyn* beat R. Lane   2-1
v Rep. of Ireland beat G. Gibson   3-0
v Northern Ireland lost to J. McLaughlin   0-3
v England beat B. West   2-1

D. May

1970–1
v England *Harringay* lost to J. Barron   1-2
v Rep. of Ireland *Port Talbot* beat D. Sheehan   3-0
1971–2
v England *Neath* lost to J. Barron   1-2
v Scotland *Edinburgh* beat D. Sneddon   2-1
v Rep. of Ireland *Dublin* beat J. Rogers   2-1
1972–3
v Rep. of Ireland *Pontygwaith* beat A. Roche   3-0
v England *Hull* beat R. Edmonds   2-1
v Scotland *Llay* lost to E. Sinclair   1-2
1973–4
v England *Garnant* lost to S. Hood   0-3

1980
v Northern Ireland *Prestatyn* beat S. Pavis   2-1
v Rep. of Ireland beat E. Hughes   2-1
v Isle of Man beat J. Radcliffe   3-0
v England lost to D. Martin   0-3
1981
v Northern Ireland *Prestatyn* lost to E. Swaffield   1-2
v Scotland beat J. McNellan   3-0
v Rep. of Ireland lost to P. Watchorn   1-2
v Isle of Man beat R. Cowley   2-1
v England lost to B. Harris   1-2

D. Meredith

1971–2
v England *Neath* beat D. French   2-1
v Rep. of Ireland *Dublin* beat D. Sheehan   3-0

D. Mountjoy

1969
v England *Port Talbot* lost to J. Barron   0-3
1970–1
v England *Harringay* lost to R. Edmonds   1-2
v Rep. of Ireland *Port Talbot* beat L. Kenna   3-0
1971–2
v Scotland *Edinburgh* beat C. Brown   3-0
v Rep. of Ireland *Dublin* lost to J. Weber   1-2
1972–3
v Rep. of Ireland *Pontygwaith* beat J. Grace   3-0
v England *Hull* lost to S. Hood   1-2
1973–4
v England *Garnant* lost to M. Wildman   1-2
v Rep. of Ireland *Dublin* beat D. Sheehan   3-0
v Scotland *Edinburgh* beat D. Sneddon   3-0
1974–5
v Scotland *Maerdy* lost to B. Demarco   1-2

Terry Parsons (right) receives the 1984 Strongbow Welsh Amateur Snooker Championship trophy

v England *Exeter* beat C. Ross ... 2-1
v Rep. of Ireland *Neath* beat P. Burke ... 2-1
1975–6
v Scotland *Edinburgh* beat M. McLeod ... 3-0
v Rep. of Ireland *Dublin* beat P. Fagan ... 2-1
v England *Merthyr* beat J. Virgo ... 2-1

S. Newbury

1976–7
v Scotland *Trealaw* beat W. McKerron ... 2-1
v England *Doncaster* lost to J. Hargreaves ... 1-2
v Rep. of Ireland *Cardiff* lost to L. Kenna ... 0-3
1977–8
v Scotland *Dublin* beat D. Sneddon ... 2-1
v Rep. of Ireland *Dublin* beat L. Kenna ... 3-0
v England *Caerphilly* beat G. Scott ... 2-1
1978
v Scotland *Prestatyn* lost to J. Donnelly ... 0-3
v Rep. of Ireland beat F. Nathan ... 3-0
v England lost to T. Meo ... 1-2
1979
v Northern Ireland *Prestatyn* beat S. Pavis ... 3-0
v Isle of Man beat M. Quine ... 3-0
v Scotland beat J. Donnelly ... 3-0
v Rep. of Ireland beat T. Langan ... 2-1
v England beat M. Watterson ... 3-0
1980
v Northern Ireland *Prestatyn* beat A. Sharpe ... 2-1
v Scotland beat P. Kippie ... 2-1
v Rep. of Ireland beat P. Watchorn ... 3-0
v Isle of Man beat M. Quine ... 3-0
v England beat J. White ... 3-0
1981
v Northern Ireland *Prestatyn* beat P. Donnelly ... 2-1
v Scotland beat J. Halcrow ... 3-0
v Rep. of Ireland beat A. Kearney ... 2-1
v England beat G. Wood ... 2-0
1982
v Isle of Man *Prestatyn* beat M. Colquitt ... 3-0
v Northern Ireland beat P. Donnelly ... 3-0
v Scotland beat J. Zonfrillo ... 2-1
v Rep. of Ireland beat M. Kane ... 3-0
v England beat N. Foulds ... 3-0
1983
v Scotland *Prestatyn* beat K. Baird ... 3-0
v Isle of Man beat P. Partington ... 3-0
v Rep. of Ireland beat J. Long ... 2-1
v Northern Ireland beat E. Swaffield ... 2-1
v England lost to S. Longworth ... 0-3

R. Oriel

1971–2
v England *Neath* beat D. Taylor ... 2-1
v Scotland *Edinburgh* beat W. McKerron ... 2-1
v Rep. of Ireland *Dublin* beat R. Brennan ... 3-0
1972–3
v Scotland *Llay* beat W. McKerron ... 2-1

T. Parsons

1969
v England *Port Talbot* lost to R. Edmonds ... 0-3
1972–3
v Rep. of Ireland *Pontygwaith* beat G. Hanway ... 2-1
v England *Hull* lost to M. Wildman ... 0-3
1974–5
v Scotland *Maerdy* beat M. Gibson ... 3-0
v England *Exeter* beat M. Wildman ... 3-0
v Rep. of Ireland *Neath* beat D. Sheehan ... 2-1
1975–6
v Scotland *Edinburgh* beat J. Phillips ... 2-1
v England *Merthyr* beat R. Andrewartha ... 3-0
1976–7
v Scotland *Trealaw* beat J. Phillips ... 3-0
v England *Doncaster* lost to G. Scott ... 1-2
v Rep. of Ireland *Cardiff* beat P. Burke ... 3-0
1977–8
v Scotland *Dublin* lost to B. Demarco ... 1-2
v Rep. of Ireland *Dublin* beat P. Burke ... 2-1
v England *Caerphilly* lost to S. Davis ... 1-2
1978
v Scotland *Prestatyn* beat E. Sinclair ... 3-0
v Isle of Man beat K. Kinrade ... 3-0

v Rep. of Ireland beat J. Rogers ... 3-0
v England lost to J. Hargreaves ... 1-2
1979
v Northern Ireland *Prestatyn* beat D. McVeigh ... 3-0
v Isle of Man beat R. Cowley ... 2-1
v Scotland lost to M. Gibson ... 1-2
v England lost to A. Knowles ... 1-2
1981
v Northern Ireland *Prestatyn* beat S. Pavis ... 3-0
v Scotland beat R. Lane ... 2-1
v Rep. of Ireland beat P. Burke ... 3-0
v Isle of Man beat P. Partington ... 2-1
v England lost to J. Hargreaves ... 1-2
1982
v Isle of Man *Prestatyn* beat C. Cooper ... 3-0
v Northern Ireland beat S. Pavis ... 2-1
v Scotland beat D. Sneddon ... 3-0
v Rep. of Ireland beat P. Ennis ... 2-1
v England beat S. Duggan ... 2-1
1983
v Scotland *Prestatyn* beat J. Rea ... 2-1
v Rep. of Ireland beat P. Ennis ... 3-0
v Isle of Man beat R. Cowley ... 3-0
v Northern Ireland beat S. Pavis ... 3-0
v England beat D. Fowler ... 2-1

J. Prosser

1972–3
v Scotland *Llay* lost to B. Demarco ... 1-2
1973–4
v England *Garnant* lost to W. Thorne ... 1-2
1975–6
v Rep. of Ireland *Dublin* lost to D. Sheehan ... 1-2
1976–7
v Scotland *Trealaw* beat D. Sneddon ... 2-1
v England *Doncaster* lost to R. Edmonds ... 1-2

E. Richards

1970–1
v England *Harringay* lost to C. Ross ... 0-3
v Rep. of Ireland *Port Talbot* beat P. Thornton ... 3-0

C. Roscoe

1980
v Northern Ireland *Prestatyn* beat E. Swaffield ... 2-1
v Scotland beat M. McLeod ... 3-0
v Rep. of Ireland lost to M. Kane ... 1-2
v Isle of Man beat W. Craig ... 3-0
v England lost to M. Watterson ... 1-2

V. Rosser

1979
v Isle of Man *Prestatyn* beat W. Craig ... 3-0
v Rep. of Ireland lost to D. Sheehan ... 1-2
1980
v Northern Ireland *Prestatyn* lost to T. Murphy ... 0-3

J. Selby

1973–4
v Rep. of Ireland *Dublin* beat F. Byrne ... 2-1
v Scotland *Edinburgh* beat B. Demarco ... 2-1
1975–6
v Scotland *Edinburgh* beat B. Demarco ... 2-1
v Rep. of Ireland *Dublin* beat L. Kenna ... 3-0
v England *Merthyr* beat J. Fitzmaurice ... 2-1
1976–7
v Scotland *Trealaw* beat B. Demarco ... 2-1
v England *Doncaster* lost to G. Foulds ... 0-3
1978
v Scotland *Prestatyn* lost to J. Zonfrillo ... 1-2
v Isle of Man beat W. Craig ... 2-1
v Rep. of Ireland lost to E. Hughes ... 1-2
v England lost to J. Johnson ... 0-3
1979
v Northern Ireland *Prestatyn* lost to E. Swaffield ... 1-2
v Isle of Man beat P. Reynolds ... 2-1
v Rep. of Ireland beat G. Sutton ... 2-1
v England lost to J. Hargreaves ... 0-3
1980
v Scotland *Prestatyn* lost to M. Gibson ... 1-2
v Rep. of Ireland beat G. Sutton ... 2-1
v Isle of Man beat P. Reynolds ... 2-1

v England beat J. Hargreaves ... 2-1
1981
v Scotland *Prestatyn* beat J. Rankeillor ... 2-1
v Rep. of Ireland lost to M. Kane ... 1-2
v Isle of Man beat M. Clinton ... 3-0
v England lost to I. Williamson ... 0-1
1982
v Isle of Man *Prestatyn* beat T. Wilson ... 3-0
v Scotland lost to J. Rankeillor ... 1-2
v England lost to B. West ... 1-2
1983
v Isle of Man *Prestatyn* beat M. Colquitt ... 2-1

J. Terry

1971–2
v Scotland *Edinburgh* lost to B. Demarco ... 0-3
1979
v Northern Ireland *Prestatyn* beat B. Harvey ... 2-1
v Scotland lost to J. Halcrow ... 1-2
v Rep. of Ireland lost to P. Burke ... 1-2
1982
v Isle of Man *Prestatyn* beat P. Reynolds ... 2-1
v Rep. of Ireland beat G. Gibson ... 3-0

D. Thomas

1971–2
v England *Neath* lost to C. Ross ... 1-2
1976–7
v England *Doncaster* lost to S. Hood ... 1-2
v Rep. of Ireland *Cardiff* beat G. Sutton ... 2-1

G. Thomas

1970–1
v England *Harringay* lost to J. Virgo ... 0-3
v Rep. of Ireland *Port Talbot* beat J. Grace ... 2-1
1971–2
v Scotland *Edinburgh* lost to E. Sinclair ... 1-2
1972–3
v Rep. of Ireland *Pontygwaith* beat J. Weber ... 2-1
v England *Hull* beat J. Barron ... 2-1
v Scotland *Llay* beat D. Sneddon ... 2-1
1973–4
v England *Garnant* lost to J. Virgo ... 1-2
v Rep. of Ireland *Dublin* beat P. Miley ... 3-0
v Scotland *Edinburgh* lost to J. Zonfrillo ... 1-2
1974–5
v Scotland *Maerdy* beat E. Sinclair ... 2-1
v England *Exeter* lost to S. Hood ... 1-2
v Rep. of Ireland *Neath* lost to J. Rogers ... 1-2
1975–6
v Rep. of Ireland *Dublin* lost to P. Burke ... 1-2
1977–8
v Scotland *Dublin* beat J. Phillips ... 2-1
v Rep. of Ireland *Dublin* beat D. Sheehan ... 3-0
v England *Caerphilly* lost to G. Foulds ... 1-2
1978
v Isle of Man *Prestatyn* beat R. Cowley ... 2-1
1979
v Northern Ireland *Prestatyn* beat J. Begley ... 2-1
v Scotland beat M. McLeod ... 2-1
v England lost to J. White ... 0-3

R. Welch

1980
v Scotland *Prestatyn* lost to E. McLaughlin ... 1-2
v Isle of Man beat C. Cooper ... 2-1

C. Wilson

1973–4
v Rep. of Ireland *Dublin* lost to D. Lenehan ... 1-2
v Scotland *Edinburgh* beat W. McKerron ... 2-1
1976–7
v Rep. of Ireland *Cardiff* beat J. Clusker ... 2-1
1977–8
v Scotland *Dublin* beat R. Miller ... 3-0
v Rep. of Ireland *Dublin* lost to J. Clusker ... 1-2
v England *Caerphilly* lost to R. Edmonds ... 1-2
1978
v Scotland *Prestatyn* beat E. McLaughlin ... 2-1
v Isle of Man beat P. Reynolds ... 3-0
v Rep. of Ireland lost to G. Sutton ... 1-2
v England beat M. Hallett ... 3-0

Amateur Circuit

In contrast to the sorry state of affairs in the 1960s and early 1970s when, apart from national championships, few amateur events offered much in status or other reward, the amateur circuit is now packed with worthwhile tournaments.

The prodigious growth in the number of new snooker centre openings has helped change the face of the amateur tournament scene; there is now a predominance of events which are decided in one or two days within the same multi-table venue.

Previously, most events had been spread over several months with players drawn home or away in their various clubs, a system which meant players spent as much time travelling to and from matches as they did playing them.

The proliferation of snooker centres also changed the balance of the amateur game. The old style billiard hall — like the one in which Tony Hancock used to claim that he had acquired his "snooker hall pallor" — tended to go out of business after the war as the public rejected its spartan facilities, and the amateur game came to be concentrated in clubs whose primary function was not snooker — Conservative Clubs, Labour Clubs, Working Men's Clubs, Church Institutes and all manner of sports and social clubs.

Snooker is still played in these places even more enthusiastically than before, and amateur leagues flourish accordingly, but the most seriously competitive players now tend to be found in the new snooker centres where they are free of any club regulations governing the amount of time members may play on the tables and where they may even be supported to some extent by the centre's proprietors.

Most open tournaments are organised by, or through, snooker centres, but among the most popular are the week-long events organised by the Pontin and Warner chains of holiday camps. Professionals may compete in certain events if prepared to concede a handicap, commonly 14, 18 or 21 points per frame.

The 1983-84 open tournament circuit included the following events:

Peradon and Fletcher South of England Open
(at Basingstoke Snooker Centre)
Semi-finals: M. Bennett (Blackwood) beat T. Chappel (Swansea) (£500) 4-2; S. Newbury (Neath) beat N. Gilbert (Bedford) (£500) 4-2
Final: Newbury (£2,000) beat Bennett (£1,000) 5-3

Silver Cue
(at International Snooker Club, Aston)
Semi-finals: R. Bales (Birmingham) beat C. Hamson (Peterborough) (£200) 5-3; T. Drago (Malta) beat N. Suthers (Rochdale) (£200) 5-3
Final: Drago (£1,000) beat Bales (£500) 7-2

Ealing Open
(at Ealing Snooker Club)
Semi-finals: *Neal Foulds (Perivale) beat M. Bradley (Worksop) (£375) 4-3; S. Newbury (Neath) beat D. Rice (Doncaster) (£375) 4-2
Final: Newbury (£2,000) beat *Foulds (£750) 4-3
* professional conceding 10 points per frame.

Pontins Autumn Open
(at Prestatyn)
Semi-finals: R. Bales (Birmingham) beat J. Kerr (Rochdale) (£300)

4-1; G. Filtness (Plaistow) beat R. Barnes (Grimsby) (£300) 4-3
Final: Bales (£1,750) beat Filtness (£750) 7-0

Beacon Open (at Charnwood Snooker Centre, Loughborough)
Final: W. Jones (Abertysswg) (£700) beat S. Newbury (Neath) (£350) 4-1

West Coast Video-Double Diamond Open
(at Pot Black Club, Plymouth)
Final: T. Drago (Malta) (£800) beat A. Snell (Exeter) (£400) 5-1

Marlborough Stones North West Open
(at Marlborough Snooker Club, Manchester)
Final: T. Chappel (Swansea) (£800) beat B. West (Rotherham) (£400) 7-4

Gordon Hamilton Trophy (at '100 Break' Snooker Club, Glasgow)
Final: S. Newbury (Neath) (£2,000) beat K. Baird (Glasgow) (£1,000) 9-1

Seiko Tallaght Open (at Colaiste Muire College, Dublin)
Semi-finals: S. Newbury (Neath) beat R. Marshall (Exeter) (IR£900) 5-3; T. Drago (Malta) beat K. Erwin (Ballymena) (IR£900) 5-3
Final: Drago (IR£3,000) beat Newbury (IR£1,800) 5-1

London Leisure Pro-Am (at Tottenham Snooker Centre)
Final: M. Smith (Ilford) (£1,000) beat *Eugene Hughes (Dublin) (£300) 4-0
*professional conceding 18 points per frame.

Warners Isle of Wight Open (at Warners, Isle of Wight)
Semi-finals: *Steve Davis (Plumstead) beat J. Grech (Malta) (£500) 4-2; *Terry Griffiths (Llanelli) beat D. Fowler (Worksop) (£500) 4-1
Final: *Davis (£5,000) beat *Griffiths (£2,000) 5-2
*professional conceding 25 points per frame.

Piccadilly Radio/Greater Manchester Open
(at Marlborough Snooker Club and Royal Exchange Theatre, Manchester)
Semi-finals: B. West (Rotherham) beat G. Lambert (Bury) (£210) 5-1; A. Hindley (Atherton) beat E. Thorpe (Atherton) (£190) 5-3
Final: West (£1,000) beat Hindley (£400) 5-1

Kingsley Classic (at Kingsley Leisure Centre, Westward Ho!)
Final: R. Connor (Shepperton) (£500) beat W. Jones (Abertysswg) (£200) 5-1

Whitbread Open (at Ashfield Snooker Centre, Nottingham)
Final: R. Marshall (Exeter) (£500) beat *Ray Edmonds (Cleethorpes) (£250) 5-2
*professional conceding 18 points per frame.

Pontins Spring Open (at Prestatyn)
Semi-finals: **Neal Foulds (Perivale) beat *Tony Knowles (Bolton) (£500) 4-1;
*Doug Mountjoy (Ewyas Harold) beat *Ray Reardon (Stoke) (£500) 4-3
Final: **Foulds (£2,500) beat *Mountjoy (£1,250) 7-4
*professional conceding 25 points per frame
**professional conceding 21 points per frame.

Warner's Open (at Warner's, Hayling Island)
Semi-finals: M. Smith (Ilford) beat *Tony Knowles (Bolton) (£500) 4-3; *Willie Thorne (Leicester) beat *Joe Johnson (Bradford) (£500) 4-1
Final: Smith (£2,000) beat *Thorne (£1,000) 4-3
*professional conceding 18 points per frame.

Bass Holidays Open (at Pontins, Brean Sands)
Semi-finals: S. Ventham (Mitcham) beat O.B. Agrawal (India) (£500) 4-1; G. Sethi (India) beat S. Sawant (India) (£500) 4-1
Final: Sethi (£2,000) beat Ventham (£1,000) 7-5

Red Rose Radio Open
Final: D. Singh (Nottingham) (£1,000) beat E. Thorpe (Atherton) (£500) 8-6

Women's Snooker

As a participant sport, women's snooker is likely to be one of the great growth areas of the next decade. Women's Championships range back to 1933 but the number of serious competitive players was very strictly limited by the social conventions which discouraged them from using public billiard halls and clubs, even when they were not formally barred. Despite its lack of emphasis on physical strength, snooker has tended to be regarded as essentially a man's game. With the arrival of large numbers of new snooker centres, which have always been open to both sexes, women have in the last five years or so taken to the game in much larger numbers.

Organisationally, not everything has run smoothly, but four women's World Championships have been promoted and in 1984 National Express sponsored a five-week grand prix series with £60,000 prize money.

Despite the discernible improvements in standards of play among the best women – Mandy Fisher's break of 62 in one of the National Express contests was the highest ever made by a woman in competition in Britain – the attempt to project women's snooker as a public entertainment was perhaps premature.

However, if more women are encouraged to participate, if regular tournaments are established at all levels of the game and their administration improved, there is no reason why women's snooker should not be a major success story.

WOMEN'S WORLD OPEN

1976 V. Selby (England)
1977–79 No contests
1980 L. McIlrath (Australia)
1981 V. Selby (England)
1983 S. Foster (England)

NATIONAL EXPRESS WOMEN'S GRAND PRIX 1984

Abertillery
Sue Foster (England) beat Georgina Aplin (England) 6-1
Leeds
Mandy Fisher (England) beat Maryann McConnell (Canada) 7-2
Basingstoke
Sue LeMaich (Canada) beat Mandy Fisher (England) 7-5
Peterborough
Sue LeMaich (Canada) beat Mandy Fisher (England) 7-5
Birmingham
Mandy Fisher (England) beat Maryann McConnell (Canada) 7-6

Mandy Fisher (right) won a total of £14,000 in prize money last season, including the £5,000 snowball prize awarded for performances spread over the five tournaments. Below: the 1983 Women's World Open Champion, Sue Foster.

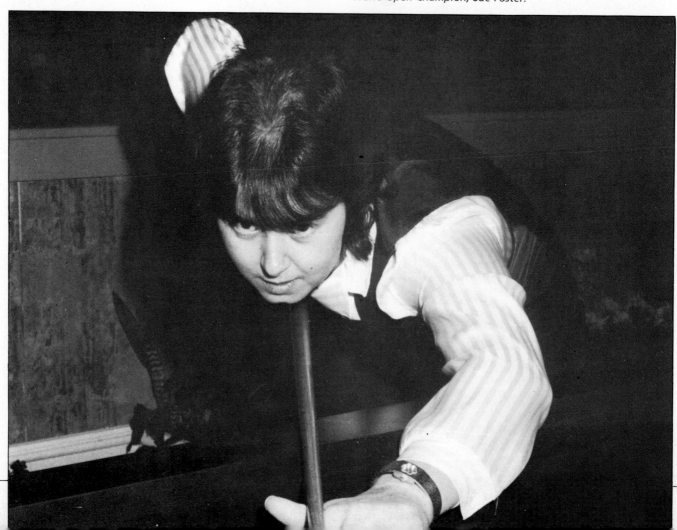

Professional Billiards

The limitation of billiards as a public spectacle is that the best players tend to make it look a great deal easier than it actually is.

This principle was extended to its logical conclusion in the 1930s when the four best players, Walter Lindrum of Australia, Joe Davis and Tom Newman of England, and Clark McConachy of New Zealand, so thoroughly mastered outwardly repetitious methods of scoring that they could reel off breaks of a thousand or more almost at will.

Billiards is therefore unique in that its best players became so good that they killed it as a public entertainment.

Though overshadowed by snooker, billiards still commands the interest of many amateurs. Entries for the English Amateur Championship, for instance, are as numerous as they were in the game's heyday and those for the British Under 16 and Under 19 Championships have recently reached record levels.

Little professional billiards has been played because it is not, for promoter or sponsor, as sound a commercial proposition as snooker, but enough enthusiasm exists among the players for expansion to be a reasonable prospect. Ironically, the standard of professional billiards has now deteriorated sufficiently to make it more interesting to watch.

The World Professional Billiards Championship, the game's senior event, became dormant in 1934 after Lindrum had retained the title in Australia. He would not travel to England to defend it and no one thought it worthwhile going to Australia to challenge him.

When Lindrum relinquished his position, McConachy beat John Barrie, the other nominated contender, for the title and held it unopposed for seventeen years until Rex Williams successfully challenged him in New Zealand in

Two of the greats: Walter Lindrum (left) and Joe Davis

1968. Williams held the title until deposed by Fred Davis in June 1980. Since then, the championship has been held each season on a tournament basis.

The 1984 event, sponsored by Strachan's, the billiard cloth manufacturers, with further financial support from the WPBSA and the promoting club, the Majestic Snooker Centre, Portsmouth, was won by Mark Wildman. In a desperately close finish to the five-hour final he beat Eddie Charlton by a mere 33 points, 1045-1012. In contrast to the commonplace thousand breaks of the pre-war era, the highest break of the championship was 319 by Charlton.

World Professional Billiards Championship

1870
William Cook beat John Roberts Jr — 1200–1083
John Roberts Jr beat William Cook — 1000–522
John Roberts Jr beat A. Bowles — 1000–759
Joseph Bennett beat John Roberts Jr — 1000–905
1871
John Roberts Jr beat Joseph Bennett — 1000–637
William Cook beat Joseph Bennett — 1000–942
1872
William Cook beat John Roberts Jr — 1000–799
1874
William Cook beat John Roberts Jr — 1000–784
1875
John Roberts Jr beat William Cook — 1000–837
John Roberts Jr beat William Cook — 1000–865
1877
John Roberts Jr beat William Cook — 1000–779
1880
Joseph Bennett beat William Cook — 1000–949
1881
Joseph Bennett beat Tom Taylor — 1000–910
1885
John Roberts Jr beat William Cook — 3000–2908
John Roberts Jr beat Joseph Bennett — 3000–1360
1889
Charles Dawson beat Joe North — 9000–4715
1900
Charles Dawson beat H. W. Stevenson — 9000–6775
1901
H. W. Stevenson beat Charles Dawson — 9000–6406
Charles Dawson beat H.W. Stevenson — 9000–5796
H. W. Stevenson (declared champion)
1903
Charles Dawson beat H.W. Stevenson — 9000–8700
1908
Melbourne Inman (declared champion)
1909
Melbourne Inman beat Albert Williams. — 9000–7662

Billiards Control Club Rules

1909
H.W. Stevenson (declared champion)
1910
H.W. Stevenson led Melbourne Inman
(match abandoned) — 13370–13212
H.W. Stevenson beat Melbourne Inman — 18000–16907
1911
H.W. Stevenson beat Melbourne Inman — 18000–16914
1912
Melbourne Inman beat Tom Reece — 18000–9675
1913
Melbourne Inman beat Tom Reece — 18000–16627
1914
Melbourne Inman beat Tom Reece — 18000–12826
1919
Melbourne Inman beat H.W. Stevenson — 16000–9468

1920
Willie Smith beat Claude Falkiner — 16000–14500
1921
Tom Newman beat Tom Reece — 16000–10744
1922
Tom Newman beat Claude Falkiner — 16000–15167
1923
Willie Smith beat Tom Newman — 16000–15180
1924
Tom Newman beat Tom Reece — 16000–14845
1925
Tom Newman beat Tom Reece — 16000–10092
1926
Tom Newman beat Joe Davis — 16000–9505
1927
Tom Newman beat Joe Davis — 16000–14763
1928
Joe Davis beat Tom Newman — 16000–14874
1929
Joe Davis beat Tom Newman — 18000–17219
1930
Joe Davis beat Tom Newman — 20198–20117
1932
Joe Davis beat Clark McConachy — 25161–19259
1933
Walter Lindrum beat Joe Davis — 21815–21121
1934
Walter Lindrum beat Joe Davis — 23553–22678
1951
Clark McConachy beat John Barrie — 9294–6691
1968
Rex Williams beat Clark McConachy — 5499–5234

In 1971, the World Professional Billiards and Snooker Association declared its autonomy in running professional championships after the Billiards and Snooker Control Council had stripped Williams of his title and declared that Lesley Driffield and Jack Karnehm, the only two professionals not then recognising the WPBSA, should play for the vacant championship. When this match took place, Driffield beat Karnehm, but the WPBSA continued to recognise Williams as champion.

1971
Rex Williams beat Bernard Bennett — 9250–4058
1973
Rex Williams beat Jack Karnehm — 8340–4336
1974
Rex Williams beat Eddie Charlton — 7017–4916
1976
Rex Williams beat Eddie Charlton — 9015–5149
1980 (June)
Fred Davis beat Rex Williams — 5978–4452

The June 1980 title match between Davis and Williams was the last to be held on a challenge basis; in November that year a tournament format was introduced.

1980 (November)*
Fred Davis beat Mark Wildman — 3037–2064
1982*
Rex Williams beat Mark Wildman — 3000–1785
1983*
Rex Williams beat Fred Davis — 1500–605
1984
Mark Wildman beat Eddie Charlton — 1045–1012

* Matches played to a points target rather than over a specified duration.

SNOOKER GLOSSARY

Break: A sequence of scoring shots.

Break off: The first shot of a frame in which the striker plays at the unbroken triangle of reds.

Clear the table: A sequence of shots in which a player pots all the balls left on the table.

Double: A shot by which a ball enters a pocket after striking one or more cushions.

Free ball: If a player is snookered after a foul shot by his opponent he may nominate any coloured ball as a red. If it is potted, he scores one and can then nominate a colour in the usual way. If all the reds have left the table, the free ball is valued at the same number of points as the lowest-valued ball on the table and the colours are then taken in sequence. (*N.B.* For the purpose of this rule a player is deemed to be snookered if he cannot hit both extremities of the object-ball.)

Maximum break: A sequence of shots in which a player takes all fifteen reds, fifteen blacks and all the colours to score 147.

Plant: A position in which the first object-ball is played on to the second object-ball in such a way as to make the second ball enter the pocket.

Safety shot: A shot in which a player makes no attempt to score but intends to leave his opponent unable to score.

Screw: Reverse spin. This is applied by striking the cue-ball well below centre.

Set: A position in which two object-balls are touching in such a way that the second ball is certain to be potted however the first object-ball is struck.

Shot to nothing: A shot in which a player attempts a pot in such a way as to leave himself in position to continue his break if successful but to leave the cue-ball in a safe position for his opponent if unsuccessful.

Side: Side spin. This is applied by striking the cue-ball to either the right or left of centre.

Snooker: A position in which the cue-ball cannot hit an object-ball because of an intervening ball.

Stun: A shot in which the cue-ball is stopped dead (if the pot is straight) by striking the cue-ball just below centre. If the pot is not straight, the stun shot is used to widen the angle the cue-ball takes after potting the object-ball.

'Only the referee is allowed to clean a ball on the table.' (official decisions)